Backpacking North Carolina

Backpacking North Carolina

The Definitive Guide
to 43 Can't-Miss Trips
from Mountains to Sea

Joe Miller

The University of North Carolina Press
Chapel Hill

A SOUTHERN GATEWAYS GUIDE

Set in Arnhem and Gotham
Manufactured in the United States of America.

The paper in this book meets the guidelines for permanence and durability of the Committee on Production Guidelines for Book Longevity of the Council on Library Resources.

The University of North Carolina Press has been a member of the Green Press Initiative since 2003.

Unless otherwise indicated, all photos are by the author.
Library of Congress Cataloging-in-Publication Data
Miller, Joe.
Backpacking North Carolina : the definitive guide to
43 can't-miss trips from mountains to sea / by Joe Miller.
    p. cm.
 Includes bibliographical references and index.
   ISBN 978-0-8078-3455-8 (cloth: alk. paper)
   ISBN 978-0-8078-7183-6 (pbk.: alk. paper)
  1. Backpacking—North Carolina—Guidebooks. 2. Hiking—
North Carolina—Guidebooks. 3. North Carolina—Guidebooks.
I. Title.
GV199.42.N66M54 2011
 796.5109756—dc22

                            2010032660

cloth   15 14 13 12 11   5 4 3 2 1
paper   15 14 13 12 11   5 4 3 2 1

To my wife, Marcy Smith, who encourages
me to do whatever crazy thing comes to mind.
Like writing a book about backpacking.

Contents

The Trips

Blue Ridge Escarpment/North

Blue Ridge Escarpment/South

Great Smoky Mountains

Appalachian Trail

Southern Mountains

Joyce Kilmer–Slickrock Wilderness

Piedmont

Coast

Acknowledgments

This guide comes about thanks to the legions of helpful folks who know far more about backpacking and the state's trails than I. Among them are Chris David, who had no qualms about sharing his favorite trips; Cindy Wooten with Cypress Group of the North Carolina Chapter of the Sierra Club; David Cook, North Carolina Division of Parks and Recreation; Chris Plummer with the Sierra Club's North Carolina Chapter/Capitol Group; the folks at Linvillegorge.net; backcountry guide extraordinaire Burt Kornegay with Slickrock Expeditions; Kate Dixon, Jeff Brewer, Chris Underhill, and Arthur Kelley with the Friends of the Mountains-to-Sea-Trail; Alan Nechemias, who managed to pick the coldest weather to go on scouting trips with me; the *News & Observer*, which offered to let me leave its employ, thereby giving me the time to finish this guide; Bill Graves, my scuba diving instructor (see Introduction); John R. Ray, lead author of the *Chunky Gal Trail and Fires Creek Rim Trail* guide, who offered suggestions for covering the Fires Creek area; the various coffee shops statewide that repeatedly revived me after bouts of camp coffee; and Mark Simpson-Vos, my editor at UNC Press, and Stephanie Wenzel, copyeditor. The only person who can truly appreciate the value of stellar editors is the writer who is constantly being saved by their keen eyes and thoughtful questions.

Backpacking North Carolina

Introduction

The best advice I ever got about backpacking came from my scuba diving instructor. It was the first day of class, and he was going over the basic requirements—about the swim test, about being able to hoist and carry the air tanks and other equipment, and about being able to swap out tanks underwater. Sensing we were becoming overwhelmed by the physical demands of diving, he stopped and smiled.

"Folks," he told us, "I am the laziest man alive, and I assure you that if I can do this, you will have absolutely no problem."

That's my philosophy toward backpacking and the philosophy that drives this guide.

Forget what you may have heard about backpacking, about carrying 40 pounds on your back for 20 miles a day, about developing blisters on top of blisters, about getting caught in a downpour and staying wet for days on end, and about bad camp coffee first thing in the morning. Backpacking isn't about enduring, it's about enjoying. It's about getting away from the masses to enjoy nature untrammeled. It's about enjoying a brilliant night sky nearly devoid of light pollution. It's about stopping and hearing only those sounds generated by nature. It's about experiencing the land as it was before our development-minded forefathers arrived. It's about escape, not exile.

More often than not, this can be accomplished without being your own beast of burden. The trips in this book are about packing in the least distance possible for the optimum backcountry exposure. Indulge me in a brief story.

One of the first backpack trips I took in North Carolina, back in the mid-1990s, was to the Shining Rock Wilderness. It was an ambitious trip: We left Raleigh after work on a Friday and arrived at the trailhead at 10:30 P.M. in a cold drizzle. Despite a planning meeting, we'd woefully miscalculated how long it would take to reach camp at Deep Gap, which was nearly 4 miles and 1,700 vertical feet up. Rather than pitching our tents around midnight as envisioned, we pulled in after 2:00 A.M. The next day was a 6-mile hike across the Shining Rock Ledge, whose rocky spine created some touch-and-go moments with a 40-pound pack (it was late November, so winter weight rules—and gear requirements—applied). The hike out on Sunday was a 9-mile slog down an old roadbed. "Incredible scenery," I thought as I drifted off to sleep on the ride home, "but man am I beat. There must be a better way to do Shining Rock."

A couple years later, I discovered there was: Hike in 4 miles from the Blue Ridge Parkway on the near-flat Ivestor Gap Trail, establish base camp at Shining Rock Gap, and explore more than 30 miles of trail from there with a day pack, a 5-pound load at most. No breaking down and setting up camp anew every day, no searching for a new tree every night to hang your food from, no crossing your fingers and hoping the campsite you covet that evening isn't taken. Best of all, minus that 40 pounds, you can cover twice as much territory. With a full pack, I feel good covering 2 miles in an hour; with a day pack, I can cover 4. Experiencing as much of nature as possible should be your goal when backpacking, not falling into an exhausted sleep on the drive home—especially if you're driving.

So why not just take a day hike, the uninitiated may ask?

I make my case in a nutshell in the last trip in this book, no. 43, Hammocks Beach State Park: Bear Island. Since I know how annoying it is to thumb to another page, I'll summarize. You backpack so you can wake up and listen to nature do a more graceful job of coming to life than you do. You backpack so you can have a breakfast free of distraction, without the paper telling you of the latest calamity, without morning DJs blathering on about last night's reality TV show, and without being asked a thousand questions by the kids before you've had your first sip of coffee. You backpack so you can explore places deep in the wild that you can't reach on a day hike. You backpack so you can have a lunch of cheese, hard salami, and gorp heavy on the M&Ms and know that it's the perfect meal, not a guilty indulgence. You backpack so you can stop at midday and take a nap in a sunny clearing. You backpack so you can take time preparing and eating a meal that may be the best thing you remember eating in your entire life. You backpack so you can lose yourself in a night sky not backlit by human habitation.

You backpack so you can clear your mind, so you can think, so you can simply be and not have to worry about being something in addition to yourself.

Even if you just backpack in a mile, it can make a huge difference. Take the East Rim trip at Linville Gorge (no. 7). Hiking up the backside of Shortoff Mountain, you can't escape the lights of the Morganton/Hickory/Lenoir triangle below. But round the bend a little over a mile in and you're suddenly atop one of the wildest, steepest gorges west of the Rockies. You're instantly transported.

This book aims to get you to these embarkation points as quickly as possible so you can, when possible, get the pack off your back, set up base camp, and explore. It is, I believe, an approach that even my lazy scuba diving instructor could embrace.

BACKPACKING THEN AND NOW

Backpacking gained popularity in the United States during the back-to-nature movement of the late 1960s and early 1970s. A sudden realization that our environment was in peril caused the public to react. One response was a demand for government action: The Environmental Protection Agency was formed in 1970, followed shortly by enactment of clean air standards, the Federal Pesticide Control Act, the Federal Water Pollution Control Act, the Ocean Dumping Act, and the ban on DDT. Another reaction was direct citizen involvement. Earth Day, launched on April 22, 1970, became an immediate success with an estimated 20 million Americans participating.

As part of this push to reconnect with the planet, we began expressing a desire to get out and "commune with nature," as we referred to it in the day. And what a compelling desire it was, considering the backpacking equipment available: canvas tents that leaked if you looked at them the wrong way, bulky and balky cookstoves, mess kits made of tin, packs that could break the back of a pack animal, and the de rigueur outdoors wear of the day, jeans and cotton T-shirts. Backpacking was fun in the 1970s—if it didn't kill you. And if it didn't kill you, you eventually got older and concluded that backpacking was for the young and durable.

If you were part of that boom and that's how you remember backpacking, you probably haven't given much thought to getting back into it. I'm not going to get into a full-blown discussion of gear—there are plenty of books (*The Backpacker's Field Manual*, by Rick Curtis [Three Rivers Press]) and websites (www.backpacker.com/gear/)—that do so in detail. Just allow me a quick observation: If we still backpacked today like we did in the 1970s, someone else would have had to write this book. I don't like being wet. I don't like being cold. And I really don't like being looked upon with pity by a pack mule.

Today's gear is lighter, dries quickly, and is designed to make you forget about the potentially uncomfortable aspects of backcountry travel. That tin mess kit has been replaced by one made of titanium, at a fraction of the weight. Canvas tents have given way to ones made of ripstop nylon that repel water, dry in five minutes, and retain heat in the winter (through thick-wall construction) or vent it in summer (via lots of mesh surface area). No self-respecting backpacker would be caught dead (actually, they might) wearing jeans. Today, only quick-drying, water-repelling, sweat-wicking materials touch our skin.

And today's cookstove has an ignito lighter (no more impotent wet matches), burns fuel from a canister (no fuel spills and minimal fumes), and can have your morning coffee ready in 3 minutes. Oh, and about that coffee: Camp coffee has kept pace with America's increasingly sophisticated taste for caffeine. You can now get a gizmo that makes camp stove espresso.

Backpacking, in short, is no longer a sufferfest. Remember spending a sleepless, rainy night in a canvas tent, fearing the surface tension keeping you dry would break and open the floodgates? Today, the sound of rain on your nylon tent, with you snuggled into your down bag atop your plush, self-inflating air mattress, is a guarantee of a good night's sleep.

I'll offer one last gear mention, at the risk of committing blasphemy in the eyes of the devout. Because cooking could be such a hassle back in the early days, we were often content to toss down a handful of gorp and some jerky and call it a meal. Today, you can buy freeze-dried meals that actually resemble what they claim to be: chicken teriyaki, beef stew, chicken breasts with mashed potatoes, pasta primavera—just about anything you'd cook at home. Heat some water, pour it in the self-cooking pouch, wait 8 minutes, and you've got dinner. And the resealable pouch makes for a handy trash container.

BACKPACKING IN NORTH CAROLINA

Like the idea of winter camping in a spruce/fir forest? Maybe you're into escaping all signs of civilization. Do you like unobscured panoramic views? Or perhaps as a city dweller it's vital that you have an emergency back-country escape within an hour's drive. And maybe you haven't thought of this, but wouldn't it be swell to have an entire island to yourself? You can do all of that in North Carolina (in order: Black Mountains, trips 1–3; Joyce Kilmer–Slickrock Wilderness, trips 32–33; Shining Rock Wilderness, trips 14–16; Raven Rock State Park, trip 40; Bear Island, trip 43.)

You'd be hard-pressed to find a place more geographically diverse than

North Carolina, a state that begins at the Atlantic Ocean and runs to Clingman's Dome, at 6,643 feet the third-highest point east of South Dakota's Black Hills, ceding the no. 1 and 2 spots to fellow Tar Heel peaks Mount Mitchell (6,684 feet) and Mount Craig (6,647 feet).

Let's start with those higher elevations. Above 5,000 feet you'll find remnants of spruce/fir forests that arrived with the last ice age 13,000 years ago and departed from lower elevations with its retreat 10,000 years ago. These relic forests—and seven trips in this guide pass through them—are less Southern Appalachia and more southern Canada. Hiking down the very same mountain topped by a spruce/fir forest, you may pass through a dozen or more ecozones. Grandfather Mountain, for instance, has 16 distinct natural communities. You'll find areas with a subtropical feel (the Joyce Kilmer–Slickrock Wilderness). You'll find mountaintop balds that afford rare—for the East—panoramic views (the Appalachian Trail) as well as passages through canyons 2,000 feet deep (Linville Gorge).

At the Blue Ridge Escarpment, the mountains give way to the Piedmont. North Carolina's Piedmont is just that, "a gentle slope leading from the base of mountains to a region of flat land," according to the Oxford College Dictionary. The mountains don't give up without a fight. Heading east, you'll find disjunct mountain ranges as old as the Appalachians but notably smaller: the South Mountains topping out at 3,000 feet (trip 34), Kings Mountains at 1,700 feet (trip 41), and the Uwharrie Mountains (trips 35–36) around 900 feet. This decline continues through the mid-Piedmont with elevations under 700 feet (Eno River State Park, trip 39) and to Umstead State Park, where the highest spots aren't much more than 400 feet. We say farewell to the Piedmont at Raven Rock State Park, where it's namesake bluff rises 150 feet above the Cape Fear River, which then meanders east into the coastal plain.

With this drop in elevation as the Piedmont rolls east, nature's allure becomes more subtle. Steep mountains are replaced by gently rolling hills, high-country creeks frothing with whitewater become meandering waterways in less of a hurry, and those northern spruce/fir forests are now maturing oak/hickory forests.

Perhaps the most unique trips in this book are at the coast. Here you'll find an upland swamp, a pine savanna, and a passage through pungent galax, all within the span of three miles and all within a whiff of salt air. That's the Croatan National Forest's 20-mile Neusiok Trail (trip 42). And how many times do you get to have a barrier island, all 892 acres, to yourself? It happens off season at Bear Island (trip 43).

Weather

As you might imagine, a state that starts at sea level and rises to almost 6,700 feet has a range of weather. On a winter's day, you can be in your shorts and a T-shirt hiking in 60-degree weather at the coast, or bundled against subzero wind-chill conditions on the Black Mountain Crest Trail. Even on the same hike you can experience radical changes: A climb up to Clingman's Dome can begin in 50-degree weather on the Noland Creek Trail and end 14 miles and 4,000 vertical feet later in blowing snow on Clingman's Dome.

Here are some attention-grabbing stats: Fifty inches of snow have fallen on Mount Mitchell (trips 1–3) in one "weather event" (the Great Blizzard of 1993); wind gusts in excess of 200 miles per hour have been recorded on Grandfather Mountain (trips 4–5)—shortly before the anemometer blew away. Lake Toxaway in Transylvania County (near Panthertown Valley, trip 28) gets about 92 inches of rain a year; Asheville, 35 crow-fly miles to the north, gets just 37 inches annually. The temperature has reached 110 degrees in Fayetteville not far from Raven Rock (trip 40), and it's dropped to 34 below zero on Mount Mitchell (trip 2).

Those facts should serve as ample supporting evidence when I say it's especially important to pack prepared in North Carolina. Regardless of season, you should always take rain gear. Few things can dampen your spirits more than being perpetually wet. Likewise, you should always take a pack cover as well. Even if it doesn't rain, passing through a tight heath passage thick with morning dew can drench you and your pack just as thoroughly as a downpour.

In the summer, you should plan your hikes to avoid ridgelines as much as possible in the afternoons. Thunderstorms tend to build during mid-afternoon, and you need only check out the blackened tree trunks on any crest trail to realize this is lightning country.

If you plan to backpack in winter, you should have a four-season tent. It needn't be expedition quality, with walls capable of bearing 3 feet of snow. But it should have minimal mesh to keep your body heat from escaping.

If you're hiking a more primitive area with lots of water, check to see if rain is in the forecast. If it is, ask yourself if you're comfortable crossing creeks with moving water that could be knee-high or higher. The Slickrock Creek Loop (trip 33), for instance, has 16 crossings that, somehow, seem to get bigger, deeper, and faster as you go *up*stream. The Wilson Creek area, especially Hunt Fish Falls (trip 8) and Harper Creek (trip 9), have multiple crossings that can become challenging when swelled by rain.

It's a terrible feeling when your trip (and safety) is jeopardized because you didn't prepare. It's a feeling of utmost satisfaction when you've got just the right equipment to deal with what nature has up its sleeve.

Hunting

Hunting is allowed in national forests in North Carolina (Croatan, Pisgah, Nantahala, and Uwharrie); it is not allowed in national parks (Blue Ridge Parkway and Great Smoky Mountains National Park) or state parks (Mount Mitchell, Grandfather Mountain, South Mountains, Umstead, Eno River, Raven Rock, Crowders Mountain, Hammocks Beach, and portions of Falls Lake).

Where hunting is allowed, the seasons vary by type of critter and by region of the state. In general, for the purposes of backpacking, the main seasons are deer and bear, both of which occur in the fall. Seasons for smaller game and birds vary as well, but most are over at the end of February. Plus, seasons can vary from year to year.

Your best bet for finding out whether a trip you have planned coincides with hunting season is to consult with the N.C. Wildlife Resources Commission through their website, www.ncwildlife.org.

TRIP PLANNING

To the novice, planning a backpacking trip can seem an overwhelming task. After all, you are venturing into the woods and need to take with you everything you'll need to survive, from prescription medicines and basic first aid supplies to food to water to water filter to kitchen utensils to clothes to your bed to the roof over your head. In essence, you're hauling a life support system on your back. You might as well be going to the moon.

Not exactly allaying your concerns, am I?

I didn't intend to, because you need to take backpacking seriously. Forgetting to pack extra underwear could just mean you'll be a little gamier at trail's end. Forgetting your water filter could have you marching peeved and parched back to the car far earlier than planned. Forgetting your fleece pullover could mean a very cold evening of stargazing. So yes, take it seriously, but also realize that planning and preparing for your trip is every much a part of the experience as actually hiking through the woods. A well-prepared backpacker is a happy backpacker.

Again, I'm not going to dwell on gear—you can get all the gear information you want on the Internet. But I'll offer a couple quick bits of advice.

Essential gear. If you're interested in backpacking, you've probably done some hiking. Thus, you're likely to have the basics: boots, clothes, water bottles, and first aid kit. Now, if you've roamed the aisles of your local REI or Great Outdoor Provision Co., you're probably aware that you can spend a small fortune on the next level of gear required. A good backpack can easily run $300; a sleeping bag, $400; a tent, $500. Fortunately, you can also rent those items at many outfitters. It might not be top-of-the-line, but it's certainly serviceable apparatus that shouldn't detract from the experience.

If you're going with an experienced group, you may not have to worry about water filters and cookstoves. If not, see about borrowing from a backpacking friend (some outfitters also rent these items). If that's not an option, you can treat water with tablets and buy an entry-level stove for as little as $30. A trip to the local mart of your choice (Wal or K, or Target) can hook you up with the rest of your basics—mess kit, cup, spork, waterproof matches, cat hole trowel, flashlight, etc.—for a pittance.

There are three pieces of gear that aren't considered mandatory but should be.

- **Hiking poles.** Hiking up Round Bald on the Appalachian Trail one summer afternoon, I met a 74-year-old man from Atlanta leaning on a pair of hiking poles. I asked how long he'd been hiking with the poles. "Not long enough," he replied good-naturedly. "I wish I'd started using them 10 years sooner." There's a silly stigma attached to hiking poles, that they're some sort of crutch. In fact, they're intended to keep you from needing crutches. The reality is that for hikers, especially those bearing a full pack, they will extend the life of your knees. They'll also speed you up, aid with stability on rocky trails, keep you from tumbling headlong on steep descents, greatly improve your odds of successfully crossing creeks, and let you cover a lot more ground. If you don't already view them as mandatory, you should.

- **Hydration bladder.** No one drinks as much water as they should on the trail. I think a lot of the problem is that water bottles, on most packs, are a pain to get to. Get a hydration bladder, fill it, store it under your pack hood, and clip the hose to your pack strap. Water when you need it. Keep hydrated and you'll be surprised at how much shorter the trail seems; dehydration will zap your strength faster than being underfed.

- **Lightweight day pack.** As I mentioned earlier, the goal of this book is to get your backpack off as quickly as possible. Pack in a short distance, set up base camp, explore. And do that exploring with one of the new breed of lightweight day packs. I've been using an REI Flashpack made of 140-denier ripstop nylon coated with polyurethane. It weighs 10 ounces, has a volume of 1,100 cubic inches, and tucks away nicely when not in use. Best of all, the newer models are bladder compatible. That size, by the way, is more than adequate to hold rain gear, an extra layer or two, lunch, first aid kit, a headlamp/flashlight, and just about any other essential you need to take on a day hike.

Pick an easy trip. More than half the trips in this guide are suitable for beginners (See "Best Trips by Category"). A popular starter is the Birkhead Wilderness loop in the Uwharrie National Forest (trip 35). It's not long (7.4 miles); the trail is easy to follow (despite being a wilderness, the trail is marked); it's not a hard hike (the elevation gains are gradual); and being mid-Piedmont, the weather is generally mild. Look for a short trip, look for a trip that doesn't gain a load of altitude, look for a trip where water should be plentiful, and try to make your first trip during a mild time of the year.

Plan, plan, plan. Get a map of the area you're going to and plot out your trip. Figure out how many miles you can cover in a day, and make sure there are campsites at the appropriate stops along the way. If it's winter, remember that you're dealing with short days; the sun may not hit some slopes in steep, shaded areas until as late as 10 A.M., and it may be dark by 5:30 P.M. Take note of water sources. Call the appropriate land manager beforehand to make sure no extenuating circumstances exist. Make a packing list. Include everything you plan to take (see the "Backpack Checklist" section). Mark items off as you load them into your pack.

How to Use This Book

In writing this guide I've tried to keep in mind the things I need to know when I go backpacking. I say that not to sound like a know-it-all. Quite the contrary. I say that because every time I head out, I feel like a novice, like I'm doing it all over again for the first time, as a backpacking Yogi Berra might say. If I write it down, I'm more likely to remember it. Thus, every trip in this book includes a detailed information box covering the key information you need. "Distance" and "No. of days" appear at the beginning of the general description for each trip.

Distance: In most cases, the distance listed is the distance to be covered wearing a full pack. In some cases, the distance is broken down into how far you'll be carrying a full pack, how far you'll be day hiking.

No. of days: Tells you how many days you should expect to spend on this trip, as described. Often a minimum is given as well as the ideal amount of time you should allot for further exploration.

Trailhead: This is where your trip begins. In most cases, it's where it ends, too. In cases where you end up elsewhere, I describe how to set up a car shuttle. And in cases where shuttle service is available, I share who provides it for backpackers.

Loop/one-way (with shuttle recommendations): Is the trail a loop, meaning your trip starts and ends at the same spot? Or do you hike a linear trail, then return via the same route or set up a shuttle? (See "Trailhead.")

Difficulty: The difficulty of a trail is subjective; one man's Bataan may be another's stroll around the lake. Some guides decline to pass judgment at all. I've elected to include difficulty ratings because I believe it provides a baseline for determining whether a trip is right for you. And as you get a few trips from this guide under your belt, you'll have a sense of how I perceive a trail and can adjust accordingly.

- *Easy*: Relatively flat, short (generally less than three miles a day), and with fairly consistent, even trail surface.

- *Moderate*: Longer (3–5 miles a day) with some elevation, usually in the form of rolling hills or gradual, sustained climbs.
- *Hard*: Length may be as short as three miles; but the trail surface is often rocky and rooty, and there is considerable elevation gain (and loss).
- *Really hard*: Could involve either long stretches between campsites or a distance as short as three miles but over extremely challenging terrain consisting of steep climbs, precipitous drops, scrambling over boulders and rock face, and possibly even removing your pack and transporting it by rope.

Campsites (with GPS coordinates): In some instances, this may mean specifically designated and marked campsites. In others, it may simply mean a spot flat enough to accommodate a tent. Do not assume that a listed campsite is near water.

Maps: For most trips in this book there is a good topographic map tailored to the area you're exploring. In cases where there isn't a tailored topo map, I've included the appropriate U.S. Geological Survey topo maps.

Follow the trail: Describes the trip shown on the accompanying map.

Fee? Gives any entrance/camping fees.

Water (with GPS coordinates): Lists reliable spots to find water. Unless otherwise indicated (in the case of springs, for instance), this is a water source that must be filtered. I've tried to avoid listing water sources known to be intermittent.

Land manager: This is the agency presiding over the land you'll be hiking. Knowing whose land a trail is on can give you a feel for the type of trail you'll be hiking. Trails in this book come under four categories of land managers:

- *N.C. Division of Parks and Recreation* Trails in North Carolina's State Parks are well marked and blazed and are generally well maintained. Creek crossings, even minor ones, are bridged. State parks trails either all or partially on state land in this guide are in Mount Mitchell State Park/Black Mountains, trips 1–2; Grandfather Mountain State Park, trips 4–5; Stone Mountain State Park, trip 12; South Mountains State Park, trip 34; Umstead State Park, trip 37; Falls Lake State Recreation Area, trip 38; Eno River State Park, trip 39; Raven Rock State Park, trip 40; Crowders Mountain State Park, trip 41; and Hammocks Beach State Park: Bear Island, trip 43.

- *National Park Service* These are possibly the best-maintained trail networks in the state. Trails are typically well groomed, well marked, and well bridged. National Park Service trails in this guide include Blue Ridge Parkway's Doughton Park: Basin Cove Loop, trip 11, and Great Smoky Mountains National Park trips 17–22.

- *USDA Forest Service* Gifford Pinchot, the father and first chief of the Forest Service, summed up the mission of his agency thus: "to provide the greatest amount of good for the greatest amount of people in the long run." Thus, the Forest Service has the challenging task of balancing recreational use with wildlife management and timber management. The Forest Service has more than 1.2 million acres to keep track of in North Carolina's four national forests—Croatan, Pisgah, Nantahala, and Uwharrie. With such a broad mission and with dwindling budgets and staff, trail maintenance isn't always at the top of the service's to-do list. Trails on Forest Service land tend to be more on the wild side, with less maintenance, fewer directional markings, and minimal safety features (bridges over creeks with thigh-deep water, for instance). Trails in wilderness areas are even more primitive. Trips with trails either all or partially on Forest Service land in this guide are Black Mountains, trips 1–3; Linville Gorge, trips 6–7; Wilson Creek, trips 8–10; Shining Rock, trips 14–16; Appalachian Trail, trips 23–27; Panthertown Valley, trip 28; Fires Creek, trips 29–31; Joyce Kilmer–Slickrock Wilderness, trips 32–33; Uwharrie Mountains, trips 35–36; and Croatan National Forest: Neusiok Trail, trip 42.

- *Private* One trip in this book is on privately owned land: no. 13, Montreat: Graybeard Mountain. The Montreat Conference Center has dedicated 2,500 of its 4,000 acres to "wilderness," which includes 13 hiking trails. Montreat trails are open to the public.

Another indicator of trail condition is whether the trail is part of a longer trail system. Backpacking on the Appalachian Trail north of Hot Springs one early November day, I met a southbound thru-hiker. "It's so nice to be in North Carolina," he gushed. "There's switchbacks, the trails are maintained, they're easy to follow. . . ."

Membership in a bigger trail network definitely has its privileges, most notably a dedicated volunteer base that keeps the trails in top condition. In this guide, you'll find trips on two major trail systems, the Appalachian

Trail and the Mountains-to-Sea Trail. When you see that a trip is on either of these systems, most likely the trail will be in good shape and short on sections where the trail goes straight up the mountain.

- Trips in this guide on the Appalachian Trail: no. 23, Carvers Gap to US 19E; no. 24, Max Patch; no. 25, Max Patch to Hot Springs; no. 26, Hot Springs to Rich Mountain Loop; and no. 27, Standing Indian Loop.
- Trips either all or partially on the Mountains-to-Sea Trail: no. 1, Black Mountains: Mount Mitchell/Colbert Ridge; no. 2, Mount Mitchell Trail; no. 7, Linville Gorge: East Rim; no. 11, Doughton Park: Basin Cove; no. 12, Stone Mountain State Park; no. 14, Sam Knob; no. 20, Smokies: Deep Creek; no. 38, Falls Lake; no. 39, Eno River; and no. 42, Croatan National Forest: Neusiok Trail.

Trip highlights: Gives reasons why you should do this hike, expressed in a sentence or two and elaborated upon in the accompanying text.

Special considerations: Mentions restrictions (e.g., nesting eagles, icy conditions that may close roads in winter) that might affect your trip.

Night hike in? Is there a campsite on the trail that you could safely get to in the dark (using a headlamp)? Especially handy if you're leaving after work and are pressed for time.

Solo? Is this a trip safely done without hiking companions? Another subjective call, true; you are the best judge of your soloing ability. My thumbs up or down is based primarily on how technically challenging the trail is and how heavily the trail is traveled (is someone likely to come along and find you if you sprain an ankle?).

Family friendly? Again, this is subjective. Grandfather Mountain may be friendly for the Swiss Family Robinson—but not many other tribes. Again, I'll share some thoughts that hopefully will help you decide if the trip is right for your clan.

Bailout options: If things don't go well—the weather goes bad, you develop a case of the mumps—are there options for abandoning?

Seasons: Gives the best seasons to explore—and seasons to avoid.

Weather: Are there special weather concerns unique to this trip?

Solitude rating: Are you far from the madding crowds? Here's the rating scale:

1—Don't come here expecting to escape your fellow man.

2—Forget your matches? You'll find someone to borrow from.

3—Mix of people and solitude.

4—Expect to see more squirrels than people.

5—Hello? *Hello!?*

Nearest outfitter: Forget something? Need something? Just want something? Here's where you can pick up anything from fuel to a sleeping pad.

Hunting allowed? Hunting is allowed on most National Forest Service lands. Hunting seasons vary by region of the state and can vary from year to year. Your best bet is to check the N.C. Wildlife Resources Commission website, www.ncwildlife.org, and click on Hunting/Seasons and Bag Limits.

More info: Where to go for additional information.

Backpack Checklist

A checklist is essential when packing for a trip. Over time, you'll tailor your list to your specific needs. For starters, here's my basic checklist:

FOOD

BREAKFAST	LUNCH	DINNER
__ oatmeal	__ bagels	__ prepackaged meal
__ pop tarts	__ cheese	__ tea
__ coffee	__ peanut butter	__ chocolate
__ nuts	__ power bars	

KITCHEN

__ stove	__ utensils	__ water filter
__ fuel	__ French press mug	__ matches
__ cookset	__ knife	__ water bottles (2)

PERSONAL

__ toilet paper	__ toothbrush	__ hand sanitizer
__ soap	__ space blanket	__ first aid kit

SHELTER

__ tent (poles, stakes, ground cloth)	__ sleeping pad
__ lantern/inside light	__ sleeping bag

MISCELLANEOUS

__ headlamp	__ rope	__ hiking poles

CLOTHES

__ thin base layer	__ camp Keens	__ fleece hat
__ midweight fleece	__ rain jacket	__ boots
__ T-shirt(s)	__ rain pants	__ hat
__ convertible pants	__ gloves	__ swim shorts
__ wool socks	__ glove liners	

Best Trips by Category

Looking for something in particular in a trip?
(Trip numbers are in parentheses.)

BEGINNER

These trips are good for folks just getting started.

1. AT: Carvers Gap to US 19E (**23**)
2. AT: Max Patch (**24**)
3. AT: Hot Springs to Rich Mountain Loop (**26**)
4. Croatan National Forest: Neusiok Trail (**42**)
5. Crowders Mountain State Park (**41**)
6. Eno River State Park: Mountains-to-Sea Trail (**39**)
7. Falls Lake: Mountains-to-Sea Trail (**38**)
8. Fires Creek: East Rim (**30**)
9. Fires Creek: West Rim (**31**)
10. Hammocks Beach State Park: Bear Island (**43**)
11. Linville Gorge: East Rim (**7**)
12. Montreat: Graybeard Mountain (**13**)
13. Panthertown Valley (**28**)
14. Raven Rock State Park (**40**)
15. Shining Rock: Ivestor Gap (**15**)
16. Shining Rock: Sam Knob Loop (**14**)
17. Smokies: Cataloochee Valley (**18**)
18. Smokies: Deep Creek Loop (**20**)
19. Smokies: Shuckstack (short) (**21**)
20. South Mountains State Park (**34**)
21. Stone Mountain State Park (**12**)
22. Wilson Creek: Hunt Fish Falls Loop (**8**)
23. Wilson Creek: Schoolhouse Ridge Loop (**10**)
24. Umstead State Park (**37**)
25. Uwharrie National Forest: Birkhead Wilderness (**35**)

HIKING IN AT NIGHT

Only have time for a weekend trip and bummed that you'll burn part of both days traveling to and from the trailhead? Buy a little extra time by leaving Friday after work, driving to the trailhead, and hiking in under the stars.

"I think it provides an interesting perspective," says 2006 Appalachian Trail thru-hiker Melissa Fleishman (trail name GA-ME). "The most important thing to note is nighttime really isn't as dark as we think it is. Especially if you're hiking into the night—hiking through sunset into dusk and then darkness, don't rush to put on that headlamp. It's amazing how well the human eye adapts to the dark, given enough time." Try to convince your hiking buddies to follow suit, she says, because once one headlamp appears, it's turn on the lights, the party's over.

This guide advises as to whether a trail is suitable for a night hike in. The recommendation is based on how challenging the trail is to the first campsites. If the trail is exceptionally steep, is narrow with sharp drops on one (or both) sides, and has lots of rocks and/or roots, it won't be recommended for a night hike in, at least for beginning backpackers.

BASE CAMP

These trips require a short backpack in, establishing a base camp, then day hiking from there.

1. Doughton Park: Basin Cove Loop (11)
2. Hammocks Beach State Park: Bear Island (43)
3. Panthertown Valley (28)
4. Shining Rock: Ivestor Gap (15)
5. Smokies: Clingman's Dome Approach (19)
6. Stone Mountain State Park (12)
7. Wilson Creek: Hunt Fish Falls Loop (8)

FAMILY

These outings are suitable for the entire clan.

1. AT: Max Patch (24)
2. AT: Hot Springs to Rich Mountain Loop (26)
3. Fires Creek: East Rim (30)
4. Hammocks Beach State Park: Bear Island (43)

TENT, SWEET TENT

After a long day on the trail, there's nothing I look forward to more than taking refuge in the comfort of a homey tent. Whether it's to curl up with a good, lightweight (in the physical, if not literary sense) book; to write in my journal; or fall immediately into a deep sleep, I like my tent to feel like an extension of my home. To that end, I like to pack a few extravagances.

LED lantern. My 4.8-ounce Black Diamond lantern casts the entire tent in a warm glow—no inky, ominous shadows beyond the glare of my headlamp.

Crocheted tent attic. My wife crochets, and she made me the coolest tent attic. It's got a tight weave to keep stuff from falling through, adds a splash of color to an otherwise dull tent, and makes me smile whenever I see it. (You can find a pattern at nchikes.com.)

A book. How often do you get a chance to curl up and indulge yourself with a good read? Nothing like a good tale in a cozy tent.

Here are a few more tips to create a homelike atmosphere:

Hang your watch from your attic. A small thing, but it adds a certain homeyness and it's easy to find.

Organize your stuff. An organized tent is a happy tent—and one that contributes to an efficient campsite.

 5. Montreat: Graybeard Mountain (13)
 6. Panthertown Valley (28)
 7. Raven Rock State Park (40)
 8. Shining Rock: Sam Knob Loop (14)
 9. Shining Rock: Ivestor Gap (15)
10. Smokies: Cataloochee Valley (18)
11. Smokies: Deep Creek Loop (20)
12. South Mountains State Park (34)
13. Stone Mountain State Park (12)
14. Umstead State Park (37)
15. Uwharrie National Forest: Birkhead Wilderness (35)
16. Wilson Creek: Hunt Fish Falls Loop (8)

SWIMMING/WATERPLAY

In the right season, is there reason to get in the water?

1. Hammocks Beach State Park: Bear Island (43)
2. Linville Gorge (6)

MAKING NICE 24/7

Even if you're hiking with your best friend, on a backpack trip you're together constantly. How do you not let your fellow campers' annoying habits—whistling the same tune incessantly, telling the same story about "that time in Glacier" over and over, or taking 15 minutes to get their boot fit "just right"—get to you?

The key is to not spend 24 hours a day together. Backpackers who do a lot of trips with groups suggest hiking at least part of the day on your own. Have a discussion over breakfast about the trail(s) you'll be taking, discuss a spot to meet for lunch and where you plan to camp that night, then proceed at your own pace. That way, if the group whistler gets stuck on the theme from *Bridge on the River Kwai* or you want to spend 20 minutes taking pictures of a flowering rhododendron, there won't be an incident. And you can share your varying perspectives on the same trip at day's end.

    3. Smokies: Deep Creek Loop (**20**)
    4. Wilson Creek: Hunt Fish Falls Loop (**8**)
    5. Wilson Creek: Harper Creek/North Harper Creek Loop (**9**)

FISHING

Should I bring a pole?

    1. Linville Gorge (**6**)
    2. Joyce Kilmer–Slickrock Wilderness: Slickrock Creek Loop (**33**)
    3. Panthertown Valley (**28**)
    4. Stone Mountain State Park (**12**)
    5. Wilson Creek: Hunt Fish Falls Loop (**8**)
    6. Wilson Creek: Harper Creek/North Harper Creek Loop (**9**)

WATERFALLS

And I mean more than just a trickle of water over a three-foot ledge.

    1. Joyce Kilmer–Slickrock Wilderness: Slickrock Creek Loop (**33**)
    2. Panthertown Valley (**28**)
    3. South Mountains State Park (**34**)
    4. Wilson Creek: Hunt Fish Falls Loop (**8**)
    5. Wilson Creek: Harper Creek/North Harper Creek Loop (**9**)

FILTERING WATER

That mountain stream may look clear, but who knows what microbes lurk within. My advice: Don't chance it. Treat your water. Here are your options:

Boiling. This is the most effective way to kill pathogens. Keep water at a full boil for at least one minute.

Chemicals. Iodine and chlorine dioxide tablets are the most common chemical treatments. Iodine was popular for years, despite the taste it leaves. (During the 1970s, a popular fix was to add Tang, the drink of astronauts.) Iodine has numerous drawbacks in addition to its disagreement with the tongue: Some people are allergic to it, and it's light-sensitive and must be stored in a dark bottle. It also isn't effective against all microorganisms, including cryptosporidium. Newer liquid treatment solutions, however, get good marks for working relatively quickly (20 minutes) and having no taste. Chlorine dioxide is a more effective chemical solution.

Filters. You have many choices for water pumps that filter out sediments and microorganisms. They're generally reliable but can be slow and tedious, and they must be cleaned regularly.

Ultraviolet light. The same method long used to sterilize hospital equipment is now being used to sterilize stream water. UV treatment systems tend to be more expensive and require batteries.

VISTAS

These trips have good views, really good views.

1. AT: Carvers Gap to US 19E (**23**)
2. AT: Max Patch (**24**)
3. AT: Max Patch to Hot Springs (**25**)
4. AT: Hot Springs to Rich Mountain Loop (**26**)
5. Black Mountains: Mount Mitchell/Colbert Ridge Approach (**1**)
6. AT: Standing Indian Loop (**27**)
7. Crowders Mountain State Park (**41**)
8. Black Mountains: Mount Mitchell Trail (**2**)
9. Black Mountains: Woody Ridge/Crest Trail (**3**)
10. Fires Creek: East Rim (**30**)
11. Fires Creek: Rim Trail (**29**)
12. Fires Creek: West Rim (**31**)
13. Grandfather Mountain: Profile Trail (**4**)

14. Grandfather Mountain: Daniel Boone Scout Trail (**5**)
15. Hammocks Beach State Park: Bear Island (**43**)
16. Panthertown Valley (**28**)
17. Shining Rock: Daniel Boone Loop (**16**)
18. Shining Rock: Ivestor Gap (**15**)
19. Shining Rock: Sam Knob Loop (**14**)
20. Smokies: Clingman's Dome Approach (**19**)
21. Smokies: Shuckstack (short) (**21**)
22. Smokies: Shuckstack (long) (**22**)

BALDS/OPEN AREAS

If you get claustrophobic, these trails are for you.

1. AT: Carvers Gap to US 19E (**23**)
2. AT: Max Patch (**24**)
3. AT: Max Patch to Hot Springs (**25**)
4. AT: Standing Indian Loop (**27**)
5. Black Mountains: Woody Ridge/Crest Trail (**3**)
6. Fires Creek: East Rim (**30**)
7. Hammocks Beach State Park: Bear Island (**43**)
8. Panthertown Valley (**28**)
9. Shining Rock: Sam Knob Loop (**14**)
10. Shining Rock: Ivestor Gap (**15**)
11. Smokies: Clingman's Dome Approach (**19**)

SPRUCE/FIR FORESTS

These trips top out high, in terrain that will make you feel you're hiking in Canada.

1. Black Mountains: Mount Mitchell/Colbert Ridge Approach (**1**)
2. Black Mountains: Mount Mitchell Trail (**2**)
3. Black Mountains: Woody Ridge/Crest Trail (**3**)
4. Grandfather Mountain: Profile Trail (**4**)
5. Grandfather Mountain: Daniel Boone Scout Trail (**5**)
6. Smokies: Clingman's Dome Approach (**19**)
7. Smokies: Mount Sterling (**17**)

NIGHT SKY: WHAT'S UP THERE?

One of the big pluses of putting a pack on your back and escaping civilization: escaping the accompanying light pollution. To stand atop Shining Rock (trips 15 and 16) or Max Patch (trip 24) or on Bear Island (trip 43) on a clear night is to experience the night sky in a whole new—and sometimes confusing—way.

Confusing, because while most of us can pick out the Big Dipper in an instant, our constellation cognition gets fuzzy from there. Remedy that by adding this to your pre-trip prep list: Download a handy night-sky viewing guide. Books are available on the subject, but books are heavy. Several websites show you not only what's in the sky, but what's in the sky on a specific night, from an exact location (you'll need your longitude and latitude). Do an Internet search for "night sky backpack chart" and you'll have several options to choose from. Less specific laminated night-sky viewing charts are also available at hiking and outdoors stores.

WILDFLOWERS

Here's where the wildflower viewing is especially good.

1. AT: Carvers Gap to US 19E (**23**)
2. AT: Max Patch (**24**)
3. AT: Max Patch to Hot Springs (**25**)
4. Raven Rock State Park (**40**)
5. Shining Rock: Ivestor Gap (**15**)
6. Shining Rock: Sam Knob Loop (**14**)
7. Smokies: Cataloochee Valley (**18**)

ESCAPING PEOPLE

You may see someone else, but probably not (especially if you hike in the recommended season).

1. Black Mountains: Mount Mitchell/Colbert Ridge Approach (**1**)
2. Black Mountains: Woody Ridge/Crest Trail (**3**)
3. Croatan National Forest: Neusiok Trail (**42**)
4. Fires Creek: Rim Trail (**29**)
5. Hammocks Beach State Park: Bear Island (**43**)

GOING SOLO

Sometimes when you want to get away from it all, you want to get away from it *all*—including people. A solo backpack trip is rewarding on several fronts, from the true sense of serenity to the knowledge that you truly are surviving on your own.

A few things to consider when heading out on your own:

Pick a popular route. True, your goal here is to escape people. But you don't want to take a trip where you won't see anyone. You'll welcome the sight of another backpacker if you run out of matches or, knock on wood, sprain an ankle.

Pick a campsite away from roads. By the same token, you want to avoid getting too close to too many people. Typically, campers who camp with such essentials as an 80-gallon cooler won't hike in beyond a mile or two. Keep your campsites beyond this perimeter and you'll increase your likelihood of camping with more like-minded folks.

Double-check your equipment. On a group trip, it's no big deal if you run out of fuel for your camp stove or your water filter breaks. On your own, it could mean cold oatmeal and taking your chances drinking straight from a stream.

Leave your itinerary with someone. You should do this even if you're hiking in a group, but it's especially important hiking solo. The more detailed you can make your itinerary, the better.

Make yourself visible. When possible, check in with a ranger or sign a trail log—anything to let someone reliable know you're on the trail.

Don't take chances. When you reach a rain-swollen stream crossing or a potentially sketchy scramble, ask yourself what will happen if you have a problem. If you don't come up with a survivable answer, don't do it.

6. Joyce Kilmer–Slickrock Wilderness: Naked Ground Loop (**32**)
7. Joyce Kilmer–Slickrock Wilderness: Slickrock Creek Loop (**33**)
8. Smokies: Clingman's Dome Approach (**19**)

WINTER

These trips either are best done in winter or have a special winter appeal.

1. Black Mountains: Mount Mitchell Trail (**2**)
2. Black Mountains: Woody Ridge/Crest Trail (**3**)
3. Croatan National Forest: Neusiok Trail (**42**)
4. Crowders Mountain State Park (**41**)

SURVIVING THE 14-HOUR NIGHT

Winter backpacking is popular in North Carolina because of the generally mild weather. But what to do about those nights that start at 5:30 P.M. and last for 14 hours?

This is less of a problem if you're hiking with a group. If your destination allows campfires (they aren't allowed in wilderness areas, FYI), the rituals of gathering fuel and keeping the fire going will pass time. A fire also keeps you warm and provides a natural gathering spot to share stories.

Early sunsets also give you time to curl up in your tent with a good book. And plenty of backpackers take their MP3 players on the trail, listening to music, catching up on podcasts, or hearing a book on tape.

Whether you're a backpacker who loves your gadgets or someone who likes to leave technology behind, don't rule out the possibility of a short night hike. This is a particularly great option if you're camping in a more open area—on or near a bald, for instance. Keep a close eye on landmarks to remind you where you are and where you've been; the last place you want to be is in a dark clearing a mile from camp, with no idea of how to get back. Night hikes are great for stargazing, and they also give your other senses a chance to excel: The sounds of the night forest do wonders to jump-start one's imagination.

5. Eno River State Park: Mountains-to-Sea Trail (**39**)
6. Hammocks Beach State Park: Bear Island (**43**)
7. Panthertown Valley (**28**)
8. Shining Rock: Daniel Boone Loop (**16**)
9. Smokies: Clingman's Dome Approach (**19**)
10. Raven Rock State Park (**40**)
11. Uwharrie National Forest: Birkhead Wilderness (**35**)
12. Uwharrie National Forest: Uwharrie Recreation Trail (**36**)

EPICS

For our purposes, a trip of 15 or more miles with a full pack on your back qualifies as epic.

1. AT: Max Patch to Hot Springs (**25**)
2. AT: Standing Indian Loop (**27**)
3. Black Mountains: Mount Mitchell/Colbert Ridge Approach (**1**)
4. Croatan National Forest: Neusiok Trail (**42**)

Resources

The following offer additional information on hiking and backpacking.

HIKING WEBSITES

Carolina Mountain Club, www.carolinamtnclub.com. Comprehensive database of hikes in the mountains.

Carolina Outdoors Guide, www.carolinaoutdoorsguide.com. Comprehensive list of public recreation lands in North Carolina; This Land, Your Land blog includes current trail news from throughout the state.

Friends of the Mountains-to-Sea Trail, www.ncmst.org. Official site of the 1,000-mile-to-be statewide trail-in-progress.

HikeWNC.com, www.hikewnc.info. Trail descriptions and news.

National Park Service, North Carolina lands, www.nps.gov/state/NC.

N.C. Division of Parks and Recreation, www.ncparks.gov. Detailed information on the state's parks, recreation areas, and natural areas.

NCWaterfalls.com, www.ncwaterfalls.com. Good source for finding hikes with waterfalls.

USDA National Forest Service/North Carolina forests, www.cs.unca.edu/nfsnc.

NORTH CAROLINA HIKING GUIDES

Statewide

de Hart, Allen. *Hiking North Carolina's Mountains-to-Sea Trail*. UNC Press, 2000.

———. *North Carolina Hiking Trails*. 4th ed. AMC Books, 2005.

Johnson, Randy. *Hiking North Carolina: A Guide to Nearly 500 of North Carolina's Greatest Hiking Trails*. 2nd ed. Falcon, 2007.

Miller, Joe. *100 Classic Hikes in North Carolina*. Mountaineers Books, 2007.

Mountains

Bernstein, Danny. *Hiking the Carolina Mountains*. Milestone Press, 2007.

Homan, Tim. *Hiking Trails of the Joyce Kilmer–Slickrock & Citico Creek Wildernesses*. 2nd ed. Peachtree, 2007.

Williams, Robert L., Elizabeth W. Williams, and Robert L. Williams III. *50 Hikes in the Mountains of North Carolina*. Backcountry Guides, 2001.

Blue Ridge Parkway

Adkins, Leonard M. *Walking the Blue Ridge*. 3rd ed. UNC Press, 2003.

Bernstein, Danny. *Hiking North Carolina's Blue Ridge Heritage*. Milestone Press, 2009.

Johnson, Randy. *Hiking the Blue Ridge Parkway*. 2nd ed. Falcon, 2010.

Great Smoky Mountains National Park

Adams, Kevin. *Hiking Great Smoky Mountains National Park*. Falcon, 2003.

Great Smoky Mountains Natural History Association. *Hiking Trails of the Smokies*. 1994.

Manning, Russ. *100 Hikes in the Great Smoky Mountains National Park*. 2nd ed. Mountaineers Books, 1999.

Piedmont

Childrey, Don. *Uwharrie Lakes Region Trail Guide: Hiking and Biking in North Carolina's Uwharrie Mountains*. Earthbound Sports, 1998.

BACKPACKING GUIDES AND WEBSITES

Backpacker.com, www.backpacker.com. Website for *Backpacker* magazine; contains trip recommendations, gear guide, advice, and more.

Berger, Karen. *Eyewitness Companions Backpacking & Hiking*. DK Publishing, 2005.

Curtis, Rick. *The Backpacker's Field Manual: A Comprehensive Guide to Mastering Backcountry Skills*. Three Rivers Press, 2005. By the director of Princeton University's Outdoor Action Program.

Kemsley, William, Jr. *Backpacker & Hiker's Handbook*. Stackpole Books, 2008. By the founder of *Backpacker* magazine.

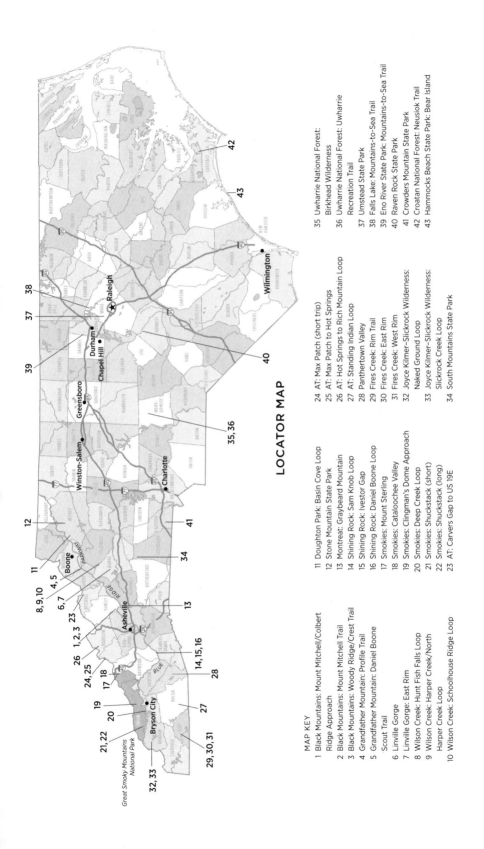

LOCATOR MAP

Great Smoky Mountains National Park

Bryson City
Asheville
Boone
Winston-Salem
Greensboro
Durham
Chapel Hill
Raleigh
Charlotte
Wilmington

MAP KEY

1 Black Mountains: Mount Mitchell/Colbert
   Ridge Approach
2 Black Mountains: Mount Mitchell Trail
3 Black Mountains: Woody Ridge/Crest Trail
4 Grandfather Mountain: Profile Trail
5 Grandfather Mountain: Daniel Boone
   Scout Trail
6 Linville Gorge
7 Linville Gorge: East Rim
8 Wilson Creek: Hunt Fish Falls Loop
9 Wilson Creek: Harper Creek/North
   Harper Creek Loop
10 Wilson Creek: Schoolhouse Ridge Loop

11 Doughton Park: Basin Cove Loop
12 Stone Mountain State Park
13 Montreat: Graybeard Mountain
14 Shining Rock: Sam Knob Loop
15 Shining Rock: Ivestor Gap
16 Shining Rock: Daniel Boone Loop
17 Smokies: Mount Sterling
18 Smokies: Cataloochee Valley
19 Smokies: Clingman's Dome Approach
20 Smokies: Deep Creek Loop
21 Smokies: Shuckstack (short)
22 Smokies: Shuckstack (long)
23 AT: Carvers Gap to US 19E

24 AT: Max Patch (short trip)
25 AT: Max Patch to Hot Springs
26 AT: Hot Springs to Rich Mountain Loop
27 AT: Standing Indian Loop
28 Panthertown Valley
29 Fires Creek: Rim Trail
30 Fires Creek: East Rim
31 Fires Creek: West Rim
32 Joyce Kilmer–Slickrock Wilderness:
   Naked Ground Loop
33 Joyce Kilmer–Slickrock Wilderness:
   Slickrock Creek Loop
34 South Mountains State Park

35 Uwharrie National Forest:
   Birkhead Wilderness
36 Uwharrie National Forest: Uwharrie
   Recreation Trail
37 Umstead State Park
38 Falls Lake: Mountains-to-Sea Trail
39 Eno River State Park: Mountains-to-Sea Trail
40 Raven Rock State Park
41 Crowders Mountain State Park
42 Croatan National Forest: Neusiok Trail
43 Hammocks Beach State Park: Bear Island

The Trips

Blue Ridge Escarpment/North

BLACK MOUNTAINS

In the Black Mountains, you can start your day in a sultry Southern Appalachian oak/hickory forest and by noon be bundled against a cold wind as you explore a spruce/fir forest straight out of the Canadian wild. From the time note-taking Europeans first found the compact range, which runs just 15 miles, the area has been a point of scientific fascination. Early botanists and naturalists—Moses Ashley Curtis, André and François Michaux, John and William Bartram—were intrigued by the range's biodiversity. Elisha Mitchell, a professor at the nascent University of North Carolina in Chapel Hill, lost his life trying to document just how high the range was. (Using the geographic instruments of the day, he determined that the range's highest peak, which would eventually bear his name, was 6,708 feet, just 24 feet off the mountain's official 6,684-foot tally.)

While the American chestnut that greeted these early explorers has long since vanished due to a blight introduced in 1900, and the crestline Fraser fir forests have been battling a pest known as the balsam woolly adelgid, the Black Mountains are as rugged as ever. The USDA Forest Service, which manages a large portion of the Black Mountains, in the Pisgah National Forest, fights an uphill battle keeping trails clear of blowdown from fierce winter storms, but most of the nearly 100 miles of trail that penetrate the Black Mountains are navigable.

The diverse plant life, the rugged geology, and the sense of being well north of the South all play a role in making the Black Mountains a popular backpacking destination. The chance for an encounter with a black bear (the timber wolves and mountain lions of the early explorers' days are long gone) also adds a thrill to the trip. Be advised that there is no "easy" in the Black Mountains, only degrees of less hard. With that in mind, I offer three routes of varying degree of less hardness.

ASHEVILLE

21.6 MILES

NO. OF DAYS: 3–4

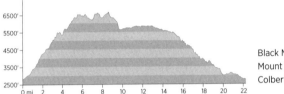

Black Mountains:
Mount Mitchell/
Colbert Ridge Approach

You can drive to the top of the highest peak east of South Dakota's Black Hills, or you can make it an epic trek. If you prefer earning your summit in a pair of Vasques rather than in a Volvo, this trip is for you.

The first half mile of Colbert Ridge Trail draws a few casual hikers, in part because it's across the South Toe River from the popular Carolina Hemlock Recreation Area, in part because it's fairly mellow. Once the true climbing begins, the crowd thins. It's a good climb, sticking to a ridgeline that starts at 2,835 feet and ends 3.9 miles later at 5,760 feet. The last mile, as the trail wraps around the southeast flank of 6,203-foot Winter Star Mountain, is treacherous as well, fumbling over rock outcrops and often obscured by downed trees. A half mile from the top, you'll hike over an intermittent seep, the last water you'll see for the next 6 miles.

Ah, but who needs water when when your thirst for adventure is slaked by bagging 6 of North Carolina's 42 peaks higher than 6,000 feet in as many miles along the Black Mountain Crest Trail? Potato Hill comes first at 6,440 feet, followed by Cattail Peak at 6,600 feet, Balsam Cone at 6,585 feet, Big Tom at 6,526 feet, Mount Craig at 6,647 feet, and, appropriately saving the biggest for last, Mount Mitchell at 6,684 feet—the highest you can get in the eastern United States. There's lots of up-and-down on this ridgeline; the climb up Big Tom includes a climbing rope anchored to help with your ascent up a steep rock face. With a full pack you should allow a good 4 hours to make this passage.

As you crest Big Tom, the solitude you've experienced will end. Some of the more adventurous visitors to Mount Mitchell State Park—and there are more than 300,000 of them annually—hike the mile and a quarter from the main parking lot to Mount Craig and Big Tom before turning back. Expect the solitude factor to evaporate completely once you hit the main parking lot and the gift shop, the snack bar, the museum, the environmental educa-

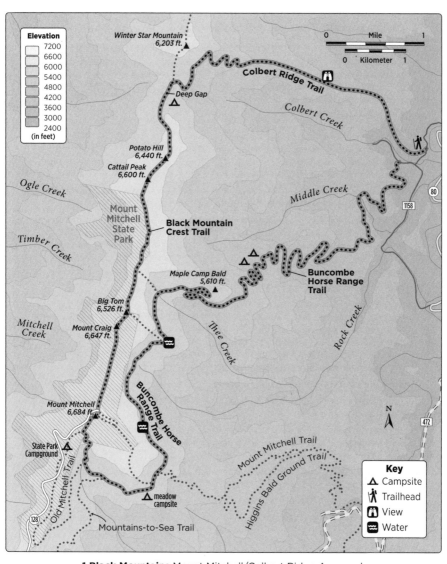

Elevation
7200
6600
6000
5400
4800
4200
3600
3000
2400
(in feet)

0   Mile   1

0   Kilometer   1

Winter Star Mountain
6,203 ft.

Colbert Ridge Trail

Colbert Creek

Deep Gap

Potato Hill
6,440 ft.

Cattail Peak
6,600 ft.

Ogle Creek

Middle Creek

Mount
Mitchell
State
Park

Black Mountain Crest Trail

Timber Creek

80

1158

Maple Camp Bald
5,610 ft.

Buncombe Horse Range Trail

Big Tom
6,526 ft.

Mitchell Creek

Mount Craig
6,647 ft.

Thee Creek

Rock Creek

Buncombe Range Trail

Mount Mitchell
6,684 ft.

N

472

State Park
Campground

Old Mitchell Trail

Mount Mitchell Trail

Higgins Bald Ground Trail

Key
△ Campsite
🚶 Trailhead
👁 View
💧 Water

128

△ *meadow campsite*

Mountains-to-Sea Trail

1 Black Mountains Mount Mitchell/Colbert Ridge Approach

1 **Black Mountains** Mount Mitchell/Colbert Ridge Approach

Trailhead: From the Blue Ridge Parkway, head north on NC 80 for nearly 6 mi.; a half mile past the Carolina Hemlocks Recreation Area go left on Colbert Creek Road/SR 1158. Trailhead parking is a half mile on the right. The trail returns a half mile up the road on SR 1158. From where the trail returns, go right on SR 1158 for a short distance, then veer left on 1158 at the split with SR 1159. Your car is a quarter mile down the road.

Loop/one-way: Loop.

Difficulty: Hard.

Campsites (with GPS coordinates): 3.9 mi., Deep Gap (N35 48.743 W82 15.121); 8.6 mi., Mount Mitchell State Park campground (N35 45.648 W82 16.248); 10.9 mi., Buncombe Horse Range Trail meadow (N35 45.284 W82 15.328); 13.9 mi. (N35 46.523 W82 15.165); 15.5 mi. (N35 47.194 W82 14.149).

Maps: "South Toe River, Mount Mitchell & Big Ivy Trail Maps," USDA Forest Service, Appalachian Ranger District, 40-ft. intervals. USGS: Mount Mitchell, Celo.

Follow the trail: From the trailhead: Hike 3.9 mi. on Colbert Ridge Trail to Black Mountain Crest Trail. Go left on the Crest Trail for 6.0 mi. to the Mount Mitchell State Park parking lot. Continue through the lot, past the concession stand/gift shop and up the paved trail to Mount Mitchell. Within 30 yds. of starting up the trail, go right on Old Mitchell Trail: the spur to the campground is 0.15 mi.; Buncombe Horse Range Trail is 0.9 mi. Go left on Buncombe for the remaining 10.1 mi.

Fee? $18 per night to camp at the Mount Mitchell State Park campground.

Water (with GPS coordinates): Water is an issue on this route. A small seep is found about a half mile from Deep Gap on Colbert Ridge Trail (N35 45.215 W82 14.267). The ridgeline is dry until Mount Mitchell State Park, about 8 mi. (N35 45.648 W82 16.428). On the return trip on the Buncombe Horse Range Trail, water can be found at two spots before the descent begins at Maple Camp Bald, at mile 11.8 (N35 47.194 W82 14.149) and mile 12.5 (N35 46.386 W82 15.466), and again as the trail reaches the valley floor and trailhead.

Land managers: USDA Forest Service; N.C. Division of Parks and Recreation.

Trip highlights: Bagging 6 of the state's 42 peaks higher than 6,000 ft. in a 6-mi. stretch; hiking the highest range along the East Coast.

Special considerations: Lack of water on the first 10 mi. of the trip; ridgeline hiking above 6,000 ft. requires attention to the weather, especially during summer when thunderstorms tend to build in the afternoon.

Night hike in? No. There are no campsites until Deep Gap, and the 3.9-mi. hike in has steep drops and is often obscured by downfall near the top.

Solo? Not recommended. Parts of this trip get little traffic and can be treacherous.

Family friendly? No. Elevation gains, total distance, and lack of water may be especially hard on kids.

Bailout options: No.

Seasons: Fall, spring, summer.

Weather: Snow and ice discourage winter hiking for all but the best prepared. Summer hikers need to keep an eye on storm clouds building after noon.

Solitude rating: 4; 1 around Mount Mitchell State Park.

Nearest outfitter: REI, Asheville, (828) 687-0918, www.rei.com.

Hunting allowed? Local seasons apply in the Pisgah National Forest portion of the hike. No hunting is allowed at the top, in Mount Mitchell State Park.

More info: Mount Mitchell State Park, (828) 675-4611, www.ncparks.gov/Visit/parks/momi/main.php; USDA Forest Service, Appalachian Ranger District, Pisgah National Forest, (828) 682-6146, www.csunca.edu/nfsnc.

At 6,647 feet, Mount Craig offers great views and is one of six 6,000-foot peaks you'll encounter on this trip.

tion center, and the new $1.1 million observation deck topping the peak. (Did I mention the restaurant?) On a summer's day when the temperature is in the 90s down the Blue Ridge Parkway in Asheville, it's likely in the 70s atop Mount Mitchell, making it an especially popular escape.

A quick word about camping: On Day 1, after you climb Colbert Ridge, Deep Gap is a good bet for spending the night. (Get up early enough on Day 2 and you can do a quick mile-long hike up Winter Star Mountain and bag your seventh 6,000-footer of the trip.) You have two options on Night 2. One is a night at the Mount Mitchell State Park campground. Advantage: This is about as high as you can camp in North Carolina. Downside: The campsites are on top of one another and they're $18 a night. Or you can camp in one of the meadows along the Buncombe Horse Range Trail, below the ridgeline and just outside the state park. There's no guarantee you won't have neighbors, but they won't be right on top of you.

If you're doing the 4-day option, there's good day-hiking off the ridgeline (the two-mile Old Mitchell Trail is good, or you can explore the Mountains-to-Sea Trail, taking it west to Balsam Gap, Walker Knob, and beyond) and entertaining people-watching at the state park's tourist attractions.

The return trip on the Buncombe Horse Range Trail begins along an old roadbed that offers some of the best views on this hike. That ends at Maple Bald—as does your ability to find the trail for the next mile or so if you're hiking it in summer when the trail becomes overgrown. Be patient, persevere, keep your compass and map in hand, and soon the trail will again become obvious.

It's all downhill from there.

2 **Black Mountains** Mount Mitchell Trail

ASHEVILLE

11.4 MILES

NO. OF DAYS: 2–3

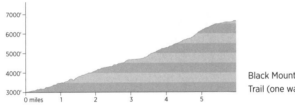

Black Mountains: Mount Mitchell Trail (one way)

Tar Heel mountaineers who complain that there's no good place to train for their expeditions out West—to the Rockies, the Sierra Nevadas, or the Cascades—apparently aren't familiar with the Mount Mitchell Trail.

You want sustained climbing? How about 5.7 miles with little in the way of respiratory respite?

You want vertical challenge? With a total elevation gain of 3,662 feet, this hike compares in gradient with some of the West's most challenging climbs. The assault on Colorado's Longs Peak, for instance, gains 5,100 feet but takes 7 miles to get there.

You want weather? The temperature has dropped to as low as -34 degrees on Mount Mitchell, wind speeds of 178 miles per hour have been recorded, and more than 4 feet of snow have fallen in a single storm (1993's Great Blizzard).

You want rugged? It was a lot more so before the trail became part of the

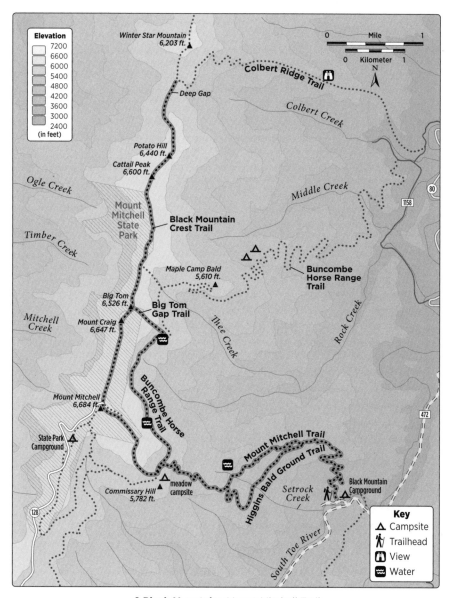

Elevation
7200
6600
6000
5400
4800
4200
3600
3000
2400
(in feet)

Winter Star Mountain
6,203 ft.

Colbert Ridge Trail

0   Mile   1

0   Kilometer   1

N

Deep Gap

Colbert Creek

80

1158

Ogle Creek

Potato Hill
6,440 ft.

Cattail Peak
6,600 ft.

Middle Creek

Mount
Mitchell
State
Park

**Black Mountain
Crest Trail**

Timber Creek

Maple Camp Bald
5,610 ft.

**Buncombe
Horse Range
Trail**

Big Tom
6,526 ft.

**Big Tom
Gap Trail**

Mount Craig
6,647 ft.

Thee Creek

Rock Creek

*Mitchell
Creek*

**Buncombe
Horse
Range
Trail**

Mount Mitchell
6,684 ft.

Mount Mitchell Trail

472

State Park
Campground

meadow
campsite

Higgins Bald Ground Trail

*Setrock
Creek*

Black Mountain
Campground

Commissary Hill
5,782 ft.

128

South Toe River

Key
△ Campsite
🚹 Trailhead
📷 View
🌊 Water

2 Black Mountains Mount Mitchell Trail

2 **Black Mountains** Mount Mitchell Trail

Trailhead: From the Blue Ridge Parkway, go north on NC 80 for 2.5 mi., then go left on FR 472. Continue 3.0 mi. to the Black Mountain Campground. Park in the lot opposite the campground (before crossing the South Toe River). Hike across the bridge and take the first left, to the Briar Bottom Campground. The Mount Mitchell trailhead is 100 yds. on the right.

Loop/one-way: One-way.

Difficulty: Hard.

Campsites (with GPS coordinates): Adjoining meadows at the intersection of Mount Mitchell Trail and Buncombe Horse Range Trail, mile 4.2 (N35 45.259 W82 14.852).

Maps: "South Toe River, Mount Mitchell & Big Ivy Trail Maps," USDA Forest Service, Appalachian Ranger District, 40-ft. intervals. USGS: Mount Mitchell, Celo.

Follow the trail: From the trailhead: Hike 4.2 mi. to the intersection with the Buncombe Horse Range Trail and the main meadow campsite. Continue 1.5 mi. on Mount Mitchell Trail to the summit. Or, go right on Buncombe Horse Range Trail for 2.5 mi. to the Big Tom Spur. Go left for 0.4 mi. to the Black Mountain Crest Trail.

Fee? No.

Water (with GPS coordinates): Water is available in the campground at the trailhead; at Setrock Creek, mile 2.9 (N35 45.424 W82 14.586); and less than a half mile north of the meadow campsite on the Buncombe Horse Range Trail (N35 45.749 W82 15.094).

Land managers: USDA Forest Service; N.C. Division of Parks and Recreation.

Trip highlight: Topping out on 6,684-ft. Mount Mitchell, the highest point on the East Coast.

Special considerations: 3,662-ft. vertical climb in 5.7 mi.; upper portions of trail also act as drainages, especially troublesome in winter when ice tends to form and remain during cold snaps.

Night hike in? No.

Solo? Yes. A fairly popular trail.

Family friendly? Not so much (see "Special considerations").

Bailout options: No.

Seasons: Fall, spring, summer. Winter is doable, but be advised that near the summit single snowfalls of 50 in. (1993) have been recorded and the temperature has dropped as low as -34. Trail near the top is often icy.

Weather: Watch for afternoon thunderstorms near the top in summer, and heed the aforementioned concerns about winter hiking.

Solitude rating: 3.

Nearest outfitter: REI, Asheville, (828) 687-0918, www.rei.com.

Hunting allowed? Local seasons apply in the Pisgah National Forest portion of the hike; no hunting is allowed at the top, in Mount Mitchell State Park.

More info: Mount Mitchell State Park, (828) 675-4611, www.ncparks.gov/Visit/parks/momi/main.php; USDA Forest Service, Appalachian Ranger District, Pisgah National Forest, (828) 682-6146, www.csunca.edu/nfsnc.

A new observation deck tops Mount Mitchell, at 6,684 feet the highest point east of South Dakota's Black Hills.

statewide Mountains-to-Sea Trail (MST), which is a good thing, because this trip is challenge enough. This is a trip for backpackers who want to earn their summit.

The Mount Mitchell Trail begins from the west end of the Black Mountain Campground, at an elevation just over 3,000 feet. You aren't on the trail long before you notice the benefits of MST membership: Strategically positioned logs steer you away from the old trail, which had a tendency to go straight up the mountain. Instead, the MST employs sensible switchbacks that save your legs and let you savor what is a surprisingly intimate hike. Much of the timbering done in the Black Mountains in the early twentieth century focused on the spruce and fir forests above 5,000 feet. Thus, for the first three miles or so you're in a rich, mature Southern Appalachian hardwood forest that affords few views down to the South Toe River Valley floor but ample opportunity for mental escape.

A quarter mile or so after you pass Setrock Creek the transition to a more northern spruce/fir forest begins. It's also where the trail can get tricky on a winter ascent. As the trail climbs, it also acts as a drainage, often harboring ice during cold weather. By the time you reach the primitive camping area, a generous meadow at the trail's intersection with the Buncombe Horse Range Trail 4.2 miles into the hike, you're firmly in more northerly climes.

Your meadow campsite makes a good base camp for exploring the highest ridgeline in the East. The top of 6,684-foot Mount Mitchell is only another mile and a half up the trail, making a good capper to your first day if time allows.

Day 2 is the highlight of this trip. From base camp, take the Buncombe Horse Range Trail north for 2.5 miles to the Big Tom Spur. This 0.4-mile trail takes you up to the gap between 6,647-foot Mount Craig and 6,526-foot Big Tom. More importantly, it emerges just about where the last of the hardier tourists to Mount Mitchell State Park have the temerity to trek. Heading north along the Black Mountain Crest Trail, you'll be well removed from the park's human influence, and in just over 3 miles you'll bag some of the state's highest peaks in Balsam Cone (6,585 feet), Cattail Peak (6,600 feet), Potato Hill (6,440 feet) and Winter Star Mountain (6,203 feet). The Crest Trail continues past Winter Star, but the short stretch north to Gibbs Mountain, though relatively flat, is overgrown in warmer months and can be a challenge to follow.

All the more reason, perhaps, to make this a winter assault.

3 Black Mountains Woody Ridge/Crest Trail

ASHEVILLE

7.4 MILES

NO. OF DAYS: 2

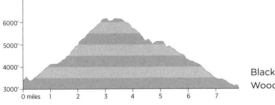

Black Mountains:
Woody Ridge/Crest Trail

From base camp at Deep Gap on the Black Mountain Crest Trail one day I decided to hike north. I'd hiked the trail heading south: 6 miles over 6 of North Carolina's 42 peaks exceeding 6,000 feet. It was a challenge at high altitude (for this part of the country) and over rocky terrain, but at least the trail was easy to follow. Beyond Deep Gap, though, where Colbert Ridge Trail comes up from the Carolina Hemlock Recreation Area, the trail was terra incognita, at least to those of us lacking Daniel Boone's tracking

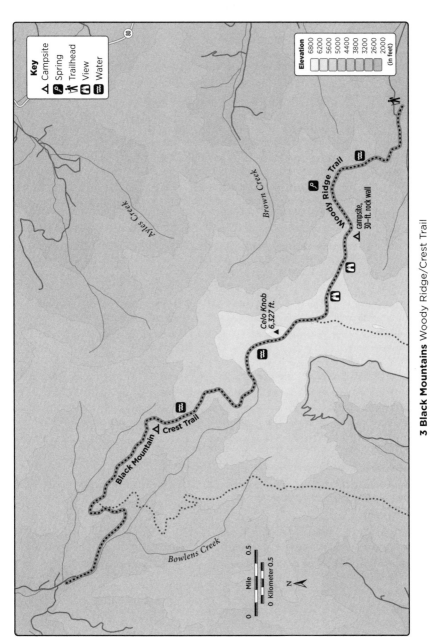

3 Black Mountains Woody Ridge/Crest Trail

Key
△ Campsite
🅿 Spring
🚶 Trailhead
📷 View
💧 Water

Elevation
6800
6200
5600
5000
4400
3800
3200
2600
2000
(in feet)

Ⓑ 80

Brown Creek

Ayles Creek

Woody Ridge Trail

Celo Knob
6,327 ft.

△ campsite,
30-ft. rock wall

Black Mountain △ Crest Trail

Bowlens Creek

Mile
0 0.5
0 Kilometer 0.5
N

3 **Black Mountains** Woody Ridge/Crest Trail

Trailhead: From the Blue Ridge Parkway go north on NC 80 for 7.5 mi. and turn left on White Oak Creek Road/SR 1157. Go 0.6 mi.; where the road Ys, veer right on SR 1156. Continue another mile to the gated trailhead.

Loop/one-way: One-way.

Difficulty: Hard.

Campsites (with GPS coordinates): 1.1 mi. (in a pinch, N35 50.659 W82 13.634); 1.2 mi. (N35 50.739 W82 13.690); 1.7 mi., beneath 30-ft. rock wall (N35 50.642 W82 14.093); 5.1 mi. (N35 51.820 W82 16.003).

Map: "South Toe River, Mount Mitchell & Big Ivy Trail Maps," USDA Forest Service, Appalachian Ranger District, 40-ft. intervals.

Follow the trail: From the trailhead, take Woody Ridge Trail 2.2 mi. to the Black Mountain Crest Trail. Go left to explore Winter Star Mountain and points south; go right to pass Celo Knob and for the 5.2 mi. to the northern end of the Black Mountain Crest Trail.

Fee? No.

Water (with GPS coordinates): This trip follows Shuford Creek for the first 0.4 mi. and Bowlens Creek for the last mile. Otherwise: 1.0 mi. (N35 50.618 W82 13.645); 1.3 mi., spring (N35 50.767 W82 13.855); 3.6 mi. (N35 51.300 W82 15.254); 4.7 mi., spring (N35 51.630 W82 15.564).

Land manager: USDA Forest Service, Appalachian Ranger District, Pisgah National Forest.

Trip highlight: Hiking a section of the 12-mi. Black Mountain Crest Trail, including 6,327-ft. Celo Knob, that's hard to get to from the more popular Mount Mitchell end of the Crest Trail.

Special considerations: There's water the first 0.4 mi. of this trip and the last mile, but little in between. Plan accordingly. The last 1.1 mi. of Woody Ridge Trail is a challenge, gaining nearly 1,700 vertical feet in just over a mile.

Night hike in? In a pinch. There's a make-do campsite a mile in, before the trail requires serious climbing.

Solo? For an experienced backpacker. Weather on the 6,000-ft. ridgeline can be difficult regardless of season.

Family friendly? No. Elevation gains, lack of water, and potentially harsh weather on the ridge have the potential to make this a not-fun hike.

Bailout options: No.

Seasons: Spring, summer, fall.

Weather: Snow and ice discourage winter hiking for all but the best prepared. Summer hikers need to keep an eye on building storm clouds after noon.

Solitude rating: 3.

Nearest outfitter: REI, Asheville, (828) 687-0918, www.rei.com.

Hunting allowed? Local seasons apply in the Pisgah National Forest.

More info: USDA Forest Service, Appalachian Ranger District, Pisgah National Forest, (828) 682-6146, www.csunca.edu/nfsnc.

The north end of the Crest Trail near Celo Knob offers wide views, few people.

skills. Come to think if it, I couldn't recall anyone I knew who had hiked beyond Deep Gap.

I soon discovered why.

Past Deep Gap the trail is difficult to find. After half an hour of fits and starts through overgrown briars, I made the 0.6 miles to 6,203-foot Winter Star Mountain. Pushing on, I was met by an ominous sign. Where one might expect trail, a red rope dangled over a 15-foot drop. That wasn't the ominous part: Beyond the rope, all I could see was ridgeline jungle, not a hint of trail. Even more frustrating: I could tell by the map that the trail for the next mile and a half to Celo Knob was nearly flat. Where the trail might snake its way through this mess was a mystery. That led to my decision to include the Woody Ridge/Crest Trail trip in this book.

I'll be upfront: Woody Ridge isn't the best 2.2-mile hike you'll ever take. It starts easy enough, with a gentle climb for the first mile and a third. After that, it plows straight uphill, gaining 1,700 vertical feet in just over a mile. (Conversely, the descent down the final 4.6 miles of the Crest Trail is a mellow ramble on an old roadbed through a mature hardwood forest.) It's a grind, but the payoff is worth it.

Approaching the 6,000-foot mark, the trail enters a landscape rare to the Southern Appalachians: a spruce/fir forest. While the Fraser fir has been in decline for the past 60 years as a result of the balsam woolly adelgid infestation, you'll still find it clinging to the ridgeline, along with red spruce, mountain ash, and yellow birch. The area is rugged in spots, requiring scrambling over and squeezing through rock outcrops and boulders. In warmer weather you'll find dense thickets of blueberry, red elder, and bush honeysuckle. You'll also find clearings that afford great views to the west, over rolling ridgelines extending into Tennessee, as well as the holy grail of backpacking: quiet and solitude.

One thing you won't find in abundance: decent campsites. Your best bet is a site 1.7 miles into the hike, beneath a 30-foot rock wall protecting you from storms approaching from the west. It's a relatively quick pack-in, then you can set up camp and spend time exploring the Crest Trail. Head south and who knows, you may even find the path to Winter Star.

GRANDFATHER MOUNTAIN

Grandfather Mountain is, curiously, best known for its mile-high swinging bridge (a mile above sea level, that is; it's only 80 feet above the ravine it spans) and its captive bears. The bridge and the bears—along with a new gift shop and other touristy draws—are in the southwest portion of this 4,000-acre park. Thus the north end is the perfect spot from which to embark on a backpack trip—and the perfect place to appreciate Grandfather for the biological marvel that it is.

As elevations ranging from 3,000 to just under 6,000 feet might suggest, there is indeed a great deal of biodiversity on this relatively small tract, so much that it has been recognized by the United Nations Educational, Scientific, and Cultural Organization as one of 553 International Biosphere Reserves worldwide. The base of Grandfather is covered by a classic Southern Appalachian hardwood forest; the top, a rugged spruce/fir forest left over from the last ice age. In all, you'll encounter 16 natural communities that support 73 rare and endangered species. Three quarters of the mountain, including 2,456 acres along the crest that became part of the North Carolina State Parks system in 2009, are preserved through conservation easements to The Nature Conservancy. Wildlife abounds, and not not all the bears on the mountain are captive.

Both trips described start at the base of the mountain and end on the 2.4-mile Grandfather Trail, which spans the mountain's crest. This is the wildest 2.4 miles covered in this book. Some climbs up jagged peaks are so severe you must use wooden ladders. Others are so slick and precipitous you hold on to an anchored cable and inch your way along. Grandfather's crest gets some of the worst weather in the state, ranging from violent afternoon thunderstorms in the summer to bitter ice storms in the winter. It has snowed as much as 2 feet in a 24-hour period here, and the temperature has dropped to 32 degrees below zero. Wind gusts of over 200 miles per hour have been recorded atop the mountain. Be especially prepared for a visit to Grandfather Mountain.

Note: Camping at Grandfather Mountain is in designated locations only, and permits are required. The permits are free. Visit www.grandfather.com for a list of locations where permits are available.

4   Grandfather Mountain Profile Trail (west approach)

BLOWING ROCK

10.8 MILES (ROUND-TRIP, INCLUDING GRANDFATHER TRAIL)

NO. OF DAYS: 2

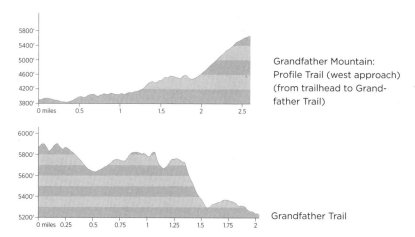

Grandfather Mountain: Profile Trail (west approach) (from trailhead to Grandfather Trail)

Grandfather Trail

Here's the camping dilemma when backpacking at Grandfather Mountain: The Profile Trail on the mountain's west flank is the more scenic route to the crest-surfing Grandfather Trail. But it's a bit of a gamble: You have one camping option, the relatively small (2–3 tents) Profile campsite, 1.8 miles up the mountain. If it's full, you'll have to climb another mile and a quarter over much more challenging terrain to the next primitive campsite. Pack

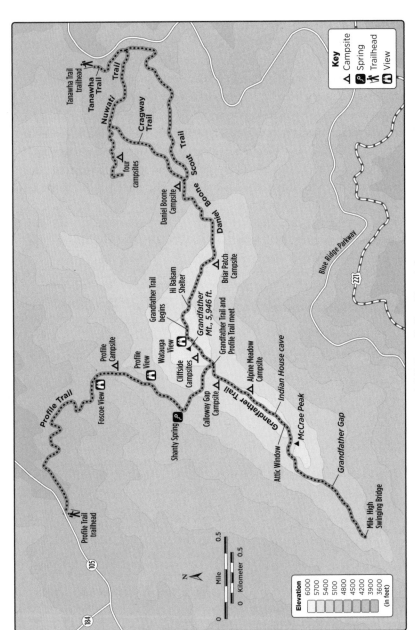

4 & 5 Grandfather Mountain

Key
△ Campsite
🅿 Spring
🚶 Trailhead
🏠 View

Tanawha Trail trailhead
Tanawha Trail
Nuwati Trail
Cragway Trail
four campsites
Daniel Boone Campsite
Daniel Boone Scout Trail
Grandfather Trail begins
Hi Balsam Shelter
Grandfather Mt., 5,946 ft.
Grandfather Trail and Profile Trail meet
Briar Patch Campsite
Watauga View
Profile Campsite
Profile View
Profile Trail
Foscoe View
Cliffside Campsites
Shanty Spring
Calloway Gap Campsite
Grandfather Trail
Alpine Meadow Campsite
Indian House cave
Attic Window
McCrae Peak
Grandfather Gap
Mile High Swinging Bridge
Profile Trail trailhead

Blue Ridge Parkway
221
105
184

N

Mile
0   0.5
Kilometer
0   0.5

Elevation
6000
5700
5400
5100
4800
4500
4200
3900
3600
(in feet)

4 Grandfather Mountain Profile Trail (west approach)

Trailhead: Trailhead parking is on the east side of NC 105, about a half mile northeast of NC 184.

Loop/one-way: One-way.

Difficulty: Moderate to campsite; moderate to hard thereafter.

Campsites (with GPS coordinates): 1.8 mi. Profile campsite (N36 07.069 W81 48.904); 3.1 mi. Cliffside campsite, north on Grandfather Trail (N36 06.603 W81 48.775), and Calloway Gap, south on Grandfather Trail (N36 06.513 W81 48.922).

Map: "Grandfather Mountain Trail Map and Backcountry Guide," 1:25,000, 100-ft. intervals.

Follow the trail: From the trailhead, take the Profile Trail 2.85 mi. to the Grandfather Trail.

Fee? No.

Water (with GPS coordinates): Seep just above the campsite runs intermittently (and is tricky to get to); Shanty Spring (N36 06.728 W81 49.124) is 0.4 mi. farther up the trail.

Land manager: N.C. Division of Parks and Recreation.

Trip highlight: 2.4-mi. Grandfather Mountain Trail along a rocky ridgeline that offers some of the most challenging—and rewarding—hiking in North Carolina.

Special considerations: Grandfather Mountain has some of the harshest weather on the East Coast, weather that can change in an instant. Grandfather Trail has some unusual . . . *aids* along the trail, including wooden ladders and anchored cables to help navigate particularly hairy spots.

Night hike in? Yes, though the Profile campsite will accommodate only 2 or 3 tents; if it's occupied, it's another 1 1/4 mi. of considerably more difficult hiking to the next campsites, Cliffside and Calloway Gap, on Grandfather Trail.

Solo? There are lots of opportunities to get in trouble on Grandfather Mountain; hiking with a partner or group is advised.

Family friendly? The top is fraught with dangerous passages—steep drops, sections that require using a cable as a guide wire over exposed rock, and ladders up especially steep sections. Not for anyone who is unsure of their outdoor skills.

Bailout options: No.

Seasons: Spring, summer, fall, though weather can quickly turn bad any time of the year.

Weather: Weather atop Grandfather, which tops out just below 6,000 ft., can vary considerably from the base. Be especially wary of thunderstorms during the summer, ice and snow in the winter.

Solitude rating: 2. The Profile Trail is a popular day hike and a favorite access route to the Grandfather Trail.

Nearest outfitter: Footsloggers, Boone, (828) 262-5111, www.footsloggers.com, and (828) 295-4453 in Blowing Rock.

Hunting allowed? No.

More info: Grandfather Mountain State Park, (828) 737-9522, www.ncparks.gov/Visit/parks/grmo/main.php; Grandfather Mountain, Inc., (800) 468-7325, www.grandfather.com.

up from the mountain's east side, from Boone's Fork off the Blue Ridge Parkway (trip 5) and you'll have your choice of campsites.

Is it worth the gamble? You be the judge.

Grandfather Mountain is often described as a diverse biosphere, and you get a good sense of that on the Profile Trail. The trail couldn't be more welcoming; the first third of a mile follows the headwaters of the Watauga River, here more of a festive creek. The trail then turns uphill in a succession of gentle switchbacks through a mature hardwood forest carpeted with ferns. Less than a mile up, the trail snuggles up to a 25-foot rock face before continuing its climb. At just over a mile and a half in, you'll get your first good view, to the town of Foscoe in the valley to the north and, on a clear day, to Mount Rogers and Whitetop, the two highest points in Virginia. There's the Profile campsite at mile 1.8, and at the 2.1-mile mark you can see the rock configuration that names both the trail and the mountain as a whole.

The hiking becomes more challenging at this point, heading up rock gullies and taking a more urgent path to the top. At the 2.6-mile mark you can take a break and slake your thirst at Shanty Spring, which pours from a black pipe at trailside. As advertised, it's the "Last Sure Water" from here on up.

At mile 3.0 you reach the crest and the 2.4-mile Grandfather Trail. If the Profile campsite is full, the Cliffside campsite is about 0.1 miles north; the Calloway Gap campsite is about the same distance south. Both locations make for a good base camp for a day exploring the Grandfather Trail, a description of which can be found in trip 5.

5 Grandfather Mountain Daniel Boone Scout Trail (east approach)

BLOWING ROCK

13.5 MILES (ROUND-TRIP, INCLUDING GRANDFATHER TRAIL)

NO. OF DAYS: 2-3

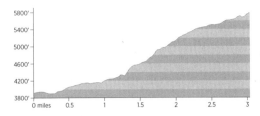

Grandfather Mountain: Daniel Boone Scout Trail (east approach) (from trailhead to Grandfather Trail)

The rocky Grandfather Trail atop Grandfather Mountain offers some of the wildest hiking in North Carolina. Photo by Helen Moss Hopper.

Your best bet for solitude at Grandfather Mountain is to start at the Boone Fork parking area at milepost 299.9 on the Blue Ridge Parkway, head south briefly on the Tanawha Trail, then go right and up the mountain on the Nuwati Trail. In less than a mile you can shed your pack and set up camp at one of 4 well-spaced campsites. Your choices range from the trailside Streamside Campsite, to the isolated Hermitage located about 5 minutes off the trail in a cozy rhododendron and pine thicket, to The Refuge, located at trail's end. These sites are an attractive option, considering that this is where the real climbing begins: Over the next 2.7 miles to the crest you'll gain more than 1,700 feet.

If you'd like to keep the pack on your back a bit longer, go left on the Cragway Trail for 0.7 miles, then hang a right on the Daniel Boone Scout Trail; in another 1.2 miles you'll be at the Daniel Boone campsite, a group area with 3 wooden platforms and space on the ground for 2 or 3 additional tents.

From here, the hiking becomes steeper and more intense. Briar Patch (1 site) and the Hi-Balsam Shelter are your last camping options before you hit the first ladder and the scrambling begins. Any of these sites will make a good base camp for exploring the top of the mountain on the 2.4-

Bad weather can descend quickly on Grandfather Mountain any time of year.

mile Grandfather Trail. Obviously, the higher you camp, the less additional climbing you'll have to deal with on your day hike along the crest. (If you're an experienced backpacker, exceptionally strong, and even more fearless, there are 4 campsites along the crest. Read on and see if you'd like to attempt to reach these with 35 pounds on your back.)

The funhouse that is the top of Grandfather Mountain starts with your first ladder shortly before you hit Grandfather Trail. It's well anchored and

5 **Grandfather Mountain** Daniel Boone Scout Trail (east approach)

Trailhead: Boone Fork parking area, milepost 299.9 on the Blue Ridge Parkway (about 5.5 mi. south of US 221 at Blowing Rock and 5 mi. north of the Linn Cove visitors center). For an alternate if the parkway is closed because of weather: From a parking area on US 221 about 1.5 mi. west of Holloway Mountain Road, pick up the 0.4-mi. Asutsi Trail, which connects to the Tanawha Trail near the Boone Fork parking area.

Loop/one-way: One-way.

Difficulty: Moderate for the first 3.5 mi., up to Briar Patch campsite; beyond that, climbing up ladders and scrambling over boulders and exposed, often steep, rock faces makes for hard going with a backpack.

Campsites (with GPS coordinates): 4 sites on a 0.5-mi. spur at mile 0.8 (sites begin at N36 07.043 W81 47.510); 1.75 mi. Daniel Boone Camp (N36 06.703 W81 47.674); 2.9 mi. Briar Patch (N36 06.556 W81 48.172); 3.9 mi. Cliffside (N36 06.603 W81 48.775); 4.5 mi. Alpine Meadows (N36 06.276 W81 49.134).

Map: "Grandfather Mountain Trail Map and Backcountry Guide," 1:25,000, 100-ft. intervals.

Follow the trail: From the trailhead, take the Tanawha Trail 0.3 mi. south to the Nuwati Trail. Go right on Nuwati for 0.6 mi.; continue straight on Nuwati to 4 campsites, or go left on the Cragway Trail. Continue a half mile on Cragway, then go right on the Daniel Boone Scout Trail. Continue 2.3 mi. to the Grandfather Trail.

Fee? No.

Water (with GPS coordinates): There are streams in two spots near the first cluster of 4 campsites on the Nuwati Trail (N36 07.043 W81 47.510) and at the Daniel Boone Scout campsite (N36 06.703 W81 47.674). There is no water along Grandfather Trail.

Land manager: N.C. Division of Parks and Recreation.

Trip highlight: 2.4-mi. Grandfather Mountain Trail along a rocky ridgeline that offers some of the most challenging—and rewarding—hiking in North Carolina.

Special considerations: Grandfather Mountain has some of the harshest weather on the East Coast, weather that can change in an instant. Grandfather Trail has some unusual aids along the trail, including wooden ladders and anchored cables to help navigate particularly hairy spots.

Night hike in? Possibly up to the first group of campsites (a mile in).

Solo? There are lots of opportunities to get in trouble on Grandfather Mountain; hiking with a partner or group is advised.

Family friendly? The top is fraught with dangerous passages—steep drops, sections that require using a cable as a guide wire over exposed rock, and ladders up especially steep sections. Not for anyone who is unsure of their outdoor skills.

Bailout options: No.

Seasons: Spring, summer, fall, though weather can turn bad on top any time of the year.

Weather: Weather atop Grandfather, which tops out just below 6,000 ft., can vary considerably from the base. Be especially wary of thunderstorms during the summer, ice and snow in the winter.

Solitude rating: 4 for most of the trip, 2 as you near the southeast trailhead for Grandfather Trail and the park's tourist draws.

Nearest outfitter: Footsloggers, Blowing Rock, (828) 295-4453, www.footsloggers.com.

Hunting allowed? No.

More info: Grandfather Mountain State Park, (828) 737-9522, www.ncparks.gov/Visit/parks/grmo/main.php; Grandfather Mountain, Inc., (800) 468-7325, www.grandfather.com.

safe, but attention-getting nonetheless. More ladders follow, taking you up the steepest rock faces. When ladders won't do, you'll find cables anchored into the rock that help you cross smooth outcrops Spiderman style. There's Attic Window, with a great view to the west; Indian House Cave (more of a deep overhang); 5,939-foot MacRae Peak (ascended via one of the less confidence-inspiring ladders on the mountain); and The Chute, which more than any other feature makes you wonder how the N.C. State Parks system, with its penchant for safety, might try to sanitize this jumble of boulders spilled down a narrow—20 feet or so—chute between two stone walls. It's some crazy hiking. At trail's end, you'll find the visitors center, the gift shop, the swinging bridge, and other touristy draws.

Grandfather Trail may be only 2.4 miles long, but it's a long 2.4 miles. Plan your day, especially the shorter days of winter, accordingly.

LINVILLE GORGE

On the surface, the compact Linville Gorge Wilderness might not seem that impressive. At just 12,002 acres, it accounts for a fraction of the nation's 109,492,591 acres of wilderness and is dwarfed by the likes of Alaska's 9.1-million-acre Wrangell–Saint Elias Wilderness and the 2.6-million-acre Frank Church–River of No Return and Gospel-Hump wilderness complex in Idaho. At Linville Gorge, it's all about what's below the surface.

From the gorge's east and west rims, it's as much as 2,000 feet down to the Linville River, which has spent hundreds of millions of years chiseling one of the deepest canyons west of the Grand Canyon. For the backpacker, that means two things: a body-jarring descent into the gorge and a vigorous climb out, and some of the most stunning scenery in the state in between. Wildlife ranges from peregrine falcons riding thermals rising from the canyon floor to rainbow and brown trout in the cool waters of Linville River. Ecozones range from dry ridgeline forests at the trailhead to a jungle of rhododendron along the river's edge. And there are the eons of geologic tumult that result in stellar views.

Experience the gorge in one of two ways: from above, along the east rim on trip 7, or by plunging into the cavernous beast itself, on trip 6.

The 13-mile Linville Gorge is one of the wildest spots on the East Coast.

6 Linville Gorge

LINVILLE FALLS

9.8 MILES

NO. OF DAYS: 2-3

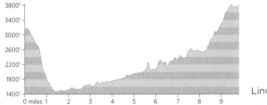

Linville Gorge

There are two main challenges to a trip into Linville Gorge. The first is the precipitous drop in on the 1.5-mile Pinch In Trail. It starts innocently—for the first couple hundred yards. Then you encounter something more common to Class IV whitewater: a horizon line. That is, a peculiar break between land and sky that makes the landscape appear Photoshopped. In fact, this abrupt disconnect between earth and air is where the trail basically drops over the edge. In the case of the Pinch In Trail, that means descending more than 800 vertical feet in a half mile.

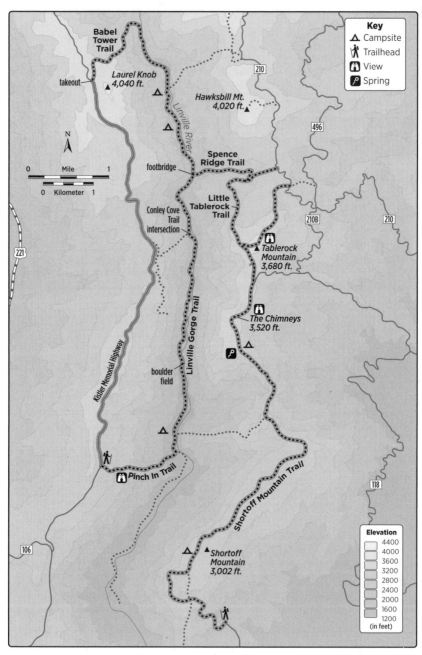

Key
- △ Campsite
- 🚶 Trailhead
- 🔭 View
- 🔑 Spring

Babel Tower Trail

takeout

Laurel Knob
4,040 ft.

Linville River

Hawksbill Mt.
4,020 ft.

210

496

N

Mile
0   1

Kilometer
0   1

footbridge

Spence Ridge Trail

221

Little Tablerock Trail

210B   210

Conley Cove Trail intersection

▲ Tablerock Mountain
3,680 ft.

Linville Gorge Trail

The Chimneys
3,520 ft.

boulder field

Pinch In Trail

118

Shortoff Mountain Trail

106

Shortoff Mountain
3,002 ft.

Elevation
- 4400
- 4000
- 3600
- 3200
- 2800
- 2400
- 2000
- 1600
- 1200
- (in feet)

6 & 7 Linville Gorge

6 Linville Gorge

Trailhead: From the junction of US 221 and NC 183 in the town of Linville Falls, head east on NC 183. After 0.7 mi., go right on the Kistler Memorial Highway. ("Highway" should be in quotes; this is a relatively well-maintained gravel road passable by car.) Parking for Babel Tower Trail (the trail's takeout) is 2.8 mi. on the left; parking for the Pinch In Trail (trailhead) is 8.5 mi. on the left.

Loop/one-way: Semi-loop. The trip begins from the west rim on Pinch In Trail, heads north along the Linville River on the Linville Gorge Trail, then retuns to the west rim on the Babel Tower Trail. There's a 5.6-mi. return along the Kistler Memorial Highway to the Pinch In trailhead. It's not a bad walk if you dump your packs at the Babel Tower lot.

Difficulty: Hard (steep 1.5-mi. drop into the gorge, unmarked trail in the gorge).

Campsites (with GPS coordinates): 1.5 mi. (N35 51.307 W81 54.093), 2.0 mi. (N35 51.698 W81 53.935), 6.3 mi. (N35 54.611 W81 54.033), 6.5 mi. (N35 54.611 W81 54.033), 6.6 mi. (N35 54.705 W81 54.068), 6.9 mi. (N35 54.927 W81 54.182), 7.7 mi. (N35 55.417 W81 54.493). From mile 3.0 (N35 52.386 W81 53.977) to mile 5.8 (N35 54.232 W81 53.842) are a series of campsites on the water that are heavily used and, alas, frequently trashed. Unless you're backpacking midweek in the off-season during cold weather, avoid these campsites. Upstream of the Spence Ridge Trail bridge crossing, the sites become smaller and more tidy. Note: Free permits are required for camping weekends and holidays between May 1 and Oct. 31. Stays are limited to 3 days, 2 nights, and group size may not exceed 10. Call (828) 652-2144 for permit information.

Maps: "Linville Gorge Wilderness, Pisgah National Forest," USDA Forest Service, 1:24,000, 40-ft. intervals; "Linville Gorge, Mount Mitchell," *Trails Illustrated*, *National Geographic*, 1:65,000, 50-ft. intervals.

Follow the trail: From the Pinch In trailhead, hike 1.5 mi. to the Linville Gorge Trail. Go left. Follow the gorge trail for 6.7 mi. to the Babel Tower Trail. Go left on Babel Tower for 1.3 mi. to the trailhead and Kistler Memorial Highway. If you haven't established a shuttle, it's a 5.6-mi. hike back to the Pinch In trailhead parking area.

Fee? No, but to limit the number of campers, camping permits are required May 1–Oct. 31. Call the district ranger's office (see "Campsites").

Water (with GPS coordinates): Water can be pumped and treated from the Linville River, which runs along the trail for about 6.5 mi., from mile 1.5 to mile 8. If you prefer to draw from smaller sources, the Linville Gorge Trail crosses small feeder streams at miles 1.3 (N35 51.258 W81 54.087), 2.0 (N35 51.657 W81 53.987), 3.6 (N35 52.799 W81 53.923), 5.0 (N35 53.757 W81 53.954) and 6.9 (N35 54.850 W81 54.197).

Land manager: USDA Forest Service, Grandfather Ranger District.

Trip highlights: Rugged landscape, great views, river with frequent pools for swimming and trout fishing.

Special considerations: Wilderness area: The trails are not blazed, nor are they officially cleared of downfall and debris. Wayfinding can be a challenge.

Night hike in? No. However, there are ample campsites along the Kistler Memorial Highway along the west rim. You can drive in at night and camp here for an early morning start into the gorge.

Solo? Only for more experienced backpackers. It's easy to get lost and into trouble.

Family friendly? No.

Bailout options: No.

Seasons: All (summer is most popular because of the water).

Weather: Weather in the bottom of the gorge can be significantly different from that on the rim some 2,000 ft. up. Be constantly aware of what's going on above you. Weather here can change in an instant.

Solitude rating: 2. Midsection of this route, near where Conley Cove and Spence Ridge trails drop in, is especially popular.

Nearest outfitter: Footsloggers, Blowing Rock, (828) 295-4453, www.footsloggers.com.

Hunting allowed? Yes. Local seasons apply.

More info: U.S. Forest Service, Grandfather Ranger District, (828) 652-4841, www.cs.unca.edu/nfsnc/recreation/linville.pd; linvillegorge.net.

It's a descent that's heck on the knees. Thus, you'll be secretly grateful for the ample opportunities to stop and take in the scenery. A particularly good vista awaits 0.6 miles in, where a knob offers views across the gorge to Shortoff Mountain to the south and The Chimneys to the north. (Your panoramic sightseeing opportunities are enhanced thanks to a wildfire that swept down the mountain in 2007.)

When Pinch In Trail reaches bottom, it gives way to the Linville Gorge Trail, which runs most of the length of the 13-mile gorge. You likely won't be aware of when this change occurs, which brings us to the second challenge: finding and keeping the trail. Since this is a wilderness, the trails here are not blazed and technically not maintained, though crews of volunteers periodically go through and clear downed trees. Still, wayfinding in this jungle of rhododendrons, downed trees (including mighty hemlocks that form impressive roadblocks), and rock slides is a challenge. A boulder field 2.7 miles into the hike is especially playful with the trail. Some simple advice to see you through: Keep your topo map handy; remember that the trail never strays too far from the river (though there are spots where you may not see it); and above all, a trail, like the person who blazed it, should follow the path of least resistance.

Along about the aforementioned boulder field, you'll discover that Linville Gorge is one loved place. Alas, not all its lovers are gentle, leave-no-trace lovers. Some subscribe to the love-it-and-leave-it school of romance, the second "it" being trash. You'll find an abundance of prime, riverside sites between miles 3 and 6 that frequently have an abundance of trash. A better bet is to camp at the more intimate sites near Pinch In on the south, or to the north, past the log footbridge over Linville River. Camp near Pinch In and you can do a day hike south on the southernmost 2 miles of the Linville Gorge Trail, a segment that sees little traffic. Camp north of the footbridge and you can take advantage of said conveyance and hike up to Tablerock on the east rim. Again, expect challenging conditions regardless.

While exploring Linville Gorge, you should expect to take your pack off more than once to get over, under, around, and through assorted natural obstacles. You should expect to fall and slide on your fanny down a muddy slope, and you should expect to bounce off so many trees that your shoulders will appear to be growing bark. Expect to return to the trailhead after emerging from the gorge on the 1.3-mile Babel Tower Trail looking like you've been on an epic adventure.

Take a picture. You earned it.

LINVILLE FALLS

14.1 MILES (ONE-WAY, INCLUDING TABLEROCK LOOP TO LINVILLE RIVER)

NO. OF DAYS: 2-3

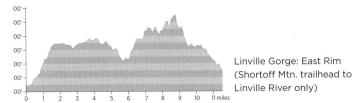

Linville Gorge: East Rim
(Shortoff Mtn. trailhead to
Linville River only)

If the Linville Gorge Wilderness, roughly 12,000 acres that's been described as some of the most rugged land in the East, can have a mellow side, the east rim would be it. In the gorge, you're constantly climbing over downed hemlocks, navigating house-sized boulders, and doing your best to follow the unblazed and indifferent trail. On the east rim, the trail never hides, never tries to break you down and make you weep.

And after a stout climb from the trailhead up the backside of Shortoff Mountain (about 1,100 vertical feet in a mile and a third), the ridge-bound trail doesn't stray far from the east rim's 3,000-foot elevation for a good 3 miles. In fact, it takes pains to let you enjoy this massive ravine that plunges 2,000 feet in spots. One of your best photo ops is from the rocky cliffs overhanging the gorge at Shortoff: There's the Linville River below, 3,537-foot Dogback Mountain across the way, and Lake James in the distance to the south.

The trail's calm turns to mild turbulence around the 4-mile mark with a general descent into Chimney Gap (a good campsite with a spring 0.3 miles down the gorge side, the only water source on the rim) and the subsequent steep climb up to The Chimneys (this steep climb is another reason Chimney Gap, 5.8 miles into the hike, isn't a bad spot to stop for the day and set up camp). The Chimneys is an exposed rock face popular with climbers but not so much with those suffering vertigo; here, the shelf trail with a steep drop is one of the few spots on the east rim demanding your focus. It's another good spot to stop and savor the view.

Just down from The Chimneys, 7.2 miles into the hike, is a flat expanse constituting the largest camping area on the east rim. Be advised that the popular Tablerock Mountain access area is just a couple hundred yards beyond, making this an especially popular spot for campers. Tablerock or Chimney Gap make for good base camps from which to launch your Day-2 day hike into the gorge.

7 **Linville Gorge** East Rim

Trailhead: From US 70 in Nebo, go north on NC 126 for just over 11 mi., past Lake James State Park. A mile after crossing the Linville River, go left on Wolf Pit Road. Take Wolf Pit 2.5 mi. to its conclusion. There's a small, usually uncrowded gravel lot at the trailhead.

Loop/one-way: One-way. To set up a shuttle, return down Wolf Pit Road to NC 126 and go left. After about a mile, veer left on Fish Hatchery Road. Go 2.6 mi. and turn left on Old Table Rock Road, which becomes Table Rock Road. The Table Rock parking area is about 22 mi. from Fish Hatchery Road.

Difficulty: Moderate.

Campsites (with GPS coordinates): There are several good campsites along this route, including Shortoff Mountain (N35 50.323 W81 53.765) 2.5 mi. into the hike, Chimney Gap (N35 51.847 W81 52.8020) at 5.3 mi., shortly before Tablerock (N35 53.043 W81 53.128) at 7.2 mi., and at 12.1 mi. (N35 54.015 W81 53.374). Note: Free permits are required for camping weekends and holidays between May 1 and Oct. 31. Stays are limited to 3 days, 2 nights, and group size may not exceed 10. Call (828) 652-2144 for permit information.

Maps: "Linville Gorge Wilderness, Pisgah National Forest," USDA Forest Service, 1:24,000, 40-ft. intervals; "Linville Gorge, Mount Mitchell," *Trails Illustrated, National Geographic*, 1:65,000, 50-ft. intervals.

Follow the trail: From the trailhead for Shortoff Mountain Trail, hike 1.6 mi. to the top of Shortoff Mountain. Continue right on Shortoff Mountain Trail, which becomes the Mountains-to-Sea Trail at this point. Continue 5.8 mi. to Tablerock Mountain, and another 1.3 mi. to Spence Ridge Trail; go left. Take Spence Ridge Trail 1.5 mi. down to the Linville River. To return, take Spence Ridge back up the mountain 0.9 mi., then go right on Little Tablerock Trail. After 1.4 mi., Little Tablerock Trail returns you to Tablerock Mountain. Return on Shortoff Mountain Trail.

Fee? No, but to limit the number of campers, permits are required May 1–Oct. 31. Call the district ranger's office (see "Campsites").

Water (with GPS coordinates): Water is scarce on this largely ridgeline hike. There's a spring near Chimney Gap (N35 51.875 W81 52.964) at mile 5.6 (on the gorge side); a creek (N35 54.190 W81 53.114) at mile 10.1; the Linville River (N35 54.132 W81 53.822) at 11 mi.; and, on Little Tablerock Trail on the return trip, a small creek at mile 12.9.

Land manager: USDA Forest Service, Pisgah National Forest, Grandfather Ranger District.

Trip highlights: Frequent and stunning views into the gorge and all points on the compass; relatively easy access to Linville River and bottom of gorge.

Special considerations: Lack of water on the ridgeline.

Night hike in? Yes. The hike to Shortoff Mountain is a good climb on open terrain, thanks to a 2007 wildfire.

Solo? Yes. This is a popular trail, though not as popular as some in the Linville Gorge Wilderness.

Family friendly? Mostly. Around The Chimneys the trail is narrow and there are some steep drops.

Bailout options: No.

Seasons: All.

Weather: Watch for thunderstorms on the ridgeline on summer afternoons. Weather in the bottom of the gorge can be significantly different from that on the rim.

Solitude rating: 2.

Nearest outfitter: Footsloggers, Blowing Rock, (828) 295-4453, www.footsloggers.com.

Hunting allowed? Local seasons apply.

More info: USDA Forest Service, Grandfather Ranger District, (828) 652-4841, www.cs.unca.edu/nfsnc/recreation/linville.pd; linvillegorge.net.

Shortoff Mountain's rocky exposure offers good views.

Quick story: The first time I descended into the gorge was in 1995, and I was stunned by the number of campers who had toted in massive 80-quart coolers and set up extensive tent cities (I'd barely managed to survive the harrowing descent from the west rim on Babel Tower Trail with a modest 35-pound pack). These guys were packing more gear than Lewis and Clark. How'd they do it?

I found out 13 years later: They came in on the east side of the gorge, on the 1.4-mile Spence Ridge Trail, which takes advantage of a dip in the ridgeline for a more gradual descent into the gorge on an old roadbed. At the bottom, a log bridge—the only bridge across the river through the 13-mile gorge and an apparent concession to the gorge's wilderness designation—makes for easy passage to the gorge's wild west side (though on a summer's day you'll likely be content to loll about on, and in, the Linville River). The return trip up Little Tablerock Trail tries to make up for your easy descent with sections that plow straight up the gorge. Yet another reason to base camp on high and day hike down low.

There are so many good views, I almost forgot Tablerock. Check it out while climbing up from the gorge. It's flat, exposed, and perhaps most importantly at this point, has several good spots for napping.

Before you think about venturing into the Wilson Creek area, ask yourself this question: Do you wish you were a duck? Or, more to the point, do you wish you were born with webbed feet?

Wilson Creek, a 13,000-acre rugged expanse at the base of the Blue Ridge Escarpment, is all about water. If you're looking for a summer trip where you can backpack in just a little ways and spend your days frolicking in rock-rimmed natural swimming holes at the base of 40-foot waterfalls, this is the place. The only trick is avoiding like-minded folk, of whom there are many.

If you're backpacking during a cooler time of year and doing 5 stream crossings—some of which involve wading thigh-deep water—in just over 3 miles (as is the case with the Harper Creek trip) is a bit more adventure than you care for, then perhaps Wilson Creek isn't for you. Of the three trips described, two involve significant stream crossings, and because the two trips—Harper Creek and Lost Cove—are in wilderness study areas, there are very few bridges—or trail markings, for that matter. And the third trip? It's an option if you show up and discover you're not as crazy about webbed feet as you thought.

Read on. I'll explain.

From this spot along the Blue Ridge Parkway, the Wilson Creek area plunges off the Blue Ridge Escarpment.

BLOWING ROCK

16.4 MILES (INCLUDING TWO DAY-HIKE OPTIONS)

NO. OF DAYS: 2–3

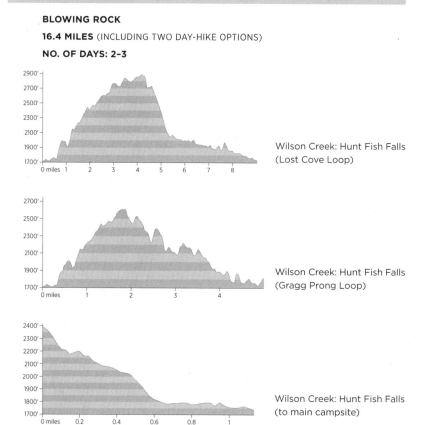

Wilson Creek: Hunt Fish Falls
(Lost Cove Loop)

Wilson Creek: Hunt Fish Falls
(Gragg Prong Loop)

Wilson Creek: Hunt Fish Falls
(to main campsite)

When I was in grade school, on the bleakest of winter days I would stare out the classroom window and dream of two things: spring training in Florida and swimming in a mountain pool rimmed by rock on a hot summer day. A variety of physical shortcomings—weak arm, poor hand-eye coordination, and a penchant for daydreaming when I needed to be focused on the ball coming at me—prevented me from making it to spring training. But I did make it to that perfect mountain swimming hole.

There's often compromise when it comes to natural swimming holes: muddy banks that make getting in and out a challenge, tannic water that keeps you from seeing what's swimming with you, and pesky flying things constantly nipping at you while you dry. At Hunt Fish Falls, there is no compromise. After dropping 8 feet, pooling briefly, then dropping

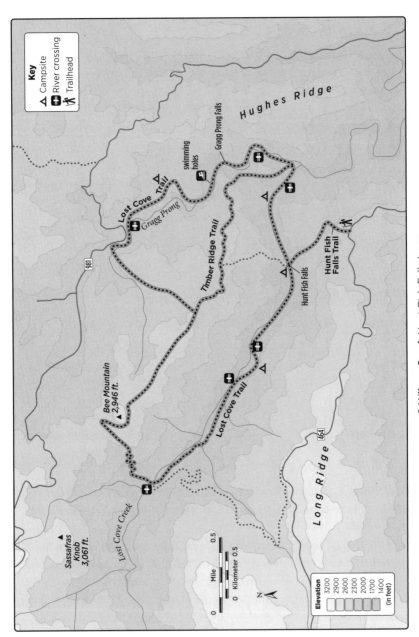

Key
△ Campsite
🚻 River crossing
🚶 Trailhead

Hughes Ridge

Gragg Prong Falls

swimming holes

Lost Cove Trail

Gragg Prong

981

Timber Ridge Trail

Hunt Fish Falls

Hunt Fish Falls Trail

Bee Mountain
▲ 2,946 ft.

Lost Cove Trail

Sassafras Knob
▲ 3,061 ft.

Lost Cove Creek

Long Ridge

464

Mile
0   0.5

Kilometer
0   0.5

N

Elevation
3200
2900
2600
2300
2000
1700
1400
(in feet)

8 Wilson Creek Hunt Fish Falls Loop

8 Wilson Creek Hunt Fish Falls Loop

Trailhead: From NC 181, go east for 4.5 mi. on Brown Mountain Beach Road, then turn left on SR 1328/ Brown Mountain Road. In Mortimer, after 8.5 mi., the road Ts into SR 90; go left. After 1.9 mi., go left again, on FR 464. Trailhead parking is 3.1 mi. on the right.

Loop/one-way: One-way (to main campsite, which is 1.4 mi.). Day-hike options include Gragg Prong Loop (7.3 mi.) and Lost Cove Loop (7.6 mi.).

Difficulty: The backpack in is easy; day hikes are moderate.

Campsites (with GPS coordinates): The main camping area, in a sizable stand of hemlocks, is 1.4 mi. in (N36 00.947 W81 47.790). If you'd like a more intimate campsite, there are 3 suitable locations on the Lost Cove Loop (hiked counterclockwise): at mile 3.4 (N36 01.431 W81 48.753), at mile 6.6 (N36 01.033 W81 49.329), and on the north bank of Lost Cove Creek just above Hunt Fish Falls (N36 00.910 W81 48.409). There is one location on the Gragg Prong Loop (hiked clockwise), at mile 3.2 (N36 01.574 W81 47.900).

Map: "Wilson Creek National Wild and Scenic River Trail Guide: Pisgah National Forest," USDA Forest Service, 1:24,000, 40-ft. intervals.

Follow the trail: To reach the main campsite: From the trailhead, go 0.8 mi. on the Hunt Fish Falls Trail to the Lost Cove Trail. Go right for 0.6 mi. to the campsite. For the Lost Cove Loop from the main campground: Hike 0.4 mi. downstream on Lost Cove Trail. Cross Lost Cove Creek and go left on Timber Ridge Trail. After 3.1 mi. go left on Lost Cove Trail. Take Lost Cove 4.1 mi. back to the campsite. For the Gragg Prong Loop, hike 0.4 mi. downstream to Timber Ridge Trail; go left. Take Timber Ridge 3.1 mi. to Lost Cove Trail and go right; descend 1.3 mi. and go right. Follow Gragg Prong 2.5 mi. back to the campsite.

Fee? No.

Water (with GPS coordinates): Water is available at the campsite (N36 00.947 W81 47.790). On the Lost Cove Loop, there is no water until the 5.5-mi. mark, at which point the trail follows Lost Cove Creek back to camp. On the Gragg Prong Loop, there is water from the 2.2-mi. mark on.

Land manager: USDA Forest Service, Grandfather Ranger District.

Trip highlights: Hunt Fish Falls and the swimming hole beneath it. There are also several good swimming holes on Gragg Prong.

Special considerations: Rain can raise water levels quickly in this steep-walled canyon. And even if it hasn't rained in a while, with multiple creek crossings you're bound to get wet.

Night hike in? Yes. The 1.4-mi. hike to the main camping area is relatively easy, though care should be taken around Hunt Fish Falls.

Solo? Yes.

Family friendly? Yes.

Bailout options: No.

Seasons: Summer and early fall, to take advantage of swimming.

Weather: Storms can quickly raise water levels in the steep canyons in the area.

Solitude rating: 2. Hunt Fish Falls is especially popular, as are the falls along Gragg Prong.

Nearest outfitter: Footsloggers, Blowing Rock, (828) 295-4453, www.footsloggers.com.

Hunting allowed? Local seasons apply.

More info: USDA Forest Service, Grandfather Ranger District, (828) 652-4841, www.cs.unca.edu/nfsnc/ recreation/linville.pd; or visit the Friends of Wilson Creek website, www.Friendsofwilsoncreek.org.

another 8 feet, Lost Cove Creek fills a rock pool carved out over millions of years. Larger than an Olympic-sized pool, it has shallow areas for wading and deeper areas for testing cooler waters on a hot day. Perhaps best of all, there's an ample expanse of smooth rock to stretch out on and catch some rays. Swim, dry, repeat. And it's just a half mile from one of the state's prime primitive camping areas, a football-field-sized flat expanse carpeted in evergreen needles and protected by towering hemlocks.

So, ideal swimming hole, great campsite just 1.4 miles from the trailhead: Why leave this little oasis? There's some good hiking here as well.

Lost Cove loop: This 7.6-mile loop gives avid hikers a chance to stretch their legs. From camp, walk downstream for 0.4 miles, cross Lost Cove Creek, then take a left on Timber Ridge Trail, which follows an old roadbed up to and along one of the many ridges that finger through the Wilson Creek area. Top out after 3.1 miles on 2,946-foot Bee Mountain (base camp is at about 1,800 feet, so it's not a bad climb), before a quick descent to the valley floor and your return along Lost Cove Creek.

Gragg Prong loop: This 7.3-mile hike begins along the same route as the Lost Cove Loop but leaves Timber Ridge after 3.1 miles. The descent is through a classic hardwood bowl, with minimal understory offering great sight lines. The true incentive for this hike, though, is perhaps the most rugged, wet-and-wild beauty throughout the Wilson Creek area. At mile 2.5 you pick up Gragg Prong, which at first looks like a lovely, if indistinct, mountain stream. That changes in just over a mile, when the trail, now clinging to the mountainside, comes upon a series of spectacular falls—highlighted by the 100-foot (in sections) Gragg Prong Falls—that cascade down the gorge. Carefully scootch out on the rock and take a moment to appreciate the rugged nature of the Blue Ridge Escarpment and how eons of weather have scoured this passage, through a lush forest, down to bedrock.

Pretty good incentive to leave, at least for an afternoon, your Hunt Fish Shangri-la.

BLOWING ROCK

13.6 MILES

NO. OF DAYS: 2–3

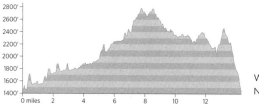

Wilson Creek: Harper Creek/
North Harper Creek Loop

In North Carolina, the Blue Ridge Escarpment marks the transition from rolling Piedmont to Southern Appalachian Mountains. It's an abrupt change, and perhaps nowhere is it more so than in the drop from Grandfather Mountain through Wilson Creek, where the elevation plunges from nearly 6,000 to 1,100 feet in less than 15 miles. You get a good sense of that upheaval backpacking in the Wilson Creek area.

Within Wilson Creek itself, the elevation differences aren't that severe. From Harper Creek to the tops of paralleling Persimmon and Long ridges, there's only a 500-foot elevation change. But that change occurs quickly, which is less a challenge for your legs—the trails into and out of the canyon on this trip are surprisingly gradual—than it is for your Gore-Tex. The Wilson Creek area is all about water and the few places it has to collect in steep terrain, which you'll quickly come to appreciate on the Harper Creek/North Harper Creek Loop.

A mile and a half in, you learn your first lesson in local hydrodynamics. Here Harper Creek, with no other options, plunges about 65 feet in three quick stages, collecting in a sweet, granite pool before moving on to its appointment with Wilson Creek 2 miles downstream. The main lesson you learn here, though, is that 90 percent of the folks who explore this trail only make it this far. Though there are numerous campsite options up to and around the falls, they fill quickly, especially in summer.

Continue upstream and, while you won't escape people, their numbers will dwindle, largely for another water-related reason. Over the next 3 miles there are 5 stream crossings along Harper Creek and North Harper Creek, which you pick up at mile 3.5. None have footbridges; some have decent rock crossings at low water. One, about 2.5 miles in, involves fording a 20-foot-wide stretch of Harper Creek where the water can reach mid-

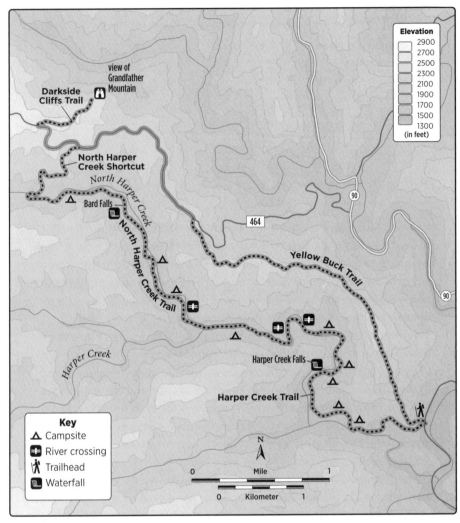

Elevation
2900
2700
2500
2300
2100
1900
1700
1500
1300
(in feet)

view of Grandfather Mountain

Darkside Cliffs Trail

North Harper Creek Shortcut

North Harper Creek

Bard Falls

North Harper Creek Trail

464

Yellow Buck Trail

90

90

Harper Creek

Harper Creek Falls

Harper Creek Trail

Key
△ Campsite
River crossing
Trailhead
Waterfall

N

0   Mile   1

0   Kilometer   1

9 Wilson Creek Harper Creek/North Harper Creek Loop

9 Wilson Creek Harper Creek/North Harper Creek Loop

Trailhead: From NC 181, go east for 4.5 mi. on Brown Mountain Beach Road. Go left on SR 1328/Brown Mountain Road. Continue another 5.5 mi. to the trailhead on the left side of the road, just past the Wilson Creek visitors center.

Loop/one-way: Loop.

Difficulty: Hard (mainly due to multiple creek crossings).

Campsites (with GPS coordinates): 0.8 mi. (N35 58.632 W81 46.509), 1.0 mi. (N35 58.715 W81 46.572), 1.7 mi. (N35 58.961 W81 46.682), 1.9 mi. (N35 59.046 W81 46.652), 2.2 mi. (N35 59.203 W81 46.698), 3.2 mi. (N35 59.244 W81 47.397), 3.8 mi. (N35 59.409 W81 47.860), and 5.7 mi. (N36 00.011 W81 48.877).

Map: "Wilson Creek National Wild and Scenic River Trail Guide: Pisgah National Forest," USDA Forest Service.

Follow the trail: Take Harper Creek Trail 3.5 mi. to a "Y"; go right on North Harper Creek Trail. Take North Harper Creek 2.6 mi. to the North Harper Creek Shortcut. Go right, 1.1 mi. to FS 464. Go left 0.7 mi. to the Darkside Cliffs Trail. Go right for 0.5 mi. to the overlook. Return to FS 464, go left, and hike 2.6 mi. to Yellow Buck Trail. Go right on Yellow Buck for 2.1 mi. The trail Ts into Harper Creek Trail. Go left for 0.1 mi. to the trailhead.

Fee? No.

Water: Water is plentiful on the first half of this trip as the trail picks up Harper Creek less than a mile in and follows it and North Harper Creek for about 6 mi. There is no water the last 7.5 mi.

Land manager: USDA Forest Service, Grandfather Ranger District.

Trip highlights: Waterfalls, beginning with Harper Creek Falls at mile 1.6 and ending with Bard Falls at mile 5.0.

Special considerations: Rain can raise water levels quickly in this steep-walled canyon. And even if it hasn't rained in a while, with multiple creek crossings, you're bound to get wet.

Night hike in? The hike to the first two campsites, both within a mile, is easy. While there are ample opportunities to pitch a tent, the area is popular. If these first areas are full, it's another 0.7 mi. to the next, smaller camping area (though no water crossing is involved).

Solo? No. Too many dicey water crossings make a solo imprudent.

Family friendly? For a family-friendly version of this hike, establish base camp at one of the first two campsites, then either play in the water and/or do day hikes.

Bailout options: No.

Seasons: All, though pay attention to rainfall, especially in winter, which can make creek crossings hazardous.

Weather: See above.

Solitude rating: 2 up to Harper Creek Falls, 4 afterward.

Nearest outfitter: Footsloggers, Blowing Rock, (828) 295-4453, www.footsloggers.com.

Hunting allowed? Local seasons apply.

More info: USDA Forest Service, Grandfather Ranger District, (828) 652-4841, www.cs.unca.edu/nfsnc/recreation/linville.pd; or visit the Friends of Wilson Creek website, www.Friendsofwilsoncreek.org.

thigh—not something you care to tackle in cold weather. (Tip on crossings that threaten to soak your boots: Take them off and slip on a pair of heavy wool socks for the crossing, then dry your feet with a chamois camp towel before putting your dry socks and boots back on. Keep your crossing socks strapped to the outside of your backpack to dry. It's a hassle when you face repeated crossings, but it's better than having wet boots the rest of the trip.)

Because the crossings do get tiresome, this trip bails on North Harper Creek shortly after Bard Falls (you can continue along along the creek for another 2 miles, taking in two more falls, Chestnut Cove Branch and North Harper Creek). Another reason to bail: about 2.3 miles of the return trip is along a gravel Forest Service road (FS 464). Frankly, after slogging along and through the creek for more than 4 miles, you'll appreciate the nontaxing foot-friendly surface.

Before heading back, take a side trip on the half-mile Darkside Cliffs Trail, which you'll pick up by hiking another half mile west on FS 464. It's an easy hike that rewards you with something non-water-related and something you don't often find in Wilson Creek.

A sweeping view, of Grandfather Mountain.

10   Wilson Creek Schoolhouse Ridge Loop

BLOWING ROCK

5.6 MILES

NO. OF DAYS: 1

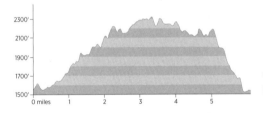

Wilson Creek: Schoolhouse Ridge Loop

This is your Plan B for Wilson Creek. Let's say the forecast calls for rain. You're hopeful that it won't be much, you make the drive, but—it's a deluge. Noah wouldn't even come out of his tent. If you've got all the right gear—head-to-toe Gore-Tex, wet suit, snorkel—and are an experienced, intrepid explorer, no big deal. But if you're like 99 percent of the rest of us, you like a Plan B. I offer this Plan B mainly to show that whether you're going to Wilson Creek, Shining Rock, the Smokies, or wherever, there's usually

Although a drier hike, you won't miss out on Wilson Creek's wet 'n' wild experience along Thorps Creek.

an option when the weather doesn't fully cooperate. Wilson Creek offers a prime spot to demonstrate this because it can be not only uncomfortable but dangerous to trek through these narrow, steep gorges in the rain.

Thus, Plan B calls for pitching your tent in the Forest Service's Mortimer Campground and exploring a portion of Wilson Creek less vulnerable to rain—after the first mile and a half, that is.

This hike begins from the north end of the campground, behind the privy. Thorps Creek is your immediate companion, treating you to a small waterfall in an intimate setting of rhododendron. Over the next mile and a half there are 13 stream crossings, nearly all of which are crossable by rocks (including the seventh crossing, in which the trail stays in the middle

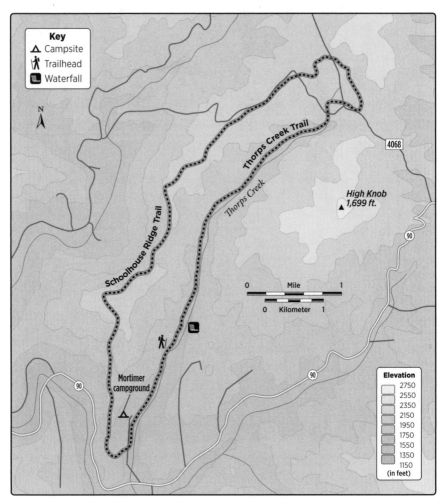

10 Wilson Creek Schoolhouse Ridge Loop

10 Wilson Creek Schoolhouse Ridge Loop

Trailhead: From NC 181, go east 4.5 mi. on Brown Mountain Beach Road. Go left on SR 1328/Brown Mountain Road. After 8.5 mi. the road Ts into SR 90 in Mortimer; go left, then take a quick right into the Mortimer Recreation Area and campground.

Loop/one-way: Loop.

Difficulty: Moderate.

Campsites (with GPS coordinates): The Mortimer campground is at the trailhead (N35 59.624 W81 45.687).

Map: "Wilson Creek National Wild and Scenic River Trail Guide: Pisgah National Forest," U.S. Forest Service.

Follow the trail: From the trailhead at the north end of the campground, take Thorps Creek Trail 2.0 mi. to FR 4068. Go left for 0.8 mi., then go left on Schoolhouse Ridge Trail. Take Schoolhouse Ridge 2.6 mi. back to the campground. (It's another 0.2 mi. back to the trailhead.)

Fee? $10 per night camping fee.

Water: Treated water is available at the campground and along the first mile and a half of trail, from Thorps Creek. There is no water the rest of the trip.

Land manager: USDA Forest Service, Grandfather Ranger District.

Trip highlight: After the first 1.5 mi., it's comparatively (for Wilson Creek) dry hiking.

Special considerations: 2.5 mi. of trail stay atop Schoolhouse Ridge; be observant for afternoon thunderstorms in summer.

Night hike in? Yes.

Solo? Yes.

Family friendly? Yes.

Bailout options: No.

Seasons: The campground is open Apr. 1–Nov. 30.

Weather: Save for the narrow Thorps Creek canyon at the beginning of the hike, this loop isn't as susceptible to sudden rains as other areas in Wilson Creek.

Solitude rating: 3. Less water means fewer people on this hike.

Nearest outfitter: Footsloggers, Blowing Rock, (828) 295-4453, www.footsloggers.com.

Hunting allowed? Local seasons apply.

More info: USDA Forest Service, Grandfather Ranger District, (828) 652-4841, www.cs.unca.edu/nfsnc/recreation/linville.pd; or visit the Friends of Wilson Creek website, www.FriendsofWilsoncreek.org.

of the stream for 20 yards). If you're worried that you'll miss out on the Wilson Creek experience, Thorps Creek, which slices through a narrow, heavily wooded canyon, will allay those concerns.

At the 2-mile mark, the trail Ts into FR 4068. If you're up for a longer hike, cross the road and pick up the Wilson Ridge Trail, which runs 11.2 miles, from the south end of the Wilson Creek Gorge north to Bank Camp Ridge. Otherwise, go left on the road for three quarters of a mile and go left again for the return trip along Schoolhouse Ridge. After 2.6 miles, the trail returns you to the south end of the Mortimer Campground.

Plan B is a nice day hike. If you're lucky, it may buy you enough time for a return of sunshine and a chance to explore Wilson Creek's true backcountry. (See trips 8 and 9.)

11   Doughton Park Basin Cove Loop

BLOWING ROCK

1.5-MILE BACKPACK; DAY-HIKE OPTIONS OF 7 TO 18 MILES

NO. OF DAYS: 2–3

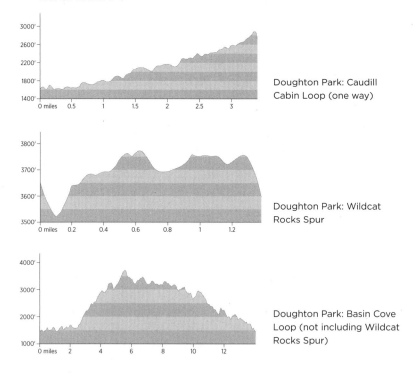

Doughton Park: Caudill Cabin Loop (one way)

Doughton Park: Wildcat Rocks Spur

Doughton Park: Basin Cove Loop (not including Wildcat Rocks Spur)

Man, is there ever a great spot to pump water at the Basin Cove camp-ground. From the information kiosk, cross the trail, then follow the worn path down to Basin Creek and you'll see the perfect rock seat to set up shop and purify some water. It's comfy, the view of trout pools downstream is relaxing, and there's a perfect pool to pump from. If you dread the usual ordeal of pumping water as much as I do, you'll feel like filling every Nalgene bottle in the campground.

When friend and fellow hiker/backpacker Chris Underhill suggested the 7.5-mile Bluff Mountain Trail for this guide, I looked at him askance. The trail parallels the Blue Ridge Parkway through Doughton Park, and you'll cross the scenic roadway twice, traipse through a parking lot, weave through a campground (which Chris suggested might make a good overnight), pass a lodge, and, conveniently for the cash-strapped National Park Service, visit an NPS-run gift shop and restaurant. It's not quite the backcountry experience most of us seek.

Then I got to thinking about the trail's other attributes: its passage over grassy balds, its side trip to the Alligator Back Overlook, and its access to Wildcat Rocks, from which you can see the tiny Caudill Cabin more than 800 vertical feet below. I got out a dog-eared copy of a Doughton Park trail map and discovered that near the base of the pie-shaped, 7,000-acre park, at the confluence of 3 trails, was a triangle next to the words "primitive campsite." Bingo! A destination was born.

The Basin Creek campground is an easy 1.5-mile hike in on the Grassy Gap Fire Road. From this base camp you can do any number of loop day hikes utilizing the park's 30 miles of hiking trail. I recommend two.

The Bluff Ridge Primitive trail, at 2.8 miles, is the quickest way up to the parkway. That also means it's the steepest, with an especially stout climb up the first mile of Bluff Ridge. Relief comes at the Bluff Mountain shelter, where you can catch your breath before heading north on the Bluff Mountain Trail over two grassy balds with stellar views. After your over-easys with grits (optional) at The Bluffs coffee shop, retrace your steps back to the Wildcat Rocks Overlook (mandatory). Peer over the edge. See that small clearing? See the tiny cabin? That's the Caudill Cabin, and it's your assignment for the next day. Continue back to the Bluff Ridge Primitive Trail, where you have two options. If the day is late and your legs are tired, head back down the Bluff Ridge Primitive Trail for a 10.6-mile day. If you're up for more, continue south on the Bluff Mountain Trail for 3.6 miles to the Flat Rock Ridge Trail, bordering the Thurmond Chatham Game Lands.

Beyond this "fat man squeeze" is open ridgeline leading to Bluff Mountain.

After 4.9 miles you'll be deposited at the Grassy Gap trailhead (need anything from the car?), for a 1.7-mile hike back to camp.

After a good night's sleep, you're in for a significantly flatter 3.4-mile hike to the Caudill Cabin. The trail plays hopscotch with Basin Creek, crossing the creek and its tributaries 16 times (unless it's been especially rainy, the crossings are relatively dry). The creek is rich with small trout pools (single hook, artificial lures, 7-inch limit, 4 per creel), and there's a particularly swell waterfall 2.5 miles up with a nice swimming hole.

The trail ends at the doorstep of the Caudill Cabin, built in the late 1890s by Martin and Janie Caudill. Walk inside (you're allowed) the one-room, 14' x 16' cabin and you might think it a cozy retreat for a young couple. Now

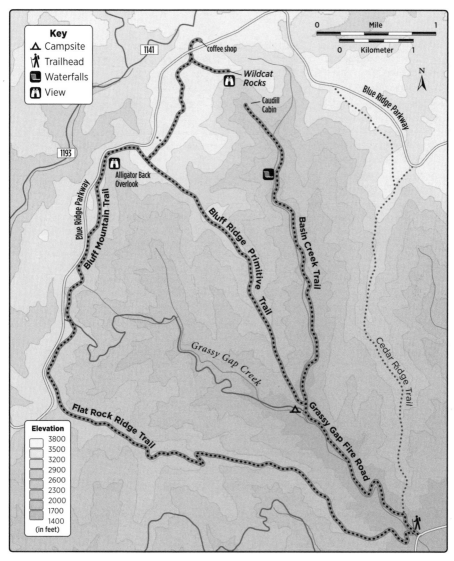

1141

coffee shop

Wildcat Rocks 🔭

Caudill Cabin

Blue Ridge Parkway

N

1193

🔭 Alligator Back Overlook

Blue Ridge Parkway

Bluff Mountain Trail

Bluff Ridge Primitive Trail

Basin Creek Trail

📖

Cedar Ridge Trail

Grassy Gap Creek

△ Grassy Gap Fire Road

Flat Rock Ridge Trail

🧍

Elevation
3800
3500
3200
2900
2600
2300
2000
1700
1400
(in feet)

0   Mile   1

0   Kilometer   1

11 Doughton Park Basin Cove Loop

11 **Doughton Park** Basin Cove Loop

Trailhead: From the Blue Ridge Parkway drive 6.6 mi. south on NC 18, then turn left (north) on, Long-bottom Road (SR 1728). Go another 6.6 mi. and cross a small bridge over Basin Creek. The trailhead is on your left; a sizable parking area is on your right.

Loop/one-way: One-way to campsite; loop and out-and-back day hikes.

Difficulty: Backpack in is easy; Bluff Ridge/Bluff Mountain/Flat Rock Ridge/Grassy Gap Loop is hard; Basin Creek to Caudill Cabin is easy.

Campsites (with GPS coordinates): Camping is only allowed at the sizable Basin Cove primitive camping area (N36 23.377 W81 09.679), with pine canopy, pine needle ground cover, and metal fire rings. Basin Creek runs by the campground.

Maps: USGS: Whitehead. A generalized map with trail distances is available at the coffee shop at milepost 241 on the Blue Ridge Parkway.

Follow the trail: To reach the primitive camping area from the trailhead on Longbottom Road, take Grassy Gap Fire Road 1.7 mi. For the Bluff Mountain/Blue Ridge Parkway day-hike loop: From the campsite, take the Bluff Ridge Primitive Trail 2.8 mi. to the Bluff Mountain shelter. Go right on the Bluff Mountain Trail for 2.5 mi. across the balds to Wildcat Rocks and the coffee shop area. Return on the Bluff Mountain Trail to the shelter. Here, you have two options: Return to camp on the Bluff Ridge Primitive Trail for a 10.6-mi. day, or boost your day to 18 mi. by continuing another 3.6 mi. on Bluff Mountain Trail to Flat Rock Ridge Trail. Go left on Flat Rock Ridge for 4.9 mi. to the Grassy Gap trailhead. Return 1.7 mi. on Grassy Gap Trail to the campsite. To reach Caudill Cabin from the campsite, take the Basin Creek Trail for 3.4 mi. Return the same way.

Fee? $9 per night. There is no self-pay kiosk at the campground. Call the District Ranger office in Laurel Springs at (336) 372-8568 to arrange payment.

Water (with GPS coordinates): Basin Creek runs by the campground and along the Basin Creek Trail to Caudill Cabin. There is water at the coffee shop (N36 26.033 W81 10.653) at milepost 241 on the Blue Ridge Parkway near Wildcat Rocks. Otherwise, there is only intermittent water on the Bluff Mountain day hike.

Land manager: National Park Service, Blue Ridge Parkway.

Trip highlights: Caudill Cabin, both from the front door and from 900 ft. almost directly above, from the Wildcat Rocks Overlook; open hiking on grassy balds on spur to Wildcat Rock.

Special considerations: Primitive camping is prohibited anywhere but the Basin Cove campground.

Night hike in? Yes. It's a flat hike to the campsite along an old road.

Solo? Yes. Some trails may not see a lot of traffic during the week, but overall, Doughton Park is a popular Blue Ridge Parkway hiking destination.

Family friendly? Yes. An easy pack-in for the kids. Basin Creek Trail is an especially good kid hike, with lots of water and a treat, the Caudill Cabin, at the end.

Bailout options: It's only a mile and a half from camp back to the car.

Seasons: All.

Weather: Ridgeline hiking can attract late afternoon thunderstorms in summer.

Solitude rating: 2.

Nearest outfitter: Footsloggers, Boone, (828) 262-5111, www.footsloggers.com.

Hunting allowed? No, although the Flat Rock Ridge Trail snuggles up to the Thurmond Chatham Game land.

More info: (336) 372-8568, www.nps.gov/blri. For more info on the Caudill Cabin: www.caudillcabin.org.

picture it with Martin, Janie, and their 14 kids. Even cozier, no? Finally, picture it on an exceptionally rainy night in 1916 when a torrential downpour sent a wall of water down Basin Creek, wiping out nearly the entire Basin Cove community (take note of the numerous stone chimneys on your hike back).

The cabin you are standing in was one of the few structures to survive.

12   Stone Mountain State Park

ELKIN

1.2 TO 3 MILES TO PRIMITIVE CAMPSITES. Devil's Garden Overlook day hike on the Mountains-to-Sea Trail is 9.6 miles roundtrip. An additional 12 miles of trail is in the park.

NO. OF DAYS: 2

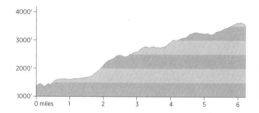

Stone Mountain State Park (trailhead to Devil's Garden Overlook)

Stone Mountain is the ideal beginner trip. The designated campsites aren't far from the trailhead, the hike in (after a quick-but-heart-thumping initial rise) is a gentle climb along old roadbed, and 4 of the 6 campsites are along water. Seclusion is guaranteed, as the sites are well spaced and out of both view and earshot of one another, and they're along a spur trail off the more-beaten path. Not only are they secluded, but they're seductive, located in big coves, on a ridgeline, and along alpine creeks. These are sites where you'd be content to hang out, get to know your gear, read a book, take pictures. Maybe write some haiku . . .

Big trees, comfy site
But I came to take a hike
Devil of a climb.

That devil of a climb would be the 5-mile hike up—more than 1,500 vertical feet up—the Mountains-to-Sea Trail (MST) to the Devil's Garden Overlook on the Blue Ridge Parkway. (The overall distance on this portion of the MST is 6 miles; you will have lopped off a little over a mile and 500 vertical

The Mountains-to-Sea Trail departs the high country and begins its descent into the Piedmont at Stone Mountain.

feet on your backpack in.) Despite following an old roadbed, this trail is steep for the first third of a mile, gaining about 600 vertical feet before better resembling the wagon path it once was. From there, it's a steady climb, with occasional saddles of relief, through a forest dominated by Piedmont hardwoods to the overlook at 3,428 feet.

As a summit destination, Devil's Garden is nothing to postcard home about. The trail's main attribute is the solitude it affords through a maturing forest. If it's postcards you're after, day hike from base camp back down the trail to Stone Mountain's varied and picturesque attractions. Most immediately, you'll encounter the East Prong of the Roaring Fork River, where single-hook, artificial-lure trout fishing is allowed; trout may be harvested only during a 4-month period (visit the N.C. Wildlife Resources Commission at www.ncwildlife.org for specifics). Elsewhere in the park, single-hook artificial lures may be used on Garden Widow's and Big Sandy creeks, both designated Wild Trout Waters, with rainbows and browns at lower elevations, brook trout higher up. (Trout were once found in North Carolina as far east as the Triangle, but warmer water temperatures have driven them back to higher elevations.)

Stone Mountain has 12 miles of less-taxing hiking. The most popular trail is the 4.5-mile Stone Mountain Loop. Hiking clockwise from the base trailhead, you might think the loop's highlight is the Hutchinson Homestead, a restoration of a mid-1800s farm that gives a keen sense of what life might have been like in this remote setting some 175 years ago. Moving

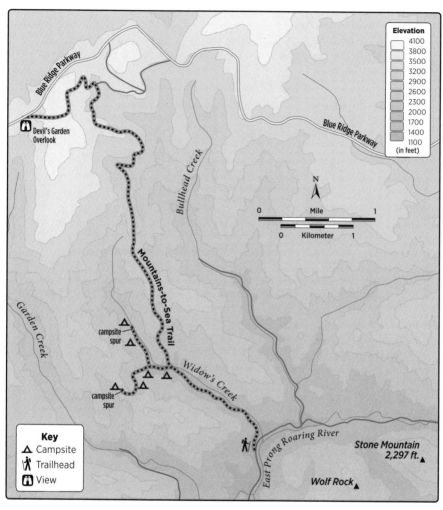

Elevation
4100
3800
3500
3200
2900
2600
2300
2000
1700
1400
1100
(in feet)

Blue Ridge Parkway

Devil's Garden
Overlook

Bullhead Creek

Blue Ridge Parkway

N

0   Mile   1

0   Kilometer   1

Mountains-to-Sea Trail

Garden Creek

campsite
spur

campsite
spur

Widow's Creek

Key

△ Campsite

🚶 Trailhead

👁 View

East Prong Roaring River

Stone Mountain
2,297 ft. ▲

Wolf Rock ▲

12 Stone Mountain State Park

12 Stone Mountain State Park

Trailhead: From US 21, go west on Traphill Road (SR 1002) for 4.4 mi. At the John P. Frank Parkway turn right and go 6.9 mi. to the park entrance, 12.8 mi. to the trailhead, a gravel parking lot on the right.

Loop/one-way: One-way.

Difficulty: Moderate backpack in; hard day hike up to Devil's Garden Overlook.

Campsites (with GPS coordinates): 6 sites, well spaced, are located off 2 spurs off the main trail, from 1.2 to 3 mi. from the trailhead. On the left spur: campsites A (N36 24.229 W81 05.055), B (N36 24.175 W81 05.221), C (N36 24.112 W81 05.232), and D (N36 24.086 W81 05.340). On the right spur: campsites E (N36 24.319 W81 05.137) and F (N36 24.544 W81 05.267).

Maps: USGS: Glade Valley. A non-topo trail map is available at the park.

Follow the trail: To reach the campsites from the trailhead, hike the Mountains-to-Sea Trail 1.2 mi. to the campsite spurs; continue another 5 mi. to the Devil's Garden Overlook.

Fee? $13 a night camping fee.

Water: Campsites A, B, E, and F are located on streams; campsites C and D are as much as a quarter mile from water.

Land manager: N.C. Division of Parks and Recreation. The day-hike option described is part of the Mountains-to-Sea Trail.

Trip highlights: Great campsites, ideal for beginners content to stay put and tinker with their new equipment. MST trail up to Devil's Garden Overlook makes for a good, long (about 10 mi. roundtrip) day hike.

Special considerations: No.

Night hike in? An easy hike on even doubletrack terrain, but the park closes at dark (9:00 P.M. May–Aug.; 8:00 P.M. Mar., Apr., Sept., Oct.; 6:00 P.M. Nov.–Feb.).

Solo? Yes. Sites are on a lesser-used portion of the park, but hikers are usually around if you get into trouble.

Family friendly? Yes. Campsites are close, and Stone Mountain State Park has 12 mi. of easy to moderate trail, including the popular 4.5-mi. Stone Mountain Trail, taking in the park's namesake attraction, a 600-ft. granite dome. Plus, there's more than 20 mi. of designated trout waters.

Bailout options: It's less than an hour's hike back to the car; the park also has a campground with water and hot showers ($18 a night) if primitive camping proves not to be your thing.

Seasons: Fall, winter, spring.

Weather: Hot summers make for not-so-hot sleeping at night.

Solitude rating: Campsites are far enough apart that you won't see your neighbors.

Nearest outfitter: Wal-Mart Supercenter, Elkin, (336) 526-2636. (Okay, Walmart isn't exactly an outfitter, but it may well have what you need.)

Hunting allowed? No.

More info: Stone Mountain State Park, (336) 957-8185, www.ncparks.gov.

on, you might think the highlight is the wooden staircase that takes you up along 200-foot Stone Mountain Falls. Topping out, you might think the highlight is the chance to skitter across the top of this granite dome, maybe catch a warm Z or two on the sun-baked rock face on an otherwise chilly late fall afternoon. Postcard opportunities all. (Pick up a trail map at the park entrance.)

Rock climbing is also permitted in the park. Several popular routes up Stone Mountain's face are detailed in *The Climber's Guide to North Carolina* (Falcon Press).

13   **Montreat** Graybeard Mountain

BLACK MOUNTAIN

8.0 MILES

NO. OF DAYS: 2

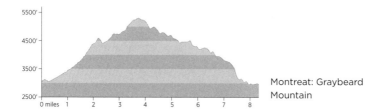

Montreat: Graybeard Mountain

Although this is a place with 20 miles of trail, not many people are familiar with the hiking at the Montreat Conference Center near Black Mountain. Perhaps that's because it exists in the shadow of its more famous neighbors, such as Linville Gorge, renowned for some of the wildest hiking in the East; or the Black Mountains, the highest mountain range east of South Dakota's Black Hills; or the greater Pisgah National Forest, with more than 800 miles of trail, a hiking playground of regional renown.

Even if the neighbors may be bigger and better known, there is much to recommend in this 2,500-acre wild area. Montreat offers something of a microcosm of its neighbors—from lush cove forest to mountain views to challenging ridgeline hiking—on the 8.0-mile Graybeard/West Ridge/Big Piney loop, a perfect 2-day trip, especially for folks who don't subscribe to the "early-to-rise-and-hit-the-trail" school of backpacking. For starters, all the campsites—and be warned that there are only 3 main ones—are within the first 2 miles. Don't end up hitting the trail until 3:00 in the afternoon? Not a problem at Montreat.

A couple of steep drops do require you and your pack to descend separately. Otherwise, West Ridge Trail is a nice ridgeline descent.

That said, don't get the idea you'll be at camp and roasting marshmallows by 4:00. The hiking here is rugged—though not, perhaps, as rugged as the descriptions on the Montreat trail map suggest. "They were done by a Boy Scout for his Eagle Scout project," the guy at the Montreat bookstore, where you'll stop for a trail map, told me. "He wasn't estimating for him; he was estimating for people like us."

The 3.25-mile climb to 5,408-foot Graybeard, an elevation gain of 2,300 feet, is estimated by the well-meaning "Boy Sprout" (the bookstore guy's bad pun, not mine) at 3 1/2 hours. Even toting a 40-pound pack and stopping to smell the galax, you should be able to knock a good half hour off that. Thus, expect a 2-hour hike to camp.

The trip begins where US 9 abruptly ends its 4-mile journey from I-40. Graybeard Trail begins its ascent up the (anything but) Flat Creek. The trail is rocky, following an old roadbed through some of the most lush terrain around. Ferns and galax carpet the forest floor, rhododendron and mountain laurel dominate the understory, and mature hardwoods provide a protective canopy in summer. Views are few, so take advantage where you can: at Pott's Cove, 1.4 miles into the hike, and at Walker's Knob, accessed via a 0.2-mile spur trail at the 2.3-mile mark.

The best camping opportunity comes 1.8 miles into the hike, at Gray-

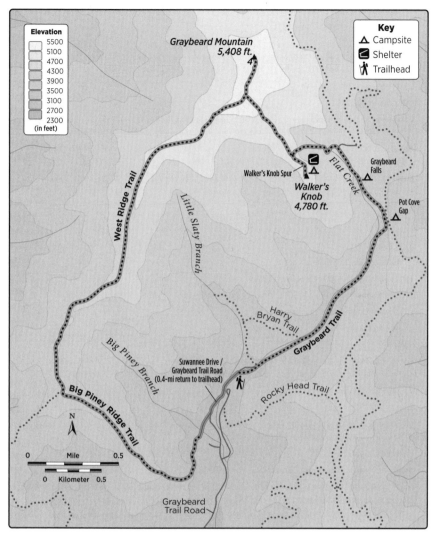

Key
△ Campsite
▣ Shelter
🚶 Trailhead

Elevation
5500
5100
4700
4300
3900
3500
3100
2700
2300
(in feet)

*Graybeard Mountain
5,408 ft.*

West Ridge Trail

Little Slaty Branch

Walker's Knob Spur

*Walker's
Knob
4,780 ft.*

Flat Creek

Graybeard
Falls

Pot Cove
Gap

Harry
Bryan Trail

Graybeard Trail

Big Piney Branch

Suwannee Drive /
Graybeard Trail Road
(0.4-mi return to trailhead)

Rocky Head Trail

Big Piney Ridge Trail

N

0   Mile   0.5

0   Kilometer   0.5

Graybeard
Trail Road

13 Montreat Graybeard Mountain

13 **Montreat** Graybeard Mountain

Trailhead: From I-40 take the Black Mountain exit on NC 9. Go north for 3.0 mi. to Lookout Drive. Take a right, park, and run into the bookstore across Lookout Drive to get a trail map. Get back on NC 9, aka Assembly Drive, and continue for 1.0 mi. to the well-marked Graybeard trailhead.

Loop/one-way: Loop.

Difficulty: Moderate.

Campsites (with GPS coordinates): 1.3 mi., Pott's Cove Gap (N35 40.275 W82 16.892); 1.8 mi., Graybeard Falls (N35 40.498 W82 17.111); 2.3 mi., Walker Knob spur, shelter (N35 40.589 W82 17.455).

Map: Montreat Trail Map, free and functional, is available at the Montreat Conference Center bookstore. A full-color, $8.95 topo version is also available at the bookstore.

Follow the trail: From the trailhead, take Graybeard Trail 3.2 mi. to the 0.3-mi. spur up to the 5,408-ft. Graybeard summit. Return to the spur/Graybeard Trail and pick up West Ridge Trail. Go 2.2 mi. to Big Piney Ridge Trail and go left. After 1.5 mi., Big Piney ends at the paved Suwannee Drive. Take Suwannee 0.3 mi., go left on Graybeard Trail Road for another 0.1 mi. to the trailhead.

Fee? No.

Water: The trail follows Flat Creek, a reliable source for treatable water, for the first 2.1 mi. There is no reliable water after that.

Land manager: Montreat Conference Center.

Trip highlights: Views from 4,780-ft. Walker's Knob and 5,408-ft. Graybeard Mountain.

Special considerations: None.

Night hike in? No. Hike in is rocky with 4 creek crossings.

Solo? Yes.

Family friendly? Yes. Campsites are not far in, making for quick reward after a good climb. Keep an eye on smaller kids on the sometimes challenging descent, especially on the West Ridge Trail.

Bailout options: No.

Seasons: All.

Weather: Not as subject to the potentially icy winter conditions and afternoon thunderstorms in summer as other spots along the Blue Ridge Escarpment.

Solitude rating: 3.

Nearest outfitter: Take A Hike Outfitters, Black Mountain, (828) 669-0811.

Hunting allowed? No, although the Montreat property brushes up against Pisgah National Forest, where hunting is allowed, at Pott's Cove Gap and atop Graybeard Mountain.

More info: Montreat Conference Center, (800) 572-2257 or (828) 669-2911; www.montreat.org/programs/outdoors.

beard Falls. Just across Flat Creek you'll find a shelf capable of comfortably holding 4 or 5 tents. There's also a camp site at Pott's Cove, and a final opportunity at a small clearing at the Walker's Knob spur (where there's also a shelter).

At the 3-mile mark you'll reach the spur to Graybeard (you'll be at Big Slaty, also known as "False Graybeard"). It's a quick 5 minutes to Graybeard's 5,408-foot pinprick summit. Mount a rock and you'll catch good views of the Craggy Mountains to the north and east.

The return trip is down West Ridge Trail, rated as "strenuous" on the trail map and upgraded to "very hard" on a trail sign. With the exception of 3 or 4 drops down steep but short, nontechnical rock faces that may require you and your pack to descend separately, this is otherwise a nice ridgeline stroll along a narrow spine. The bigger challenge comes where you leave West Ridge for the descent down Big Piney Ridge, a trail that loses more than 1,000 feet in 1.2 miles. This stretch can be especially perilous during wet weather, when the clay tread gets telemarketer slick.

If you've been debating whether hiking poles are a worthy companion, this stretch should convince you to make the commitment.

Blue Ridge Escarpment/South

According to the Wilderness Act of 1964, "A wilderness, in contrast with those areas where man and his own works dominate the landscape, is hereby recognized as an area where the earth and its community of life are untrammeled by man." Ironically, the Shining Rock Wilderness might not exist were it not for an act of blatant trammeling by man.

In the early 1900s, intense logging began that would soon strip the area of much of its native red spruce, Fraser firs, hemlocks, and hardwoods. Left in the wake were heaps of slash, forest-fire fuel waiting to be ignited. On October 19, 1925, a wildfire started in the vicinity of Black Balsam Knob. Within three days, it had torched 25,000 acres, burning so intensely in areas that all organic matter was destroyed 10 to 12 inches deep, well into the rooting zone. Those trees that did manage to battle back were destroyed in a subsequent fire in 1942.

In their place today, for the most part, are vast balds. As a result, Shining Rock, a member of the nation's inaugural 1964 class of wilderness areas, is one of the few spots in the Southern Appalachians where open terrain and wide vistas are the norm. This abundance of open space makes the 18,483-acre wilderness extremely popular with backpackers and day hikers alike. Adding to its allure is the fact that much of the area sits atop ridgelines and high plateaus, generally from 5,000 to 6,200 feet, and is surprisingly flat. Save the climb up from the Daniel Boone Boy Scout Camp to Shining Rock Ledge, a gain of more than 1,500 feet in 3.7 miles, the area is devoid of grueling climbs. From a scenery-for-sweat perspective, it's hard to top Shining Rock.

Described here are 3 trips: the popular summer hike in from Ivestor Gap to Shining Rock; the main winter option, a 16-mile loop from the Daniel Boone Boy Scout Camp; and a lesser-known 8.2-mile loop that skirts the crowds but doesn't scrimp on scenery.

BREVARD

8.2 MILES

NO. OF DAYS: 2

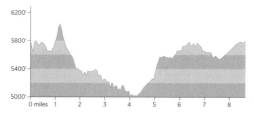

Shining Rock: Sam Knob Loop

As the masses fill the generous Forest Service parking lot at Black Balsam Knob, lace up their boots, strap on their packs, and begin marching in lockstep out the Ivestor Gap Trail, resist the urge to lemming along. Instead, stay back, give a wave, then duck behind the outhouse for an 8.2-mile, 2-day loop of solitude. For it's Shining Rock that gets written up in *Backpacker* and other outdoors magazines, Shining Rock that's on the itinerary of every scout troop and youth group in need of a wilderness experience, and Shining Rock that, despite being a wilderness area, has a Web cam. Meanwhile, Sam Knob and its understudy Little Sam Knob sit just to the west, just outside the designated wilderness, basking in relative solitude.

This is a bit of a mystery. The Sams offer many of the same treats you'll find at Shining Rock: great views from mountaintop balds, open heath meadows teaming with wildflowers, isolated sky islands of black balsam copses, and a waterfall or two—without the crowds. And unlike at Shining Rock, your odds of scoring a primo backcountry campsite are good no matter when you visit.

After your stealth departure behind the privy (it's actually about 15 feet north of the loo) on Sam Knob Trail, you descend through a heath meadow rich with blueberries. After just over a half mile the trail reaches the base of Sam Knob. Take the 0.8-mile spur to the 6,050-foot summit, where you'll find 3 cozy yet exposed campsites on the false summit (on the knob's east side).

More good sites await as you descend and continue on the main trail down to Flat Laurel Creek, where you'll pick up the eponymously named trail. The trail leaves the creek after 0.4 miles and follows an agreeable old roadbed for the next 2 miles, to Flat Creek Trail's southwest terminus at NC 215. Here you'll encounter the only ugliness on this loop: a short, 0.2-mile

The descent from Little Sam Knob to Flat Laurel Creek.

stretch along the wimpy shoulder of curvy NC 215. Keep your ears perked for oncoming traffic.

Resume the backcountry portion of the hike with a left turn onto the Mountains-to-Sea Trail (MST). For the next couple of miles the trail changes complexion, exchanging the region's open expanse for tight passage through rhododendron and mountain laurel. Resilient, if small, stands of black balsams dot the way. This ends as you leave the MST on Little Sam Trail, which descends from the ridgeline down to Flat Laurel Creek Trail. The last mile or so of the loop may be the highlight, as it hugs the southeast rim of a bowl dominated by blueberries and assorted wildflowers. It's akin to Graveyard Fields, the popular Blue Ridge Parkway pullout attraction a ridge to the east, but again, without the crowds.

Emerge from near the privy and brace for your return to wilderness civilization.

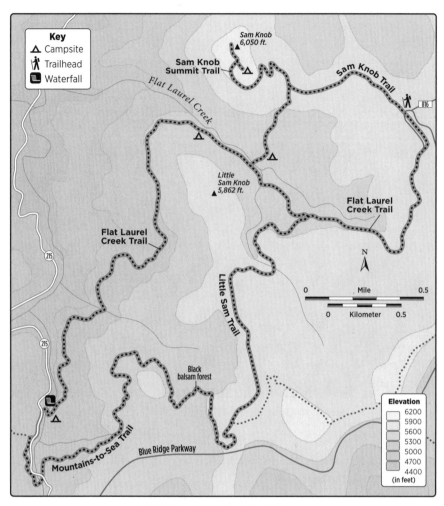

Key
△ Campsite
🥾 Trailhead
🖼️ Waterfall

Sam Knob
6,050 ft.

**Sam Knob
Summit Trail**

Flat Laurel Creek

Sam Knob Trail

816

*Little
Sam Knob
5,862 ft.*

**Flat Laurel
Creek Trail**

**Flat Laurel
Creek Trail**

N

215

Little Sam Trail

215

0   Mile   0.5

0   Kilometer   0.5

Black
balsam forest

Mountains-to-Sea Trail

Blue Ridge Parkway

Elevation
6200
5900
5600
5300
5000
4700
4400
(in feet)

14 Shining Rock Sam Knob Loop

14 Shining Rock Sam Knob Loop

Trailhead: From milepost 420 on the Blue Ridge Parkway, go north on FS 816; the road ends after a mile, in the trailhead parking lot. Trailhead is at the gate just north of the outhouse.

Loop/one-way: Loop.

Difficulty: Moderate.

Campsites (with GPS coordinates): *Distances are on main route, not including spur to Sam Knob.* 0.9 mi. (N35 19.417 W82 53.541), 1.2 mi. (N35 19.446 W82 53.763), 3.2 mi. (N35 18.469 W82 54.5250). Also, 0.7 mi. up the Sam Knob spur (about 1.3 mi. from the trailhead) are 3 compact campsites on the knob's false summit (N35 19.685 W82 53.653).

Map: "Shining Rock & Middle Prong Wilderness," Pisgah National Forest, USDA Forest Service, 1:24,000, 50-ft. intervals.

Follow the trail: From the trailhead, take the Sam Knob Trail. At the 0.6-mi. mark is the 0.8-mi. Sam Knob Summit Trail; continue on Sam Knob Trail 0.4 mi. to Flat Laurel Creek Trail. Go right. After 2.3 mi., Flat Laurel Creek ends at NC 215; go left along the shoulder of NC 215 for 0.2 mi., then go left onto the Mountains-to-Sea Trail. Stay on the MST for 1.9 mi., then go left on Little Sam Trail. After 1.6 mi., Little Sam Ts into Flat Laurel Creek Trail; go right for 1.1 mi. back to the trailhead.

Fee? No.

Water (with GPS coordinates): Water is available from Flat Laurel Creek from mile 1.0 to mile 1.4. Beyond that: miles 2.0 (N35 19.069 W82 54.005), 2.5 (N35 18.846 W82 54.267), 3.1 (N35 18.527 W82 54.438), 3.2 (N35 18.469 W82 54.525), 4.0 (N35 18.394 W82 54.220), 5.4 (N35 18.351 W82 53.720), 6.6 (N35 18.994 W82 53.508), and 7.4 (N35 19.056 W82 52.999).

Land manager: USDA Forest Service, Pisgah Ranger District.

Trip highlight: More solitude than you'll find next door at Shining Rock, but with similar open terrain.

Special considerations: Main trailhead is off the Blue Ridge Parkway, which is not maintained during winter and closes due to snow and ice. There's a secondary access, with parking, on the east side of NC 215 less than a mile north of the parkway. The loop also includes a 0.2-mi. stretch along NC 215, which is curvy and has a minimal shoulder. Be alert.

Night hike in? Yes (from primary trailhead). Trail is open and well maintained. Do not hike the 0.2-mi. stretch on NC 215 in the dark.

Solo? Yes.

Family friendly? Yes. Trip splits into 2 mid-length days. There are views and water to keep kids entertained. Again, take extra care on the 0.2-mi. stretch along NC 215.

Bailout options: Loop can be shortened to less than 3 mi. by going left on Flat Laurel Creek Trail at the 1.0-mi. mark.

Seasons: All, though see "Special considerations."

Weather: Ice and snow can prevent access to primary trailhead in winter. High altitude, exceeding 6,000 ft., makes area susceptible to afternoon thunderstorms in summer.

Solitude rating: 3.

Nearest outfitter: Backcountry Outdoors, Brevard, (828) 884-8670, www.backcountryoutdoors.com.

Hunting allowed? Yes. Consult N.C. Wildlife Resources Commission for local seasons.

More info: USDA Forest Service, Pisgah Ranger District, (828) 257-4200, www.cs.unca.edu/nfsnc/recreation/shining_rock.pdf.

BREVARD

**4.0 MILES TO BASE CAMP; 3.3-MILE OUT-AND-BACK DAY HIKE
ALONG SHINING ROCK RIDGE; VARIOUS ADDITIONAL DAY HIKES**

NO. OF DAYS: 2–4

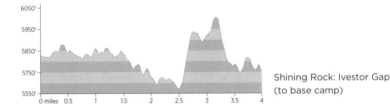

Shining Rock: Ivestor Gap
(to base camp)

Having knocked Ivestor Gap in trip 14 as the Disney of Shining Rock, the attraction everyone comes to see, how can I recommend it? Just as there's good reason folks flock to Disney Land/World, there's good reason they make the pilgrimage along Ivestor Gap to Shining Rock.

For starters, it's a dang easy hike. At 4 miles, it gains just 92 feet of altitude—that's if you stick with the easier Ivestor Gap Trail the entire way. While I recommend coming back that way, the trip is more interesting (and not that much more taxing) if you pick up the Art Loeb Trail at mile 1.7. Art Loeb takes you up 6,050-foot Grassy Cove Top, a tight passage through rhododendron, mountain laurel, blueberries, and the other close-knit members of the heath community. There's a funhouse maze element to this half-mile passage that's amusing in dry weather but can dampen the pack in wet. A pack cover is advised.

Your prime campsites are found between Ivestor Gap and Shining Rock Gap. On busy summer and fall weekends you might have to settle for a trailside spot along this mile and a half stretch. Pay close attention, though, and you'll likely be able to set up camp in a balsam cove, an open gap, or a heath clearing. Keep in mind that the lone water source is just south of Shining Rock Gap, at mile 3.9.

A good campsite is key because this will be your base camp for the next day or two or three. A popular strategy: Hike in, establish camp, then explore Shining Rock for the remainder of the day. Shining Rock is a playground of massive white quartz blocks jutting from the south end of Shining Rock Ledge, the wilderness area's spine. There's good scrambling here and even better views, especially to the west. It's a great spot to catch the

The Art Loeb Trail has wonderfully wide-open stretches near Shining Rock.

sunset (provided you remember to pack a headlamp and bread crumbs for the trip back to camp).

In addition to the natural beauty of this trip is the beauty of its conceit. Quick backpack in, establish camp, do day hikes. Such as

Shining Rock Ledge to Cold Mountain, 3.5 miles. The first 2 miles or so of this hike are a cozy ridgeline hike, flat hiking through a forest of firs and mountain ash and other hardwoods. Then the trail gets interesting, wedging through rock crevasses when it's not climbing over them. An occasional break in the trees offers a glimpse of the world below. The climb from Deep Gap to Cold Mountain is a stout one, gaining more than 1,000 feet in less than a mile and a half.

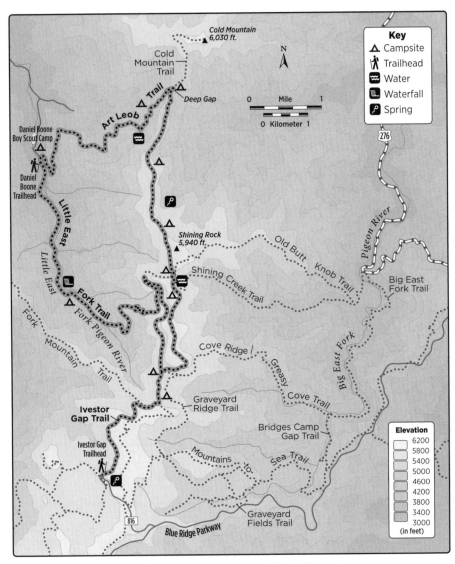

Key

- △ Campsite
- 🚶 Trailhead
- 🌊 Water
- 💧 Waterfall
- 🔑 Spring

Cold Mountain
6,030 ft.

Cold Mountain Trail

Deep Gap

N

Mile

0 — 1

0 — Kilometer — 1

Art Leob Trail

Daniel Boone Boy Scout Camp

Daniel Boone Trailhead

Little East

Little East Fork Trail

Fork Pigeon River

Fork Mountain Trail

Shining Rock
5,940 ft.

Shining Creek Trail

Old Butt Knob Trail

Pigeon River

276

Big East Fork Trail

Big East Fork

Cove Ridge

Greasy Cove Trail

Ivestor Gap Trail

Graveyard Ridge Trail

Bridges Camp Gap Trail

Ivestor Gap Trailhead

Mountains to Sea Trail

816

Blue Ridge Parkway

Graveyard Fields Trail

Elevation

	6200
	5800
	5400
	5000
	4600
	4200
	3800
	3400
	3000
	(in feet)

15 & 16 Shining Rock Ivestor Gap and Daniel Boone Loops

15 **Shining Rock** Ivestor Gap

Trailhead: From milepost 420 on the Blue Ridge Parkway, go north on FS 816. The road ends after a mile, in the trailhead parking lot. The Ivestor Gap Trail begins at the gate north of the parking area.

Loop/one-way: One-way.

Difficulty: Backpack to base camp is easy; day hike along Shining Rock Ledge is moderate; Shining Rock Ledge/Little East Fork loop is hard; Old Butt Knob, Shining Creek Trail loop is hard; Graveyard Ridge to Graveyard Fields is moderate; Black Balsam Knob is moderate.

Campsites (with GPS coordinates): (Note: Included are campsites along the 21-mi. Ivestor Gap/Art Loeb/ Little East Fork loop.) 1.0 mi. (N35 20.217 W82 52.651); 1.9 mi., Ivestor Gap (N35 20.528 W82); 2.2 mi. (N35 20.713 W82 52.030 52.079); 3.5 mi. (N35 21.434 W82 51.868); 4.0 mi., Shining Rock Gap (N35 21.799 W82 51.833); 4.5 mi. (N35 22.286 W82 51.939); 5.7 mi. (N35 23.134 W82 52.161); 7.2 mi. (N35 23.935 W82 51.864); 8.5 mi., in a pinch (N35 23.609 W82 52.657); 12.9 (N35 21.770 W82 53.519); 17.7 mi. (N35 21.449 W82 51.935).

Map: "Shining Rock & Middle Prong Wilderness," Pisgah National Forest, USDA Forest Service, 1:24,000, 50-ft. intervals.

Follow the trail: From the trailhead, take the Ivestor Gap trail 1.7 mi. There, pick up the Art Loeb Trail, which veers right. Take Art Loeb 5.6 mi. to Deep Gap (where you can take the 1.4-mi. spur to Cold Mountain), then continue 3.7 mi. to the Daniel Boone Boy Scout Camp. There, go left along the road through camp for 0.2 mi. and pick up the Little East Fork Trail. Stay on it for 5.5 mi., until it reaches Ivestor Gap Trail. Go right for 4.5 mi. back to the trailhead.

Fee? No.

Water (with GPS coordinates): (Note: Water locations are for the 21-mi. Ivestor Gap/Art Loeb/Little East Fork loop.) 0.1 mi., spring (N35 19.590 W82 52.790); 3.5 mi., seep, but dammed (N35 21.644 W82 51.752); 3.9 mi., just below trail (N35 21.765 W82 51.852); 8.7 mi. (N35 23.509 W82 52.653); 9.0 mi. (N35 23.303 W82 52.811); 11.4 mi. (N35 23.303 W82 52.811); water is available from Little East Fork for next 2.7 mi.

Land manager: USDA Forest Service, Pisgah Ranger District.

Trip highlights: Expansive grass and heath balds offering some of the best views in the state and some of the most exposed hiking; Shining Rock quartz outcrop.

Special considerations: Trailhead is off the Blue Ridge Parkway, which is not maintained during winter and closes due to snow and ice. If that's the case, consider the Daniel Boone option (see trip 16).

Night hike in? Yes. Flat, easy trail.

Solo? Yes.

Family friendly? Yes. You can set up camp in a number of good spots between 1 and 4 mi. in. There are easy day-hike options, and Shining Rock is fun scrambling for kids (though there are some steep and abrupt drops, so keep a close eye on them).

Bailout options: Hike out is short and easy if things don't go well.

Seasons: Spring, summer, fall.

Weather: Ice and snow can prevent access to primary trailhead in winter. High altitude, exceeding 6,000 ft., makes area susceptible to afternoon thunderstorms in summer.

Solitude rating: 2.

Nearest outfitter: Backcountry Outdoors, Brevard, (828) 884-8670, www.backcountryoutdoors.com.

Hunting allowed? Yes. Consult N.C. Wildlife Resources Commission for local seasons.

More info: USDA Forest Service, Pisgah Ranger District, (828) 257-4200, www.cs.unca.edu/nfsnc/ recreation/shining_rock.pdf.

Shining Rock Ledge/Little East Fork loop, 13 miles. For a more robust hike, follow Shining Rock Ledge to Deep Gap (see above description), then drop down on the Art Loeb Trail to the Daniel Boone Boy Scout Camp and return up Little East Fork. An especially attractive option on a hot summer day, considering the abundance of pools and waterfalls on Little East Fork. A rigorous hike.

Old Butt Knob, Shining Creek Trail loop, 7 miles. If you're into historical fiction, then you'll like this option. Shining Rock's Cold Mountain is indeed the Cold Mountain at the crux of Charles Frazier's 1997 National Book Award–winning bestseller. Re-create the homestretch of W. P. Inman's epic journey home during the Civil War by trudging through Daniels Cove, up Bearpen Ridge, and on to Shining Rock Ledge.

Graveyard Ridge to Graveyard Fields, 11.1 miles. Graveyard Fields may be the coolest part of the Shining Rock area (it's actually just outside the wilderness, in the Pisgah National Forest). The 1925 and 1942 fires that devastated the area seem to have had the longest-lasting effect here; the tree stumps that once dominated this bowl (and resembled gravestones) have since been covered over; the heath community that survives gives the area an eerie "Hound of the Baskervilles" feel.

Black Balsam Knob, 7.5 miles. This hike sticks with the Art Loeb Trail from Shining Rock Gap to the knob's 6,214-foot summit. Grass balds and heaths dominate this trail.

16   Shining Rock Daniel Boone Loop

BREVARD

16.8 MILES

NO. OF DAYS: 2–5

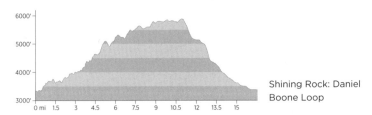

Shining Rock: Daniel Boone Loop

The 16.8-mile Daniel Boone Loop beginning and ending at the Daniel Boone Boy Scout Camp near Lake Logan is one of the most popular winter backpack trips in the state. In part, that's because intrepid backpackers from the state's major metropolitan areas—Charlotte, the Triad, and the Triangle—can do it in a weekend, without taking time off from work.

I say "intrepid" backpackers can do this trip in a winter weekend because if you're leaving after work, you will be doing your hike-in in the dark. Now, if you look at the information box for this trip, you'll notice that it's not recommended for a night hike-in—unless, that is, you are intrepid. And by intrepid I mean someone who doesn't mind climbing straight up in the dark (the 3.7-mile hike from the trailhead to Deep Gap gains about 1,700 vertical feet), doesn't mind occasionally hurdling a downed tree in the dark, and doesn't mind not knowing that in places the side of the trail that isn't hugging a hillside is disappearing into an abyss. On one night assault of this stretch years ago, my Raleigh climbing party hit the trail at 10:30 P.M. and didn't get to our campsite at Deep Gap until 2 A.M.

It was well worth the push, though, because what you get in return are 2 days to explore Shining Rock under cold but typically sunny winter skies. Wake up Saturday morning and take a 1.4-mile (and 1,000-foot vertical) day hike up to the Cold Mountain made famous by author Charles Frazier. Return to camp and throw on your pack for the 3.7-mile trek across Shining Rock Ledge. There's a hairy scramble or two in the first half mile, but nothing but enjoyable, relatively flat ridgeline hiking after that. The views through a naked canopy (and from the occasional rocky perch) are stellar on a clear winter's day.

Set up camp at Shining Rock Gap (if it's full, you should be able to find something within the next quarter mile on the Art Loeb), then spend the rest of the afternoon scrambling atop Shining Rock, an outcrop rich with white quartz giving the impression of perpetual snowcover. It's a great place to catch the sunset as well, though remember in winter that dark can come as early as 5:30 P.M.; bring a headlamp and watch your step on the trip back down to camp.

Sunday's return trip, 6.6 miles, is all downhill, nearly all of it along an old rail- and roadbed, the last 3.3 miles of which parallel the Little East Fork of the Pigeon River. The waterway is replete with deep pools and waterfalls, though access down the steep banks can be tricky.

Water is a consideration on this trip. You'll hit a small source less than 2 miles into the hike, then no more for another 5 miles. Fortunately, the sources near the campsites at Shining Rock Gap are generally reliable.

16 **Shining Rock** Daniel Boone Loop

Trailhead: From NC 215 in Lake Logan, go east on SR 1236/Little East Fork Road for 3.5 mi. to the trailhead opposite the Daniel Boone Boy Scout Camp. Park along the road.

Loop/one-way: Loop.

Difficulty: Hard.

Campsites (with GPS coordinates): Hiking clockwise: 3.7 mi., Deep Gap (N35 23.935 W82 51.864); 5.1 mi. (N35 23.134 W82 52.161); 6.2 mi. (N35 22.286 W82 51.939); 6.8 mi., Shining Rock Gap (N35 21.824 W82 51.833); 7.4 mi., Flower Gap (N35 21.434 W82 51.868); 8.7 mi., Ivestor Gap (N35 20.713 W82 52.030).

Map: "Shining Rock & Middle Prong Wilderness," Pisgah National Forest, USDA Forest Service, 1:24,000, 50-ft. intervals.

Follow the trail: From the trailhead, take the Art Loeb Trail 3.7 mi. to Deep Gap (go left for the 1.4-mi. spur up Cold Mountain). Continue along the Art Loeb 5.3 mi. to Shining Rock Gap and Ivestor Gap. At Ivestor Gap go right on Ivestor Gap Trail for 1.2 mi. to Little East Fork Trail. Take the latter 6.6 mi. back to the trailhead.

Fee? No.

Water (with GPS coordinates): 1.8 mi. (N35 23.303 W82 52.811); 6.9 mi. (N35 21.765 W82 51.852); 7.3 mi., water seep, but dammed (N35 21.644 W82 51.752); 13.4 mi., pick up Little East Fork of the Pigeon River (N35 21.293 W82 52.852), which you'll follow for the remaining 3 mi. of the trip.

Land manager: USDA Forest Service, Pisgah Ranger District.

Trip highlights: Ridgeline views in winter; Shining Rock quartz outcrop.

Special considerations: This is the recommended winter route for Shining Rock; the Ivestor Gap trailhead becomes inaccessible when ice and snow close the Blue Ridge Parkway.

Night hike in? No.

Solo? Yes. A popular route, even in winter.

Family friendly? No. Steep; scrambling required in spots; sharp drops.

Bailout options: No.

Seasons: Most popular in winter.

Weather: Since this is the preferred winter route, be aware that conditions can change radically from the 3,300-ft. base to 6,001-ft. Shining Rock.

Solitude rating: 2.

Nearest outfitter: REI, Asheville, (828) 687-0918, www.rei.com.

Hunting allowed? Yes. Consult N.C. Wildlife Resources Commission for local seasons.

More info: USDA Forest Service, Pisgah Ranger District, (828) 257-4200, www.cs.unca.edu/nfsnc/recreation/shining_rock.pdf.

Great Smoky Mountains

GREAT SMOKY MOUNTAINS NATIONAL PARK (SMOKIES)

It's true that the Great Smoky Mountains National Park is the nation's most popular national park, drawing 9.4 million visitors in 2007. It's also true that about 9.39 million of those visitors don't venture more than a few yards from their cars. Despite the Smokies' popularity, there's a surprising amount of solitude to be had on the 900 miles of trail that penetrate the half-million-acre park shared by North Carolina and Tennessee. And there's so very much to see.

With elevations ranging from 875 feet to 6,643 feet atop Clingman's Dome, there's a remarkable amount of ecodiversity. Start your day in a subtropical climate and end it 20 degrees cooler in a climate more suitable to Canada. Wildlife is abundant: An estimated 1,500 bears live in the park; wild boars roam here; and in 2001, elk were reintroduced, in the Cataloochee Valley. Like wildflowers? More than 1,660 kinds of flowering plants have been identified in the Smokies—so far. Waterfalls are abundant—and well fueled with more than 85 inches of rainfall a year at the higher elevations—and the park features a variety of native trout streams. And evidence of the history of humans in the park, dating back at least 9,000 years, is everywhere. In fact, most of the trails you'll walk on are old roadbeds from the Smokies' pre-park past.

The 6 trips that follow promise to expose you to all of this and more.

17 Smokies Mount Sterling

WAYNESVILLE

18.1 MILES

NO. OF DAYS: 2-3

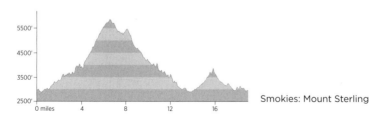

Smokies: Mount Sterling

The first 4 miles of this trip are a lovely ramble through the Big Terrain that represents much of the half-million-acre Great Smoky Mountains National

Pretty Hollow Creek requires some innovative crossings at points.

Park: Big Hillsides, Big Drainages, and Big Hardwoods led by the ramrod-straight, sky-piercing yellow poplar. Then, something magical happens.

You begin the steep climb to Mount Sterling.

It is steep, though never ridiculously so, because the trail follows, for the most part, an old railbed. You'll notice the climb, which gains more than 1,700 feet in 2.2 miles, less on those occasions when you look up to see that you're climbing into one of the more grand balsam fir forests in the park. At times, the trail is consumed by towering firs and red spruce that ward off heat in summer and add to the mountain's northern feel in winter. Be consoled that the climbing on this trip is largely over when you reach the Mount Sterling Ridge Trail and take a right for the final assault up 5,823-foot Mount Sterling.

That said, your summit is a bit anticlimactic, thanks to the observation tower (climb at your own risk) and communications equipment gracing the peak. Still, 2 of the 3 camping spots atop Mount Sterling at campsite 38 are mostly secluded from this pox of progress. A night spent atop Mount

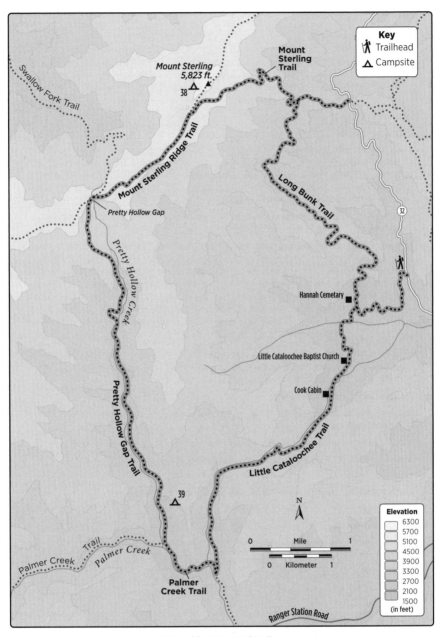

17 **Smokies** Mount Sterling

Trailhead: From I-40 west of Canton take exit 20, US 276. Loop under the overpass, and after 0.3 mi. go right on Cove Creek Road, which becomes gravel after 5 mi. Continue past the gate to the Great Smoky Mountains National Park at mile 6.2. At mile 10.9, fill out a backcountry camping permit at the kiosk on the left side of the road. Head back the way you drove in, and after 1.4 mi. go left on the road to Big Creek. The trailhead is 5.5 mi. on the left.

Loop/one-way: Loop.

Difficulty: Moderate.

Campsites (with GPS coordinates): Camping is allowed only at designated sites in the Great Smoky Mountains National Park. There are two designated sites on this route: campsite 38 atop Mount Sterling at mile 6.4 (N35 42.183 W83 07.368) and campsite 39 at mile 12.0 (N35 38.616 W83 07.702). Reservations are required in advance for campsite 38; call (865) 436-1231. See "Trailhead" for getting a backcountry camping permit, which is free.

Map: "Great Smoky Mountains National Park," Tennessee/North Carolina, *Trails Illustrated*, *National Geographic*, 1:70,000, 50-ft. intervals.

Follow the trail: From the trailhead, take Long Bunk Trail 1.1 mi. to the intersection with Little Cataloochee Trail; continue to the right to stay on Long Bunk another 3.1 mi. to Mount Sterling Trail and go left. Take Mount Sterling Trail 1.7 mi. to its intersection with the Mount Sterling Ridge Trail. Go right for 0.5 mi. to the Mount Sterling summit. Return down the Mount Sterling Ridge Trail 1.8 mi. to Pretty Hollow Gap and take the Pretty Hollow Gap Trail left. After 4.2 mi., Pretty Hollow Gap Trail Ts into Palmer Creek Trail; go left. After 0.7 mi., go left on Little Cataloochee Trail for 4.1 mi., to its intersection with Long Bunk Trail. Go right on Long Bunk for a 1.1-mi. hike back to your car.

Fee? No.

Water (with GPS coordinates): 0.9 mi. (N35 40.403 W83 05.601), 1.6 mi. (N35 40.705 W83 05.702), 2.2 mi. (N35 41.067 W83 06.013), 2.8 mi. (N35 41.286 W83 06.369), 3.0 mi. (N35 41.382 W83 06.496). Between miles 9.7 and 14.2 the trail follows streams.

Land manager: National Park Service.

Trip highlight: The climb up to 5,823-ft. Mount Sterling passes through an evergreen forest with some of the park's tallest fir trees.

Special considerations: Trailhead access is on a windy gravel road that could pose problems in winter.

Night hike in? No. It's more than 7 mi. of climbing to the first campsite.

Solo? Yes.

Family friendly? Climbing up Mount Sterling may be a bit much for smaller hikers.

Bailout options: No.

Seasons: Year-round.

Weather: Watch for severe weather, both summer afternoon thunderstorms and snow and ice in winter, atop Mount Sterling.

Solitude rating: 3.

Nearest outfitter: REI, Asheville, (828) 687-0918, www.rei.com.

Hunting allowed? No.

More info: Great Smoky Mountains National Park, (865) 436-1200, www.nps.gov/grsm.

Sterling, even in summer, is a night spent in a rare aerie of the Southern Appalachians.

Leaving Mount Sterling, the 1.8-mile ridgeline hike to Pretty Hollow Gap is a gradual descent that stays in evergreen country much of the way. And the 4.2-mile run down Pretty Hollow Gap Trail goes pretty fast, especially with Pretty Hollow Creek as company. What begins as an intimate relationship with a small stream ends with you 100 feet above a frolicking waterway slicing through a canyon of rhododendron and hemlocks.

Campsite 39 is near the end of this stretch, and if you have the time, you'd be wise to spend a second night here and set up base camp for a day hike. One option: Continue another 2 miles downstream, along Pretty Hollow Creek, which shortly becomes Palmer Creek, and hike into the Cataloochee Valley, where structures from the valley's heyday in the early 1900s—including Palmer Chapel, Beech Grove School, and the Caldwell House—are open for touring. The wide meadow to the east is ideal for viewing the elk herd reintroduced to the valley in 2001. Early morning and evening are best for catching a glimpse of the elk.

You'll want to leave ample time for your return trip to the car along the 4.1-mile Little Cataloochee Trail. This trail goes through Little Cataloochee, an offshoot settlement where apple orchards helped create a thriving community. Remnants of the orchard are visible, as are cabins once belonging to the Cook and Hannah families, as well as the Little Cataloochee Baptist Church.

Nearly all the trail on this trip is on old roadbeds that the Cooks, the Hannahs, and other pioneering families cleared and used more than a century ago to create thriving communities that are slowly returning to nature.

18 Smokies Cataloochee Valley

WAYNESVILLE

9.5 MILES

NO. OF DAYS: 2-3

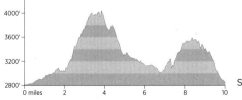

Smokies: Cataloochee Valley

Explore the past, including the old Caldwell barn, on a trip through Cataloochee Valley.

The highlights of this trip aren't found along the trail, they're found before you reach the trailhead.

Visiting the Cataloochee Valley is a little like watching one of those *Twilight Zone* episodes where a couple comes upon a town in which everything looks normal except for one thing: There are no people, and time appears to have stopped 75 years ago. In fact, the Cataloochee Valley, as evidenced by the surviving homes, church, and school, was once a bustling community. White settlers began moving into the area in the early 1800s. By mid-century the narrow valley had a healthy population, and by 1910 the census counted 1,251 people in Cataloochee and the smaller Little Cataloochee, a ridgeline to the north. While agriculture—corn, apples, wheat, oats, and rye, for starters—in the rich valley was Cataloochee's main economic engine, there was tourism even back then: The prominent Palmer family charged visitors 50 cents to fish for rainbow trout in their creek. The valley in the early 1900s was one bustling place.

By 1938, nearly everyone was gone.

A close mountain encounter of the third kind would make a better movie plot, at least for a summer blockbuster. The reality, though, is more documentary: The valley's residents left because the federal government was buying land to create the Great Smoky Mountains National Park. Fortunately, it was an orderly retreat that left a handful of the 200 buildings that once dotted the valley intact and open today for your perusal. Exploring the remaining structures is a real trip—a trip back in time.

Stand in the back bedroom on the second floor of the Caldwell House, built between 1903 and 1906, and you'll get a sense of what might have made the pages of *Home & Garden* in the early twentieth century: wallpaper made of old newspaper ads featuring bonnets for $1.49 and wool for 59 cents a yard. Stand inside the 2-room Beech Grove schoolhouse, the sun and the sound of a playful, trout-bearing Palmer Creek streaming in through its windows, and you have to wonder what the truancy rate was on those first warm days of spring. Settle into a pew in Palmer Chapel and you can almost hear one of the circuit preachers extolling the virtues of hard work and service to the Lord. When you leave the church, check the long meadow to the east for the elk herd reintroduced to the valley in 2001.

Eventually, you'll remember that you are here to backpack. Good thing the first designated campsite on this 9.5-mile loop is a flat, 1.5-mile hike in. You should have just enough time to set up camp before dark (unless you get distracted by the Woody House, which is a tenth of a mile before the campsite).

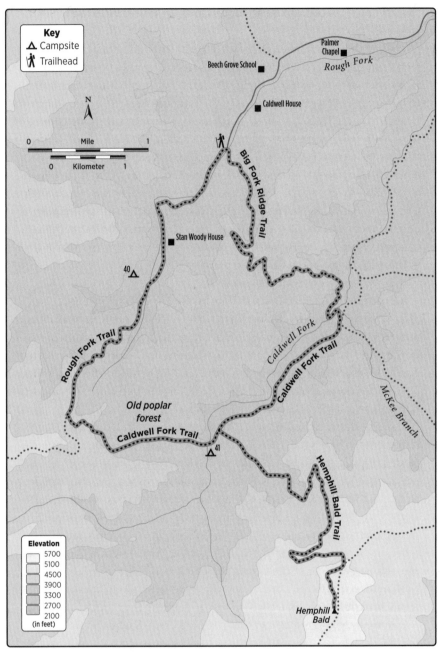

Key
△ Campsite
🚶 Trailhead

N

0 — Mile — 1

0 — Kilometer — 1

Rough Fork

Palmer Chapel

Beech Grove School

Caldwell House

Big Fork Ridge Trail

Stan Woody House

40 △

Rough Fork Trail

Caldwell Fork

Caldwell Fork Trail

McKee Branch

Old poplar forest

Caldwell Fork Trail

△ 41

Hemphill Bald Trail

Elevation
5700
5100
4500
3900
3300
2700
2100
(in feet)

Hemphill Bald

18 Smokies Cataloochee Valley

18 Smokies Cataloochee Valley

Trailhead: From I-40 west of Canton take exit 20 for US 276. Loop under the overpass, and after 0.3 mi. go right on Cove Creek Road, which becomes gravel after 5 mi. Continue past the gate to the Great Smoky Mountains National Park at mile 6.2. At mile 10.9, fill out a backcountry camping permit at the kiosk on the left side of the road. Continue through the Cataloochee Valley to the trailhead, at the end of the road.

Loop/one-way: Loop.

Difficulty: Moderate.

Campsites (with GPS coordinates): Camping is allowed only at designated sites in the Great Smoky Mountains National Park. There are two designated sites on this route: campsite 40 at mile 1.5 (N35 36.097 W83 07.861) and campsite 41 at mile 4.8 (N35 35.156 W83 07.222). Reservations are not required for either location, though a backcountry permit is. See "Trailhead" for information on where to obtain a permit.

Map: "Great Smoky Mountains National Park," Tennessee/North Carolina, *Trails Illustrated*, *National Geographic*, 1:70,000, 50-ft. intervals.

Follow the trail: From the trailhead, take the Rough Fork Trail for 1.6 mi. to campsite 40. Continue on Rough Fork for another 1.6 mi., then go left on Caldwell Fork Trail. At the 1.5-mi. mark is Hemphill Bald Trail and campsite 41. Continue another 1.9 mi. and go left on Big Fork Ridge Trail. After 3.0 mi., Big Fork Ridge spits out on the road through Cataloochee Valley; your car and the trailhead are 75 yds. to the left.

Fee? No.

Water (with GPS coordinates): There is water the first 2 mi., from Rough Fork and Hurricane Creek, and at miles 4.6 (N35 35.058 W83. 07.338), 4.8 (N35 35.156 W83 07.222), 5.5 (N35 35.352 W83 06.761), 5.8 (N35 38.654 W83 06.521), and 6.5 (N35 35.930 W83 06.226).

Land manager: National Park Service.

Trip highlights: Sightseeing in Cataloochee Valley—a handful of structures from the once-thriving community remain. Also, an elk herd reintroduced in 2001 that grazes early morning and late afternoon in the valley meadows.

Special considerations: None.

Night hike in? No. Gate into Cataloochee Valley closes at sunset.

Solo? Yes.

Family friendly? Yes. Exploring old buildings from a century ago, including Beach Grove School, should entertain the troops.

Bailout options: No, but the first campsite is just 1.5 mi. in, on a flat trail.

Seasons: Year-round.

Weather: Lower elevation hike avoids most severe weather.

Solitude rating: 3.

Nearest outfitter: REI, Asheville, (828) 687-0918, www.rei.com.

Hunting allowed? No.

More info: Great Smoky Mountains National Park, (865) 436-1200, www.nps.gov/grsm.

Day 2 is a short 3.2-mile hike to campsite 41, a good base camp for a day hike up to Hemphill Bald. If you're feeling particularly adventuresome, there's a 13.7-mile loop that takes in Hemphill, Polis Gap, and some old-growth forest. There's little water on this route, so plan accordingly.

Your hike out on Day 3 is a short 4.7-mile return to the car. That should leave plenty of time to swing by Palmer Chapel and give thanks for a good trip.

19 Smokies Clingman's Dome Approach

BRYSON CITY

26.2 MILES

NO. OF DAYS: 3

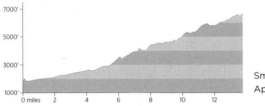

Smokies: Clingman's Dome Approach (one way)

Who among us hasn't read of an epic mountaineering expedition—to the top of Everest, perhaps, or Denali—and thought, "Man, wouldn't I love to do a trip like that!" Only maybe not up such a big mountain. And in a little less time—like a weekend, rather than a month or two. And without the possibility of having body parts freeze and fall off.

Being a mere mortal lacking the Ed Viesturs gene doesn't mean you have to give up on your big mountain dreams. You just need to focus on a slightly less-big mountain. Instead of Himalayas, think Appalachians. Instead of Everest, think Clingman's Dome.

Clingman's Dome is Everyman's answer to Everest. At 6,643 feet, it's the third-highest point in the eastern United States, only slightly lower than 6,684-foot Mount Mitchell and 6,647-foot Mount Craig to the east in the Black Mountains. You don't need a month or more to climb it: 3 days is ideal, 2 is doable. You won't need bottled oxygen (though at 6,600 feet your breathing may be more labored than at the base). And you don't need to pay a guide $70,000 to get you to the top. The price of this book is all the guide fee you'll need.

The even more important advice you get from this book: Do this climb

The top of Clingman's Dome is that much more special when the world below is socked in.

between December 1 and March 31 when the road to Clingman's is closed and you'll likely have this normally touristy summit to yourself.

Like the trip to Everest, the trip up to Clingman's begins in a much warmer clime. At the Noland Creek Trailhead, elevation 2,100 feet, the temperature may well be 20 degrees warmer than atop Clingman's Dome. Don't be deceived by relatively balmy weather when you head out.

Though there are 2 designated campsites on this route, no. 64 at 4 miles in makes for a better base camp. It's a mellow hike, gaining about 650 vertical feet, and allotting 3 days for this trip gives you plenty of time on Day 1 to establish base camp.

Day 2 of your trip is the day-hike assault on Clingman's Dome. Over 10 miles, you'll gain nearly 4,000 feet. That sounds like a lot, and it is. But the route—up 2.8-mile Springhouse Branch Trail, then 6.3 miles along Forney Ridge—is a steady climb with no spirit-breaking sections where the trail goes straight uphill (this is a well-heeled national park, remember). For-

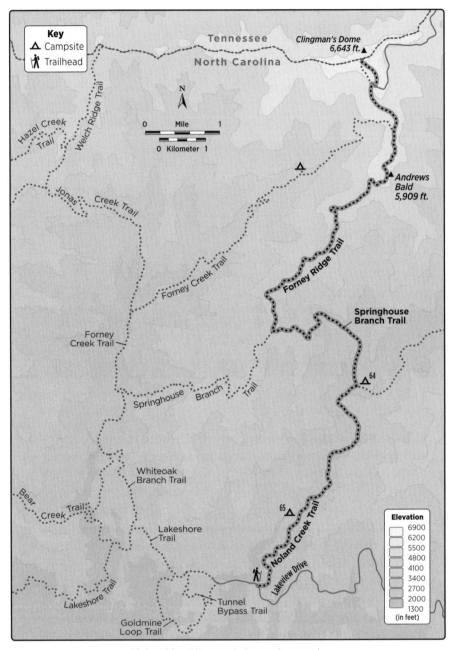

△ Campsite

🚶 Trailhead

Tennessee

North Carolina

Clingman's Dome
6,643 ft. ▲

N

0   Mile   1

0   Kilometer   1

Welch Ridge Trail

Hazel Creek
Trail

Jonas   Creek Trail

Andrews
Bald
5,909 ft.

Forney Creek Trail

Forney Ridge Trail

Springhouse
Branch Trail

Forney
Creek Trail

Springhouse   Branch   Trail

△ 64

Whiteoak
Branch Trail

Bear   Creek   Trail

△ 65

Noland Creek Trail

Lakeshore
Trail

Lakeview Drive

Lakeshore Trail

Tunnel
Bypass Trail

Goldmine
Loop Trail

Elevation

6900
6200
5500
4800
4100
3400
2700
2000
1300
(in feet)

19 Smokies Clingman's Dome Approach

19 Smokies Clingman's Dome Approach

Trailhead: From downtown Bryson City at Depot Street, go north on Everett Street, which becomes Fontana Road shortly after leaving town. At 2.8 mi. from Everett Street, the road enters the Great Smoky Mountains National Park and becomes Lakeview Drive. Reach the trailhead, on your left, at 8.0 mi.

Loop/one-way: One-way.

Difficulty: Easy to campsite; moderate to hard day hike to Clingman's Dome.

Campsites (with GPS coordinates): campsite 65, 1.0 mi. (N35 28.186 W83 31.143); campsite 64, 4.0 mi. (N35 29.892 W83 30.222).

Map: "Great Smoky Mountains National Park," Tennessee/North Carolina, *Trails Illustrated*, *National Geographic*, 1:70,000, 50-ft. intervals.

Follow the trail: From the trailhead, take Noland Creek Trail 4.0 mi. to campsite 64. Go left on the Springhouse Branch Trail for 2.8 mi. to Forney Ridge Trail. Stay on Forney Ridge Trail for 4.6 mi., then go right on Clingman's Dome Bypass Trail for 0.8 mi. before catching the 0.9-mi. paved trail to the summit.

Fee? No.

Water: Water is available from Deep Creek for the first 4.0 mi. and along Springhouse Branch for the next 2.0 mi. Beyond that, as the trail follows ridgelines to the top, there is no reliable water source.

Land manager: National Park Service.

Trip highlights: 360-degree view from the top of Clingman's Dome and, during winter, the season recommended for this trip, the opportunity to have one of the top destinations in the country's most popular national park all to yourself.

Special considerations: Weather can change radically on this trip, from warm and dry at the 2,100-ft. base to winterlike atop 6,643-ft. Clingman's Dome. Don't let the weather at the base dictate what gear and clothing you'll need up top. Also, before setting out on assault day, figure out your turn-around time—that is, the time at which you need to start heading back down the mountain to avoid hiking after sunset. The return trip is downhill and will be faster, but don't underestimate how long it will take to get down.

Night hike in? Yes. The 4-mi. hike to base camp is along a foot-friendly old roadbed.

Solo? Weather conditions at the top can be severe in winter; best to do this one with a companion.

Family friendly? Probably not. The 9.1-mi. day hike to the top is long and gains about 4,000 ft. And there's the 9.1-mi. return trip, all in one day.

Bailout options: No.

Seasons: Dec. 1–Mar. 31 (when the paved road to Clingman's Dome is closed).

Solitude rating: 5, during the recommended season.

Nearest outfitter: Lester's Sports & Variety, 146 Everett St., Bryson City, (828) 488-6311, has an eclectic selection of basic camping gear.

Hunting allowed? No.

More info: Great Smoky Mountains National Park, (865) 436-1200, www.nps.gov/grsm/index.htm.

ney Ridge is particularly enjoyable, actually following the ridgeline for the most part, rather than tracking below it. There's a nice payoff at 5,909-foot Andrews Bald, 7.7 miles into the hike. You'll know you're coming up to the bald when the forest transitions from southern hardwoods to spruce/fir and the trail briefly becomes uncharacteristic of the National Park Service by following a path of small rocks and boulders that doubles as a drainage after a rain. Above Andrews Bald the trail mellows considerably, as it's maintained to accommodate sneaker-clad summer tourists descending from the Clingman's Dome parking lot 2 miles above. When you reach the lot, it's another half mile to the top, up a macadam path, which is, ironically, the steepest part of the climb.

Take a moment to savor the silence and the view from atop Clingman's Dome. If you're lucky, you'll hit it on a clear day when visibility can exceed 100 miles. If you're even luckier, you'll hit it on a day when the world below 5,000 feet is enveloped in clouds and you're treated to isolated mountain-top islands poking through a fluffy carpet of white.

And take a moment, too, to bask in the glory of conquering your own Everest.

20 **Smokies** Deep Creek Loop

BRYSON CITY

13.5 MILES

NO. OF DAYS: 2

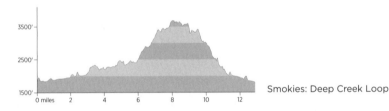

Smokies: Deep Creek Loop

Hiking Deep Creek Trail, it's easy to wax poetic about how idyllic life in the pre-park Great Smoky Mountains must have been. Easy because this mellow trail follows an old roadbed up Deep Creek, a classic mountain stream that crashes through boulder fields, collects in dark green pools, then squeezes through, over, and around another jumble of rocks cleaved from high above. Rising on either side and straight ahead is a mature forest of basswood, magnolia, ash, beech, and other hardwoods common to a Southern Appalachian cove forest.

Sunkota Ridge Trail catches some welcome winter afternoon sun.

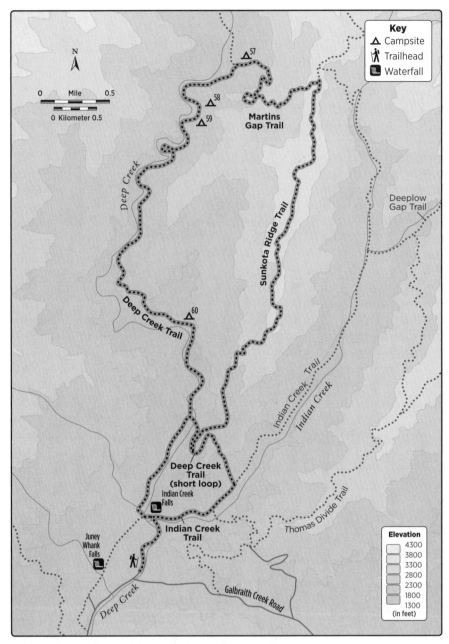

Key
△ Campsite
🚶 Trailhead
🖼 Waterfall

N

0   Mile   0.5

0 Kilometer 0.5

△ 57

△ 58

△ 59

Martins
Gap Trail

Deep Creek

Sunkota Ridge Trail

Deeplow
Gap Trail

Deep Creek Trail

△ 60

Indian Creek Trail

Indian Creek

**Deep Creek
Trail
(short loop)**

Indian Creek
Falls 🖼

**Indian Creek
Trail**

Thomas Divide Trail

Juney
Whank
Falls 🖼

🚶

Deep Creek

Galbraith Creek Road

Elevation
	4300
	3800
	3300
	2800
	2300
	1800
	1300
(in feet)

20 Smokies Deep Creek Loop

20 **Smokies** Deep Creek Loop

Trailhead: From the train depot on Everett Street in downtown Bryson City, go right on Depot Street. After a tenth of a mile, Depot Ts into what shortly will become W. Deep Creek Road; go left. The road ends at the trailhead parking area, at 2.8 mi.

Loop/one-way: Loop.

Difficulty: Moderate.

Campsites (with GPS coordinates): Camping is allowed only in designated sites in the Great Smoky Mountains National Park. There are 4 sites on this trip: no. 60, 2.6 mi. (N35 29.584 W83 25.505); no. 59, 5.0 mi. (N35 30.677 W83 25.539); no. 58, 5.4 mi. (N35 30.850 W83 25.515); and no. 57, 6.0 mi. (N35 31.078 W83 25.215).

Map: "Great Smoky Mountains National Park," Tennessee/North Carolina, *Trails Illustrated*, *National Geographic*, 1:70,000, 50-ft. intervals.

Follow the trail: From the trailhead, take Deep Creek Trail 6.2 mi. to the Martins Gap Trail; go right. Reach the gap after 1.6 mi., then go right on the Sunkota Ridge Trail. After 3.7 mi., Sunkota Ridge Ts into a Deep Creek Trail spur; go left for 0.5 mi., to the Indian Creek Trail and go right. Indian Creek Ts into Deep Creek Trail after 0.8 mi.; go left on Deep Creek for the final 0.8 mi. to the trailhead.

Fee? No.

Water (with GPS coordinates): Water is available from Deep Creek for the first 6.2 mi., and from Indian Creek from mile 12.3 to mile 13.0. There is a spring 1.7 mi. into the trip, about 10 yds. upstream from the bridge over Deep Creek, on the left side of the river looking upstream (N35 29.089 W83 25.443).

Land manager: National Park Service.

Trip highlight: A surprisingly easy trip for Smokies scenery.

Special considerations: In warm weather, Deep Creek is popular with tubers; expect lots of company for the first three quarters of a mile (tubing is prohibited upstream from this point).

Night hike in? Yes. Trail follows a foot-friendly old roadbed to the designated campsites.

Solo? Yes.

Family friendly? Yes. Opportunities to play in Deep Creek make this trip especially popular with kids.

Bailout options: No.

Seasons: All.

Weather: Lower elevations make weather less of an issue on this trip.

Solitude rating: 2. The lower portions of this trail are popular year-round with local hikers and runners. And there are the tubers.

Nearest outfitter: Lester's Sports & Variety, 146 Everett St., Bryson City, (828) 488-6311, has an eclectic selection of basic camping gear.

Hunting allowed? No.

More info: Great Smoky Mountains National Park, (865) 436-1200, www.nps.gov/grsm/index.htm.

In such a picturesque setting it's easy to imagine children of the Ani-Yunwiya (dubbed by Europeans the Cherokee) playing in those deep pools and rapids on a hot summer's day, or early farmers taking a bumper crop to market, or loggers around the turn of the twentieth century using this very road to supply a rapidly growing nation with lumber. Yup, life must have been good along the Deep Creek drainage. And I'm guessing that even on the not-so-good days before parkhood—the days when bad weather kept the kids cooped up in their wattle-and-daub homes, when the crop wasn't bumper, and when the danger of being a sawyer hit a little too close to home (or your humerus)—residents along this drainage outside Bryson City still had plenty to be thankful for.

Today, it's difficult to imagine hard times along the Deep Creek Trail. This 13.8-mile route is about as forgiving as any backpacking trip you can take in the Smokies. In fact, you're a good 6.5 miles into the hike before you notice any appreciable climbing. That would be at campsite 57, the fourth and last designated camping area on the loop. Here the trail leaves Deep Creek, hanging a right for the 1.3-mile, 800-vertical-foot climb up to Martins Gap. From there it's another three quarters of a mile (and 400 vertical feet) of climbing up Sunkota Ridge before 5 miles of gradual downhill back to the trailhead.

You might be thinking that a trail this good is going to be crowded, and you'd be partially right. In summer, the first three quarters of a mile is a tuber's paradise, something you'll perhaps gather from the tube-rental concessions lining W. Deep Creek Road on the drive in. A mile up the trail, most of the day-hiker traffic peels off on the Deep Creek short loop. Beyond that, it's just you and the other hard cores.

Though I recommend a 2-day, 1-night trip, a base camp at campsite 57 offers various day-hike options. Continue up Deep Creek to the Fork Ridge Trail for an 8.7-mile trip to the crest of the Smokies, take the Pole Road Creek Trail west and explore the Noland Creek and Noland Divide areas, and continue east past Martins Gap and you'll have various loop options along creek and ridge.

Deep Creek offers a good introduction to the Smokies for the novice backpacker.

FONTANA VILLAGE

11.6 MILES (trip 21), **28.8 MILES** (trip 22)

NO. OF DAYS: 2 (trip 21), **4** (trip 22)

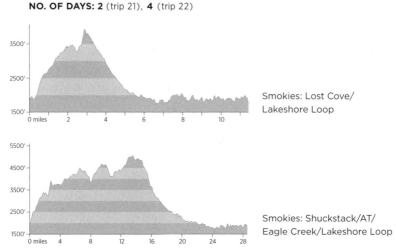

Smokies: Lost Cove/
Lakeshore Loop

Smokies: Shuckstack/AT/
Eagle Creek/Lakeshore Loop

Fittingly for the Great Smoky Mountains National Park, we have a mama bear and a papa bear trip from the same trailhead. One is a nearly 12-mile loop that climbs 2,280 feet in 3.5 miles, drops through a 3-mile-long cove, then returns on the Lakeshore Trail, a shoreline roller coaster not to be confused with the flat greenway circling your local city lake. The other trip is a 3-day, 29-mile loop that follows the Appalachian Trail up to 5,000 feet, then returns along one of the Smokies' longest drainages.

Both trips begin on the Appalachian Trail (AT) shortly after it crosses Fontana Dam, a Tennessee Valley Authority project from the early 1940s that created a reservoir 29 miles long. (One of its many fingers will keep you company on your return to the trailhead.) And both trips begin on the steady climb up the AT from Fontana Dam. At mile 3.5 there's a short spur up to the fire tower atop 4,020-foot Shuckstack Mountain. On a clear day, the climb up this rickety, retired watchtower is worth it.

At Sassafras Gap, 3.7 miles up the AT, these trips part ways. Trip 21 goes right on Lost Cove Trail, the trail the National Parks System seems to have forgotten; where most of the 900 miles of trail in the Smokies are well-designed (many follow old roadbeds from the park's civilian days three quar-

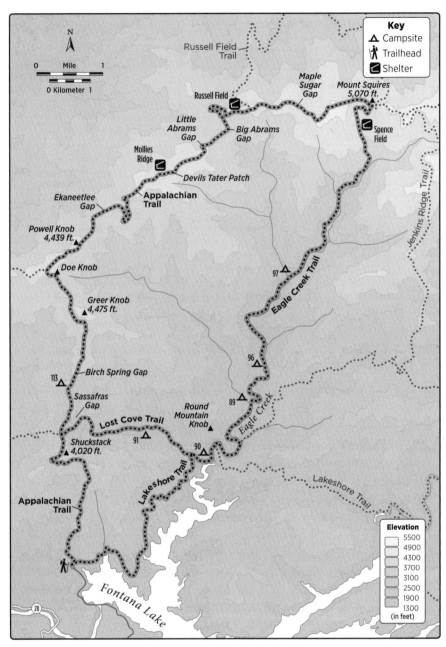

Key
△ Campsite
🚶 Trailhead
🏠 Shelter

N

Mile
0   1

0   Kilometer   1

Russell Field
Trail

Maple
Sugar
Gap

Mount Squires
5,070 ft.

Russell Field

Little
Abrams
Gap

Big Abrams
Gap

Spence
Field

Mollies
Ridge

Devils Tater Patch

Ekaneetlee
Gap

**Appalachian
Trail**

Jenkins Ridge Trail

Powell Knob
4,439 ft.

Doe Knob

Greer Knob
4,475 ft.

Eagle Creek Trail

97

Birch Spring Gap

113

Sassafras
Gap

96

Lost Cove Trail

Round
Mountain
Knob

89

Eagle Creek

Shuckstack
4,020 ft.

91

90

Lakeshore Trail

Lakeshore Trail

**Appalachian
Trail**

Elevation
5500
4900
4300
3700
3100
2500
1900
1300
(in feet)

28

Fontana Lake

21 & 22 Smokies Shuckstack

21 Smokies Shuckstack/Lost Cove/Lakeshore (short loop)

22 Smokies Shuckstack/AT/Eagle Creek/Lakeshore (long loop)

Trailhead: From NC 28 1.4 mi. east of Fontana Village, go left on Fontana Dam Road/SR 1245. There's parking at 1.4 mi., at the visitors center. If the dam road is open, veer right just past the dam and proceed another 1.4 mi. to the trailhead parking lot. Pick up the trail at the kiosk.

Loop/one way: Loops.

Difficulty: Trip 21: moderate; trip 22: hard.

Campsites (with GPS coordinates): There is one designated campsite for trip 21: no. 91, mile 6.0 (N35 29.532 W83 47.398). For the longer trip 22 there are five designated campsites and three shelters: campsite 113 at mile 3.5 (30.07399940490723, 48.83000183105469); Mollies Ridge Shelter, mile 8.5 (32.8129997253418, 47.74800109863281); Russell Field Shelter, mile 10.0 (33.7599983215332, 45.88800048828125); Spence Field Shelter, mile 12.5 (33.79899978637695, 43.83100128173828); campsite 97, mile 16.3 (31.61100006103516, 45.26800155639648); campsite 96, mile 18.2 (30.34700012207031, 45.67599868774414); campsite 89, mile 18.9 (29.95700073242188, 45.84799957275391), campsite 90, mile 21.1 (29.10600090026855, 46.59000015258789).

Map: "Great Smoky Mountains National Park," Tennessee/North Carolina, *Trails Illustrated*, *National Geographic*, 1:70,000, 50-ft. intervals.

Follow the trail: For trip 21: From the trailhead, take the Appalachian Trail 3.7 mi. north to Sassafras Gap. Go right for 2.7 mi. on Lost Cove Trail, then right on Lakeshore Trail, for the 5.2-mi. return to the trailhead. For trip 22: From the trailhead, take the Appalachian Trail north for 15.4 mi. On Mount Squires, go right on the Eagle Creek Trail, which Ts into Lakeshore Trail after 8.2 mi. Go right on Lakeshore for the final 5.2 mi. back to the trailhead.

Fee? No.

Water (with GPS coordinates): There is no water along the Appalachian Trail for the first 4 mi. of both trips. For trip 21: Water is available from mile 6 to mile 7 from Lost Cove Creek. Lakeshore Trail crosses small creeks at mile 7.3 (N35 28.927 W83 46.922), 8.3 (N35 28.638 W83 47.364), 8.9 (N35 28.468 W83 47.529), 9.5 (N35 28.119 W83 47.517), 9.9 (N35 27.909 W83 47.570), and 11.1 (N35 27.911 W83 48.169). For trip 22: Water is available at springs located near Russell Field Shelter, mile 10.0 (33.7599983215332, 45.88800048828125); Spence Field Shelter, mile 12.5 (33.79899978637695, 43.83100128173828); and along Eagle Creek from mile 13 to mile 21. Water is also available at Lakeshore Trail locations mentioned for trip 21.

Land manager: National Park Service.

Trip highlight: View from Shuckstack Tower at mile 3.7.

Special considerations: For trip 21, Lost Cove Creek crosses its namesake creek 9 times; some of the crossings near the bottom may require shucking the boots and wading up to your knees. Care should be taken on the ridgeline portion of trip 22 during the summer afternoon thunderstorm season. Also on trip 22, bears can be especially active around the shelters; Spence Field and Russell Field shelters have bear fences.

Night hike in? No. On either hike, it's a long way up to the first campground.

Solo? Yes.

Family friendly? Even on the shorter trip, there's lots of climbing.

Bailout options: No.

Seasons: All.

Weather: Lower elevations on trip 21 mean fewer potential weather issues; watch for summer afternoon thunderstorms on higher reaches of trip 22.

Solitude rating: 3. The AT portion of these trips adds to their popularity.

Nearest outfitter: Nantahala Outdoor Center, Wesser, (888) 905-7238, www.noc.com.

Hunting allowed? No.

More info: Great Smoky Mountains National Park, (865) 436-1200, www.nps.gov/grsm/index.htm.

ters of a century ago), Lost Cove more or less goes straight down the mountain. Further, when the trail begins playing hopscotch with its namesake creek, the park's signature log footbridges with a single handrail are nowhere to be found. This is not a problem initially, but as the stream gains momentum, you may find yourself shedding your boots and wading.

The final 5.2 miles of this trip are along the Lakeshore Trail. For the most part, this trail negotiates a series of coves, dropping in, climbing out, going up, coming down. Watch for the long-abandoned, *Untouchables*-era cars a little over 10 miles into the trip. Because this is a national park and camping is restricted to designated sites, your options here are limited to campsite 91 6 miles into the hike (about the midpoint of the trip) and campsite 90 on the Lakeshore Trail just north of the intersection with Lost Cove Trail.

The longer route continues up the AT at Sassafras Gap for another 11.7 miles, taking in various knobs (Greer, Doe, Powell, and McCampbell), gaps (Birch Spring, Buck, Ekaneetlee, Little and Big Abrams, and Maple Sugar) and a bald (Little). There are 3 AT shelters along the way (Mollies Ridge at mile 8.5, Russell Field at mile 10, and Spence Field at mile 12.5). At 5,070-foot Mount Squires, this trip departs the AT and descends, sharply at first, for 8.2 miles along Eagle Creek, where you'll find campsites at mile 16.3 (no. 97), 18.2 (no. 96) and 18.9 (no. 89). The trail meets the Lakeshore Trail, described above, near campsite 90, for the last 5.2 miles back to the trailhead.

Appalachian Trail

APPALACHIAN TRAIL (AT)

On its 2,178-mile journey from Springer Mountain, Georgia, to Mount Katahdin, Maine, the Appalachian Trail spends about 288 miles in North Carolina. (Technically, it shares about 200 of that total with Tennessee, straddling the border from the Great Smoky Mountains National Park north.) From the moment the AT enters the state from the south, at Bly Gap, the trail quickly climbs above 5,000 feet. The North Carolina section is known for having the highest elevations on the AT (Clingman's Dome, at 6,643 feet, is the highest point on the trail); some of its most lush forests; and balds that offer great panoramic views.

Despite the rugged nature of the land it traverses, the AT in North Carolina is also known for having some of the most hiker-friendly trail. Switchbacks abound to help you make it up the relentless barrage of peaks, the trail is well marked, and the tread is uniformly in foot-friendly condition, thanks largely to the efforts of the three hiking clubs responsible for maintaining this stretch: the Carolina Mountain Club, Smoky Mountains Hiking Club, and the Nantahala Hiking Club.

The following five trips (as well as trips 21 and 22, originating from Fontana Dam in the Great Smoky Mountains National Park) give you a good sense of the AT in North Carolina.

23 AT Carvers Gap to US 19E

BURNSVILLE

14.0 MILES

NO. OF DAYS: 2–3

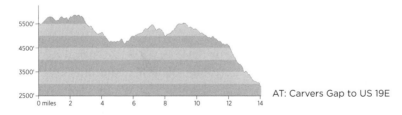

AT: Carvers Gap to US 19E

The traverse of the high balds of Hump Mountain, Yellow Mountain, and the entire eastern portion of Roan Mountain is one of the most spectacular parts of the entire Trail, with superb views from treeless meadows above 5,000 feet.

That's not me talking about this postcard-perfect 14-mile stretch of the

Looking west into Tennessee from Hump Mountain.

AT; that's the Appalachian Trail Conservancy (ATC), which generally tries not to pick favorites when discussing its 2,178-mile footpath. Yet as anyone who's been on this stretch knows, it's impossible not to gush over what's arguably the best hiking in North Carolina (and, to be fair, Tennessee; much of this stretch straddles the border, and the last 3 miles are in the Volunteer State). The main reason: those high balds.

Not a third of a mile in, you're on the first, 5,826-foot Round Bald, offering a panorama that includes 6,285-foot Roan High Knob and its extensive rhododendron garden, which blazes pink in June. Within a half mile you're on Jane Bald, and within another half mile—during which you may come across a herd of bald-maintaining grazing goats, part of the Baa-tany Goat Project—there's the short spur up to Grassy Ridge Bald, at 6,165 feet the highest point on this trip. Wowed as you may be, the best is yet to come. Don't get ahead of yourself, though, or you'll miss the surprise of this trip.

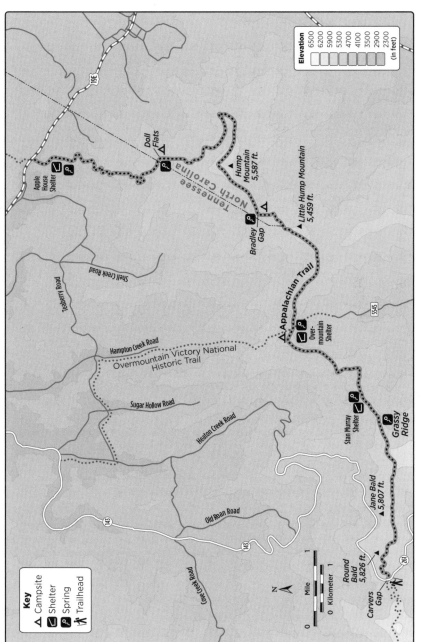

Key
△ Campsite
▣ Shelter
P Spring
人 Trailhead

19E

Apple
House
Shelter

Doll
Flats

Tennessee
North Carolina

Hump
Mountain
5,587 ft.

Bradley
Gap

▲ Little Hump Mountain
5,459 ft.

Shell Creek Road

Teaberry Road

Appalachian Trail

5545

Hampton Creek Road

Overmountain Victory National
Historic Trail

Over-
mountain
Shelter

Sugar Hollow Road

Heaton Creek Road

Stan Murray Shelter

Grassy
Ridge

Old Roan Road

143

143

Jane Bald
5,807 ft.

Cove Creek Road

N

Round
Bald
5,826 ft.

Carvers
Gap

261

0   Mile   1

0   Kilometer   1

Elevation
6500
6200
5900
5300
4700
4100
3500
2900
2300
(in feet)

23 AT Carvers Gap to US 19E

23 AT Carvers Gap to US 19E

Trailhead: From the intersection of NC 226 and NC 261 in downtown Bakersville, go north on NC 261 for 7 mi. to Carvers Gap on the North Carolina/Tennessee line. Park in the lot to the left; the trailhead is just across NC 261, on the east side of the road.

Loop/one-way: The trip described is one-way, out-and-back. You can also set a shuttle on the east end of this section by driving from Carvers Gap 12.6 mi. north on TN 143 to US 19E, then turning right and driving 4.0 mi. to a small (2–3 cars, depending on how friendly the first two park) pullout at the end of this stretch.

Difficulty: Moderate.

Campsites (with GPS coordinates): There are several good spots along the way. Those with water include Grassy Ridge Bald, 2.3 mi. (N36 06.044 W82 04.858); Stan Murray Shelter, 3.4 mi. (N36 06.746 W82 03.942); Overmountain Shelter, 5.0 mi. plus a 0.3-mi. hike off the trail (N36 07.414 W82 03.271); Bradley Gap, 6.8 mi. (N36 07.647 W82 01.616); Doll Flats, 10.7 mi. (N36 09.043 W82 00.657); and Apple House Shelter, 13.4 mi. (N36 10.319 W82 00.669).

Maps: Appalachian Trail Conservancy, Tennessee–North Carolina, map 2, 1:63,360, 100-ft. intervals, and the accompanying guide.

Follow the trail: From the trailhead, take the white-blazed Appalachian Trail east and north for 14 mi. to US 19E.

Fee? No.

Water: Because the trail follows a ridgeline, all water is from springs, which are located near the above-mentioned camping areas. While water from springs is often safe to drink without boiling or treating, because of cattle grazing in the area (in part to maintain the balds), the ATC recommends treating all water.

Land manager: USDA Forest Service, Pisgah National Forest, Toecane Ranger District.

Trip highlights: The balds—all of them, but especially 5,587-ft. Hump Mountain, which provides a rare panoramic view that's especially stunning to the west, over Tennessee.

Special considerations: This trail is popular, especially with groups. If possible, plan your trip midweek or early or late in the season.

Night hike in? Yes. Trail is well maintained, and bald hiking for the first 2 mi lets you take advantage of available moonglow.

Solo? Yes. You're rarely alone on this stretch.

Family friendly? Yes. Despite the elevations (approaching 6,200 ft. if you take the Grassy Ridge spur), there are few places for kids to get in trouble. Plus, there's always something to look at.

Bailout options: No.

Seasons: Fall, spring, and summer. Year-round if you're looking for a winter hike; the area is one of the few cross-country skiing destinations in the area.

Weather: Snow in the winter, typically unpredictable mountain weather in the summer (clear and cloudless one minute, rain and lightning the next).

Solitude rating: 2.

Nearest outfitter: Footsloggers, Boone, (828) 262-5111, www.footsloggers.com.

Hunting allowed? Local seasons apply.

More info: www.hikewnc.info/.

Coming off Grassy Ridge, your 2 miles of exposure end as the trail enters the first of several passages through copses of mountain ash. Some of the most exposed trail in the Southeast suddenly gives way to a cozy passage. It's a pattern repeated often, on ridgelines and through gaps alike en route to US 19E as the trail trades extreme exposure for the canopied comfort of a southern deciduous forest.

But again, we're here for the balds, and 9 miles into the hike you come to the belle of the balds, Hump Mountain. Round and Jane may be higher, but the view from 5,587-foot Hump is unparalleled. Says the ATC guide: "From here there is a magnificent panoramic view of Doe River Valley to the northwest, Whitetop and Mount Rogers in Virginia to the northeast, Beech Mountain to the east-northeast, and Grandfather Mountain with multiple peaks to east. Nearby and to west-southwest are Grassy Ridge and Roan High Knob." On a mildly hazy midsummer afternoon I counted 11 ridgelines disappearing west into Tennessee. Perhaps most amazing, of the 360 degrees viewable, perhaps 280 afforded no sign of human development. Plan to spend some time on Hump Mountain.

You can set a shuttle on this trip (see info box), but a good way to approach this route is to backpack midway, set up base camp, then spend a day day-hiking. If you're into shelters, Overmountain, a two-story barn, is 5 miles in. Or there's an especially nice camping spot at Bradley Gap, at mile 6.8. Both have spring water nearby.

24 AT Max Patch (short trip)

HOT SPRINGS

5.7 MILES

NO. OF DAYS: 2

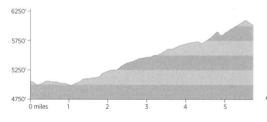

AT: Max Patch (short trip)

Hoping to hook your kids on backpacking—and don't mind employing a devious tactic or two? This trip should do the trick. Here's why.

Max Patch's open, mountaintop exposure offers panoramic views.

1. You don't want to overdo it their first time out. At 5.7 miles over relatively gentle terrain, the 2-day trip from Lemon Gap to Max Patch is
   ideal.
2. You need a carrot, and as carrots go in backpacking, you can't beat
   a bald. And as balds go, it's hard to beat Max Patch. Max Patch is a
   350-acre open-air playground at 4,629 feet. Created years ago by Native Americans who burned the area for hunting purposes, the bald is
   maintained today by grazing, and a fleet of Lawn-Boys couldn't keep
   the mountaintop meadow grass shorter. Kids will love the notion
   of running free atop Max Patch and perhaps flying a kite (a popular
   Patchtime). Adults marvel at the 360-degree view, which includes

Mount Mitchell, at 6,684 feet the highest point east of South Dakota's Black Hills, to the east and the Great Smokies to the south.

3 It's got cool history. For starters, you've got the bald concept itself. (Native Americans and fire? Doesn't get any cooler for an 8-year-old.) You've got the fact that Max Patch was once privately owned and that the owner charged hikers a nickel to climb to the top. Or, for a quarter, you could drive to the top.

4. It's got backcountry intrigue. When you hike into camp at the Roaring Fork Shelter, the kids will want to know what's up with the crazy wires with pie tins strung between the trees. That, you can tell them, is how you'll be storing your food at night—in bags suspended 12 feet in the air—to keep it from the *bears*!

5. It's got water. To drink and cook with, sure. But you also need it for entertainment. The trail spends a good bit of time along Roaring Fork Creek and crosses some smaller tributaries.

6. It offers you the potential for getting lost. Starting around the Roaring Fork Shelter, the trail plays tag with the U.S. Forest Service's Buckeye Ridge Trail as well as some old roadbeds. This being the Appalachian Trail, it's always marked with the distinctive 2" x 6" white rectangular blaze. But sometimes you need to take a moment, stop, get out your map and your compass, and look around before you can spot the blaze.

7. It's got stuff your kids may have never experienced. On this section of the AT, which manages to distance itself from both paved roads (the nearest is 5 miles distant) and civilization (the nearest town, Hot Springs, is 15 miles up the trail), that would be both quiet and, on a cloudless night, a star-studded sky.

About the aforementioned "devious tactic." To get to the trailhead, you must pass Max Patch and the parking area (here's where you'll drop a car if you're running a shuttle). As you do, point out the window to the enticing bald and tell the kids, "That's it, kids! That's Max Patch. That's where we'll be . . . *tomorrow*."

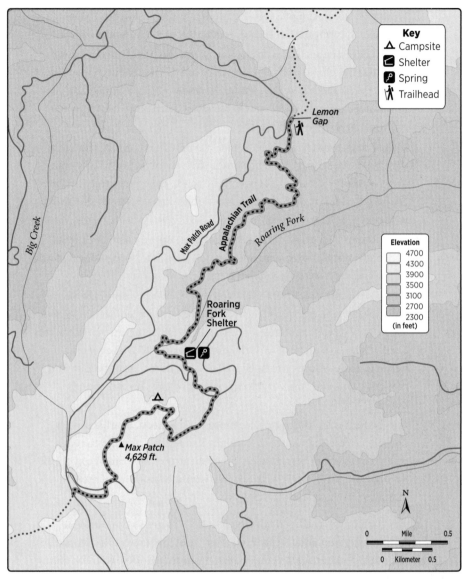

24 AT Max Patch (short trip)

24 AT Max Patch (short trip)

Trailhead: From NC 209 about 7 mi. south of Hot Springs, go west on Meadow Fork Road/SR 1175 for 5.5 mi. At Little Creek Road, go right (shortly the road appears to T, but in fact it continues to the left). Continue 3.6 mi. to Max Patch Road; go right. The Max Patch parking area is 2.6 mi.; Lemon Gap is another 3.6 mi. beyond that. You can either leave a shuttle car at the Max Patch parking area, or if there's a fleet-footed driver in your group for whom hiking 5.7 mi. isn't enough, that person can hike/jog back to Lemon Gap for the car.

Loop/one-way: One-way.

Difficulty: Easy.

Campsites (with GPS coordinates): 3.1 mi., Roaring Fork Shelter (N35 48.262 W82 56.948); 4.3 mi., ridgeline campsites just below Max Patch (N35 48.000 W82 57.095).

Map: "Appalachian Trail Guide to Tennessee–North Carolina," map 4, Appalachian Trail Conservancy, 1:63,360, 100-ft. intervals, and the accompanying guide.

Follow the trail: From Lemon Gap, take the white-blazed Appalachian Trail southwest for 5.7 mi. to Max Patch.

Fee? No.

Water (with GPS coordinates): 0.4 mi. (N35 49.341 W82 56.350); 2.8 mi. (N35 48.314 W82 57.126); 3.1 mi., spring at Roaring Fork Shelter (N35 48.262 W82 56.948); 3.3 (N35 48.094 W82 56.768).

Land manager: USDA Forest Service, French Broad Ranger District.

Trip highlight: 360-degree views from Max Patch on a clear day.

Special considerations: When you encounter a campsite or shelter with bear cables for hanging food—whether it's on the AT here at the Roaring Fork Shelter, in the Great Smokies, or anywhere else—use them. They're a sign that bears have discovered this spot as a source of food.

Night hike in? Can be done. There's a passable campsite 0.3 mi. into the trail (N35 49.387 W82 56.302). There's also room for an overnight camp at Lemon Gap.

Solo? Yes.

Family friendly? Yes. Hike is gently uphill, much of it along Roaring Creek. And there's a great payoff at the end in Max Patch.

Bailout options: No.

Seasons: Year-round, though access to the trailhead on gravel roads could be an issue in winter.

Weather: Be alert to rapidly changing weather conditions atop exposed Max Patch.

Solitude rating: 1 on Max Patch, a popular destination for day hikers; 3 on the rest of the trip.

Nearest outfitter: Bluff Mountain Outfitters, Hot Springs, (828) 622-7162, www.bluffmountain.com.

Hunting allowed? Yes; local seasons apply.

More info: USDA Forest Service, French Broad Ranger District, (828) 622-3202; www.ncnatural.com/NCUSFS/Pisgah/index.html.

HOT SPRINGS

20.8 MILES

NO. OF DAYS: 2–3

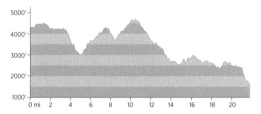

AT: Max Patch to Hot Springs

The 20.8-mile stretch from Max Patch to Hot Springs is classic southern Appalachian Trail. It begins atop a Southern Appalachian bald, rambles through hardwood forests, snakes up 4 peaks (only one of which, Bluff Mountain, is of consequence to a load-bearing, northbound backpacker) dips through 6 gaps, and ends in one of the AT's quintessential trail towns, Hot Springs. To hike the stretch of trail between Max Patch and Hot Springs is to get a good feel for the AT in North Carolina.

Starting at Max Patch may seem like having dessert before the main course. This 350-acre bald is one of the highlights of the southern Appalachian Trail. On a clear day from its 4,629-foot summit you can look east to the highest mountain range on the East Coast, the Black Mountains featuring 6,684-foot Mount Mitchell; look south to the Great Smoky Mountains; and perhaps most impressive, look west and see the Southern Appalachians dissolve, in a series of successively distant ridgelines, into Tennessee's Cumberland Plateau.

From here the trail offers moments on a more intimate scale. Creekside passages through tunnels of rhododendrons and ridgeline rambles under cover of young hardwoods, even stripped bare in winter, create a snug lane. Recurring drainages with little understory offer ample opportunity to stop, listen, and look for wildlife. For the patient, it's an especially good chance to see a black bear. The 3-mile descent down the east slope of 4,686-foot Bluff Mountain offers a big mountain feel on a hike otherwise characterized by gradual ups and downs (save for the precipitous drop the last 2 miles into Hot Springs).

Such solitary moments underscore another highlight of this trip: the quiet. Remote as many trails in North Carolina may seem, it's unusual to stop for 5 minutes and not hear a dog barking or a truck passing in the val-

The Walnut Mountain Shelter is a welcome sight to hikers after a day on the trail.

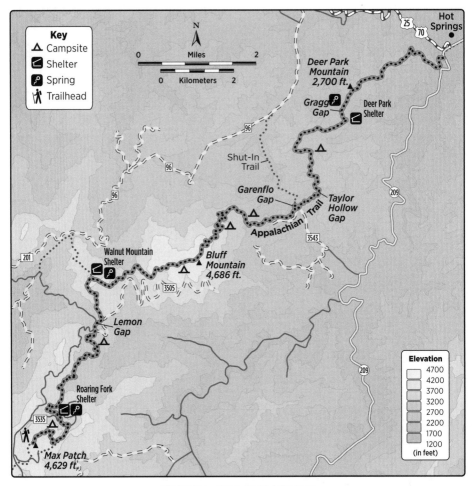

Key
- △ Campsite
- ◿ Shelter
- ⚷ Spring
- 🧍 Trailhead

N

Miles
0 — 2

Kilometers
0 — 2

Hot Springs

25 · 70

Deer Park
Mountain
2,700 ft.

Gragg
Gap

Deer Park
Shelter

96

Shut-In
Trail

Garenflo
Gap

Taylor
Hollow
Gap

209

96

96

Appalachian Trail

3543

201

Walnut Mountain
Shelter

Bluff
Mountain
4,686 ft.

3505

Lemon
Gap

Elevation
- 4700
- 4200
- 3700
- 3200
- 2700
- 2200
- 1700
- 1200
(in feet)

209

Roaring Fork
Shelter

3535

Max Patch
4,629 ft.

25 AT Max Patch to Hot Springs

25 AT Max Patch to Hot Springs

Trailhead: From NC 209 about 7 mi. south of Hot Springs, go west on Meadow Fork Road/SR 1175 for 5.5 mi. At Little Creek Road, go right. Continue 3.6 mi. to Max Patch Road; go right. The Max Patch parking area is 2.6 mi.

Loop/one-way: One-way. To set a shuttle, return to NC 209 and head north to Hot Springs. Turn left on Serpentine Street and park in the gravel U.S. Forest Service lot at the trailhead. Shuttle service is also available through Bluff Mountain Outfitters in Hot Springs, with a minimum 2-day notice (see "Nearest outfitter," below).

Difficulty: Moderate (heading northbound).

Campsites (with GPS coordinates): There are 3 shelters: Roaring Fork, mile 2.7 (N35 48.262 W82 56.948); Walnut Mountain, mile 6.9 (N35 50.196 W82 56.194); and Deer Park, mile 17.4 (N35 52.580 W82 51.751). Good campsites are at miles 1.1 (N35 48.000 W82 57.095), 5.4 (N35 49.387 W82 56.302), 9.2 (N35 50.406 W82 54.723), 11.0 (N35 50.989 W82 54.032), 12.8 (N35 51.089 W82 53.078), and 15.8 (N35 52.031 W82 52.299).

Map: "Appalachian Trail Guide to Tennessee–North Carolina," map 4, Appalachian Trail Conservancy.

Follow the trail: From the trailhead, follow the white-blazed Appalachian Trail for 20.8 mi. north to Hot Springs.

Fee? No.

Water (with GPS coordinates): Springs are located at Roaring Fork Shelter, mile 2.7 (N35 48.262 W82 56.948); Walnut Mountain Shelter, mile 6.9 (N35 50.196 W82 56.194); and Deer Park Shelter, mile 17.4 (N35 52.580 W82 51.751). Stream water is available at miles 2.5 (N35 48.094 W82 56.768), 2.9 (N35 48.314 W82 57.126), 3.7 (N35 48.628 W82 56.936), 5.4 (N35 49.321 W82 56.363), and 6.4 (N35 49.975 W82 56.205).

Land manager: USDA Forest Service, French Broad Ranger District.

Trip highlights: 360-degree views from Max Patch on the south end; descent into the quintessential AT town of Hot Springs (which does have hot springs) on the north.

Special considerations: Water is plentiful for the first 7 mi. of this trip, but over the last 13 mi. there's only one reliable source, the spring at mile 17.4.

Night hike in? Yes. Good ridgeline campsites just past Max Patch, at mile 1.1.

Solo? Yes.

Family friendly? The hike is long, and while it's generally downhill, even in 3 days it could be a challenge for smaller backpackers.

Bailout options: No.

Seasons: Year-round, though access to trailhead on gravel roads could be an issue in winter.

Weather: Watch for afternoon thunderstorms on Max Patch, Bluff Mountain, and Deer Park Mountain in summer.

Solitude rating: 1 at Max Patch and on the drop into Hot Springs; 3 in between.

Nearest outfitter: Bluff Mountain Outfitters, Hot Springs, (828) 622-7162, www.bluffmountain.com.

Hunting allowed? Yes; local seasons apply.

More info: USDA Forest Service, French Broad Ranger District, (828) 622-3202.

ley below. On this stretch of the AT, you're sometimes 5 or more miles from the nearest paved road, and the nearest town of consequence (the *only* town of consequence) is Hot Springs, population 638. The trail's distance from civilization has another key benefit for the backpacker: minimal light pollution, giving motivation to stay outside the tent on those long winter nights and search the sky for constellations. (For stargazers, the Deer Park Shelter and campsites just before Garenflo Gap offer particularly good night viewing.)

One word of caution: Water is abundant the first 7 miles of this trip, but there's only one reliable source the last 13 miles—the spring near the Deer Park Shelter.

One last pitch: Hiked as suggested, from south to north, the trek requires only 1,800 feet of total climbing (as opposed to 5,800 feet if hiked north to south).

Classic Appalachian Trail *and* it's mostly downhill. You can't beat that.

26 AT Hot Springs to Rich Mountain Loop

HOT SPRINGS

12.7 MILES

NO. OF DAYS: 2

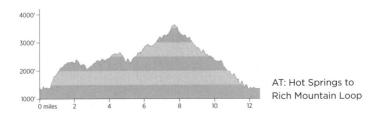

AT: Hot Springs to Rich Mountain Loop

This is the ideal weekend trip for a Boy Scout troop. It's a good weekend length: 2 days (3 if you want to explore connector trails). There's lots of cool stuff, from hiking along the shallow but wide French Broad River, to outcrop overlooks, to a rickety fire tower. And less than 3 miles in you might get an idea for your Eagle Scout project.

Even if you're not a scout, it's hard to beat a trip that begins and ends in one of the Appalachian Trail's best-known trail towns. In just a few short blocks along Hot Springs's Bridge Street, down which the AT passes, you can eat at one of several grills/diners/sandwich shops/restaurants, find just about any vital gear you can imagine at Bluff Mountain Outfitters (and

The view back toward Hot Springs on the climb up to Lovers Leap Ridge.

score organic coffee as well), and mend your trail-ravaged body in the hot springs for which the town is named. Fittingly, the first retail establishment to greet southbound hikers on their way into town is The Wash Tub, a laundromat.

This trip begins just across the river from Hot Springs, with a 0.3-mile warm-up walk along the east bank of the French Broad. If you're doing this trip in the summer, hang around a few minutes and you may catch sight of a raft of tourists careening down the river. A series of tight switchbacks climbs more than 500 feet in less than three quarters of a mile; three increasingly higher rock outcrops give you good reason to pause and check out the French Broad, Hot Springs, and surrounding mountains to the north and west.

The trail continues to climb, but along a ridgeline that shows mercy and, in winter through a naked canopy, more views of the French Broad below. At Pump Gap, mile 2.8, take a minute to read about the efforts of Taylor Michael and fellow members of Boy Scout Troop 374 in Raleigh. They treated

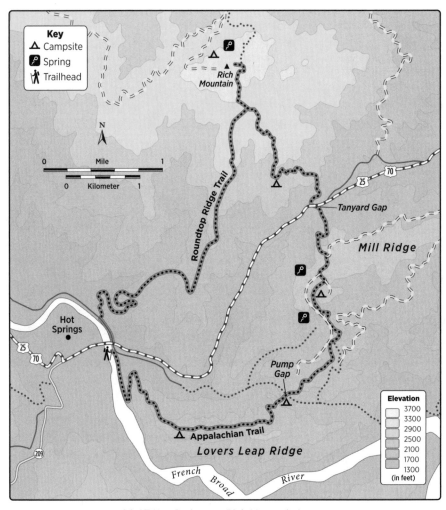

Key
△ Campsite
🔲 Spring
🚶 Trailhead

N

0   Mile   1

0   Kilometer   1

Roundtop Ridge Trail

Rich Mountain

Tanyard Gap

Mill Ridge

25   70

Hot Springs

25
70

Pump Gap

209

Appalachian Trail

Lovers Leap Ridge

French Broad River

Elevation
3700
3300
2900
2500
2100
1700
1300
(in feet)

26 AT Hot Springs to Rich Mountain Loop

26 AT Hot Springs to Rich Mountain Loop

Trailhead: From downtown Hot Springs, take US 25/70 across the French Broad River, then take the first left just past the bridge, which takes you down to River Road. Go left, under the US 25/70 overpass. Park to the right; pick up the Appalachian Trail heading upstream along the French Broad.

Loop/one way: Loop.

Difficulty: Moderate.

Campsites (with GPS coordinates): 1.5 mi. (N35 53.111 W82 48.869), 2.7 mi. (N35 53.282 W82 47.845), 4.2 mi. (N35 54.007 W82 47.537), 6.3 mi. (N35 54.904 W82 47.902), 7.8 mi. (N35 55.626 W82 48.299).

Map: "Appalachian Trail Guide to Tennessee–North Carolina," map 4, Appalachian Trail Conservancy.

Follow the trail: From the trailhead, take the white-blazed Appalachian Trail for 7.7 mi. to the 0.2-mi. spur, left, to Rich Mountain. Retrace your steps from the summit for 0.8 mi. to Roundtop Ridge Trail; go right. After 3.5 mi., the trail feeds into Reservoir Road, which heads down the mountain 0.3 mi. to River Road. Go left on River Road for another 0.3 mi. to your car.

Fee? No.

Water (with GPS coordinates): Springs are at 3.1 mi. (N35 53.439 W82 47.534) and 7.6 mi. (on the AT, about 50 yds. beyond the spur up to Rich Mountain (N35 55.692 W82 48.176). Streams with water are at 5.1 mi. (N35 54.440 W82 47.417) and 12.1 mi. (N35 54.035 W82 49.417).

Land manager: USDA Forest Service, French Broad Ranger District.

Trip highlights: Great views of Hot Springs, the French Broad River, and points north on the climb up to Lovers Leap Ridge; panoramic views from the fire tower atop Rich Mountain.

Special considerations: Water is scarce on this trip. Be sure to fill up when you can.

Night hike in? Probably not. The hike up to the first campsites involves close cliff encounters of the precipitous kind.

Solo? Yes.

Family friendly? The first 8 mi. of this trip are a steady climb, from about 1,500 ft. to nearly 3,700 ft., but with enough diversions to keep the whimpering to a minimum. And everyone loves a downhill finish.

Bailout options: US 25/70 crosses the trail at mile 5.6, offering a quick return to Hot Springs.

Seasons: Year-round.

Weather: Relatively low elevations mean this loop may escape winter weather that makes trekking treacherous at higher elevations.

Solitude rating: 3. Proximity to hiking mecca Hot Springs and encounters with various Forest Service trails means you'll likely encounter day hikers.

Nearest outfitter: Bluff Mountain Outfitters, Hot Springs, (828) 622-7162, www.bluffmountain.com.

Hunting allowed? Yes; local seasons apply.

More info: USDA Forest Service, French Broad Ranger District, (828) 622-3202.

a nearby stand of hemlocks with "soil-applied pesticides" in an effort to rid the trees of the dreaded hemlock woolly adelgid that is ravaging hemlocks throughout the Southeast. It's hoped that the treatment will spare the trees until a natural predator for the invasive insect is discovered.

There's history, which you get a sense of when a concrete dam suddenly appears, a mile and a half up the trail. The dam is responsible for a mountain pond signaling the beginning of the Mill Ridge area, which once produced tobacco and hay. In 1970 the Forest Service acquired the land, which today is used for a variety of recreational uses.

The trail drops into Tanyard Gap, crosses US 25/70, then begins the 2.0-mile climb to Rich Mountain. A mile into that climb the trail traces a ridgeline that has several campsites, especially good for watching the sun set over Tennessee.

Rich Mountain, at 3,635 feet, offers a fitting summit for a pack of eager boys or avid shutterbugs. The view is elevated by a fire tower that is more solid than some abandoned fire towers but still requires the watchful eye of an authority type who doesn't mind yelling when yelling is called for.

About now the troops will realize the hike has been pretty much "up" to this point. Nip potential whining in the bud with the promise that the return trip on 4.5-mile Roundtop Ridge Trail is all downhill.

You might mention, too, that there's an ice cream shop back in Hot Springs.

27 AT Standing Indian Loop

FRANKLIN

30 MILES

NO. OF DAYS: 3

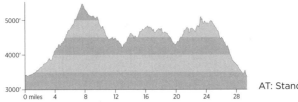

AT: Standing Indian Loop

A loop hike on the Appalachian Trail? The dickens you say: Isn't the AT a point-to-point—as in Springer Mountain, Ga., to Mount Katahdin, Maine —trail?

Stumbling upon some "trail magic" sprinkled for thru-hikers is one of the joys of hiking the Appalachian Trail.

It is, but on occasion the AT finds it necessary to take an oxbow route, nearly doubling back on itself. Shortly after passing into North Carolina from Georgia, the AT finds itself facing one of those rare occasions. And thanks to a developed network of Forest Service trails in the Standing Indian Basin, you can make a tidy 30-mile loop by starting at Rock Gap and hiking 20.7 miles south to Deep Gap, then taking the 3.7-mile Kimsey Creek Trail down to the Standing Indian Campground, and then taking the 2.0-mile Long Branch Trail back up to the AT for a return 2.6-mile trip to your car. A rare AT section hike with no pesky shuttle.

If you take this trip between April 1 and November 30, you can lop about 5 miles off the total by starting in the Standing Indian Campground (and paying a $2-per-day use fee to park your car) and hiking the 2.0-mile Long Branch Trail up to the Appalachian Trail at Glassmine Gap. In the off-season, when the campground is closed, you'll need to start from the small parking area at Rock Gap and hike 2.6 miles to Glassmine Gap. I suggest making this trip in the first couple weeks of April and hiking the AT south-

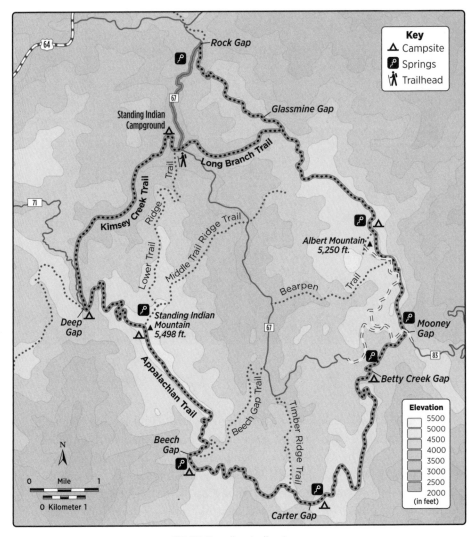

Rock Gap

Glassmine Gap

Standing Indian
Campground

Long Branch Trail

Kimsey Creek Trail

Ridge Trail

Lower Trail

Middle Trail Ridge Trail

Albert Mountain
5,250 ft.

Bearpen Trail

Deep
Gap

Standing Indian
Mountain
5,498 ft.

Mooney
Gap

Appalachian Trail

Betty Creek Gap

Beech Gap Trail

Timber Ridge Trail

Beech
Gap

N

Elevation
5500
5000
4500
4000
3500
3000
2500
2000
(in feet)

0 Mile 1

0 Kilometer 1

Carter Gap

27 AT Standing Indian Loop

27 AT Standing Indian Loop

Trailhead: From US 441/23 south of Franklin, go 12.0 mi. west on US 64 to Old US 64/West Old Murphy Road. Turn left. After 1.8 mi., turn right on the Forest Service access road. The Rock Gap parking area is 0.5 mi. on your left; the Standing Indian Campground parking area is 1.8 mi. on your right. The Long Branch trailhead is another 0.2 mi. down the road, on your left.

Loop/one-way: Loop.

Difficulty: Moderate.

Campsites (with GPS coordinates): Primary camping areas from Glassmine Gap southbound: Big Spring Shelter, mile 3.2 (N35 03.555 W83 28.814); Betty Creek Gap, mile 9.0 (N35 01.709 W83 28.695); Carter Gap Shelter, mile 9.6 (N34 59.965 W83 29.663); Beech Gap, mile 12.8 (N35 00.610 W83 31.542); Standing Indian Shelter, mile 17.2 (N35 02.121 W83 32.276); Deep Gap, mile 18.1 (N35 02.522 W83 33.240).

Maps: "Appalachian Trail Official Map: Nantahala National Forest, Bly Gap to Fontana Dam," Appalachian Trail Conference, 1:63,360, 40-ft. intervals, and the accompanying guide; "Southern Nantahala Wilderness and Standing Indian Basin, Nantahala National Forest and Chatahoochee National Forest," USDA Forest Service.

Follow the trail: In the off-season, from the Rock Gap trailhead hike 2.6 mi. to Glassmine Gap on the white-blazed Appalachian Trail. If starting from the Standing Indian Campground between Apr. 1 and Nov. 30, start at the blue-blazed Long Branch Trail. From Glassmine Gap, follow the AT for 18.1 mi. south to Deep Gap. At Deep Gap, take the blue-blazed Kimsey Creek Trail 3.7 mi. to the Standing Indian Campground. If hiking in the off-season, either take the road left for 1.4 mi. to the Rock Gap trailhead, or hike the 2.0-mi. Long Branch Trail to the AT, then go left and hike 2.6 mi. to Rock Gap.

Fee? $2 per day use fee if you park inside the Standing Indian Campground between Apr. 1 and Nov. 30.

Water (with GPS coordinates): Water is available from streams along the 2.0-mi. Long Branch Trail leading up to the AT and the 3.7-mi. Kimsey Creek Trail descending from Deep Gap. Along the AT heading southbound from Glassmine Gap, springs or reliable water sources are found at Big Spring, mile 3.2 (N35 03.555 W83 28.814); Betty Creek Gap, mile 9.0 (N35 01.709 W83 28.695); Carter Gap, mile 9.6 (N34 59.965 W83 29.663); Beech Gap, mile 12.8 (N35 00.610 W83 31.542); Standing Indian Shelter, mile 17.2 (N35 02.121 W83 32.276); and Deep Gap, mile 18.1 (N35 02.522 W83 33.240).

Land manager: USDA Forest Service, Nantahala National Forest, Wayah Ranger District.

Trip highlight: Views from atop 5,498-ft. Standing Indian Mountain.

Special considerations: None.

Night hike in? Yes.

Solo? Yes.

Family friendly? Trip has various shorter options, taking trails off the horseshoe-trending AT that return to the trailhead. The shortest of these options is about 10 mi., taking the 27-mi. route suggested, up Kimsey Creek to Deep Gap, then heading north, then returning to the trailhead on Lower Trail Ridge Trail.

Bailout options: 10-mi. trip described above is your best bet.

Seasons: Year-round.

Weather: With lots of ridgeline hiking on the AT, be aware of thunderstorms building during late afternoon in the summer.

Solitude rating: 4.

Nearest outfitter: Three Eagles Outfitters, Franklin, (828) 524-9061.

Hunting allowed? Yes.

More info: USDA Forest Service, Nantahala National Forest, Wayah Ranger District, (704) 524-6441.

bound; that way, you'll catch the first wave of thru-hikers on their way from Springer Mountain, Ga., the AT's southern terminus, 2,176 miles north to Mount Katahdin, Maine. There's always an entertaining tale to be heard when you encounter a thru-hiker, and from Glassmine Gap to Deep Gap you'll have nearly 21 miles to hear some trail tales.

You'll have some sweet hiking as well. The trail, for the most part, follows a ridgeline, cresting the occasional peak—most notably 5,250-foot Albert Mountain and 5,498-foot Standing Indian Mountain—and dipping into frequent gaps (Bearpen, Mooney, Betty Creek, Carter, Coleman, and Beech). There's a fire tower atop Albert and great views to the east into the Coweeta Hydrologic Laboratory, where the University of Georgia, the National Science Foundation, and the Forest Service are studying the relationship between trees and water. There's a nice putting-green surface atop Standing Indian, making for a great campsite during calmer weather. The camping is especially good at Beech Gap, where plenty of good sites are nestled inside the rhododendrons.

At Deep Gap, the trail returns to the Standing Indian Campground via the blue-blazed 3.7-mile Kimsey Creek Trail (the Forest Service trails here are all blazed blue; the AT, its traditional white). Three miles down Kimsey Creek, do not be deceived by a double blaze suggesting a switchback: This will take you on a nutty 0.8-mile connector trail uphill to the Park Ridge Trail, which then takes you back down the mountain 1.8 miles to the campground. Stick with Kimsey Creek, a shorter (0.7 miles) and more pleasant way to end your trip.

Southern Mountains

CASHIERS

1.0 MILE BACKPACK IN, ABOUT 30 MILES OF DAY HIKING WITH

NUMEROUS LOOP OPTIONS (the 6.0-mile loop shown on the map covers
a good cross section of Panthertown).

NO. OF DAYS: 2–4

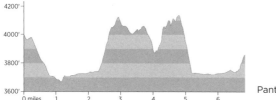

Panthertown Valley

I'm going to start with something I rarely do: a little hand-holding—but
just to get you to base camp. After that, you're on your own. Worry not,
you'll be fine.

The hand-holding is necessary because Panthertown can be a bear to get
around, and no one likes walking in circles with 40 pounds on their back.
Park in the gravel lot at the gate at the area's west entrance (see "Trailhead"
for directions). Hike 0.6 miles down the Salt Rock Trail to Panthertown
Creek Trail (stopping after less than a half mile to take in a view of the valley from Salt Rock). At Panthertown Creek Trail, go left for 0.3 miles, then
take a right at Mac's Gap Trail and go less than 0.2 miles before you start
running into a bonanza of camping options. You should find something to
your liking here; if not, continue another two-thirds of a mile—cross the
bridge over Panthertown Creek, then hang a right on Granny Burrell Falls
Trail—to a second generous camping area (with an A-frame shelter) on the
other side of Panthertown Creek, just above Granny Burrell Falls.

Now you're on your own, because while it is easy to become . . . momentarily displaced in Panthertown, you will never be momentarily displaced
for long. While there are more than 30 miles of trail in the valley, none goes
particularly far before T-boning into another trail or spitting you out onto
an overlook where you can quickly regain your bearings. Since there are
fewer than 6,700 acres contained in a tidy natural arena, it's hard to become officially lost. It's also hard to grow bored.

Panthertown is sometimes referred to as the Yosemite of the East.
There is a resemblance, with an abundance of waterfalls and exposed
granite faces. But it's more accurate to think of 6,700-acre Panthertown

Little Green Mountain's slickrock exposure makes for a scenic spot to stop for lunch.

as a diorama of 1,200-square-*mile* Yosemite—of Little Green Mountain's exposure as replicating Yosemite's Half Dome, of Schoolhouse Falls as a portrait in miniature of Yosemite Falls, and of Panthertown's collection of white pines as table-top versions of Yosemite's giant Sequoias.

While the Yosemite analogy may be a stretch, Panthertown may offer the most diversity per mile hiked of any spot in the state. The valley floor is unusually flat for the Southern Appalachians and is home to at least 11 natural communities, according to The Nature Conservancy. Among them is a rare Southern Appalachian forest-bog community. Here you'll also find a variety of rare plants, including Cuthbert's turtlehead, Canada burnet, marsh bellflower, climbing fern, and spinulose wood fern. Panthertown Creek offers some of the state's best fly-fishing for trout, in part due to an abundance of large pools that allow for unrestricted casts. Those pools and

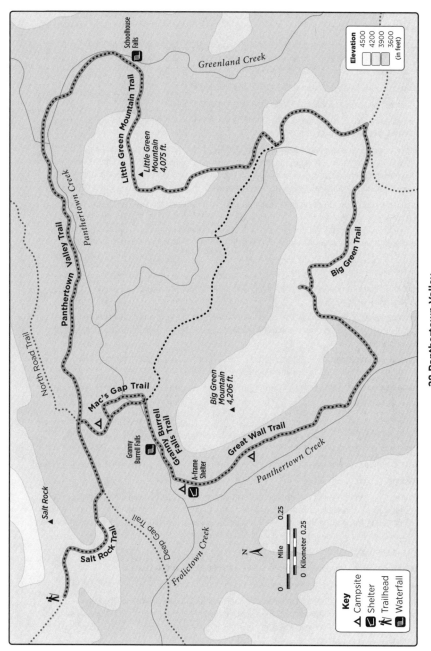

Key

△ Campsite

🏚 Shelter

🏃 Trailhead

📖 Waterfall

N

Mile 0.25

0 Kilometer 0.25

0.25

0

Schoolhouse Falls

Greenland Creek

Little Green Mountain Trail

▲ Little Green Mountain 4,075 ft.

Big Green Trail

Panthertown Creek

Panthertown Valley Trail

North Road Trail

Big Green Mountain ▲ 4,206 ft.

Mac's Gap Trail

Granny Burrell Falls

Granny Burrell Falls Trail

△ A-frame Shelter

Great Wall Trail

Panthertown Creek

Salt Rock ▲

Salt Rock Trail

Deep Gap Trail

Frolictown Creek

Elevation

4500 | 4200 | 3900 | 3600

(in feet)

28 Panthertown Valley

28 Panthertown Valley

Trailhead: 2.0 mi. east of the intersection of US 64 and NC 107 in Cashiers, go left on Cedar Creek Road/SR 1120. Go 2.2 mi. and go right on Nicholson Lane/SR 1121. Continue 3.4 mi. to paved parking, another 0.4 mi. to gravel trailhead parking.

Loop/one-way: One-way backpack in, various day-hike loops.

Difficulty: Backpack in is easy; day hikes range from easy to moderate.

Campsites (with GPS coordinates): 1.0 mi. (N35 09.921 W83 01.707), 1.6 mi. (N35 09.666 W83 01.929), 1.9 mi. (N35 09.470 W83 01.800).

Maps: *A Guide's Guide to Panthertown, Bonas Defeat, and Big Pisgah*, by Burt Kornegay, owner of Slickrock Expeditions, $12. Available at local outfitters or at www.slickrockexpeditions.com. A Forest Service map is available in PDF form at www.cs.unca.edu/nfsnc/nepa/highlands/panthertown/panthertown.htm and may be available in print as well.

Follow the trail: To get to the main camping sites, hike 0.6 mi. down the Salt Rock Trail to Panthertown Creek Trail; go left. After 0.3 mi., go right at Mac's Gap Trail and go less than 0.2 mi. before you start running into campsites. Additional sites are located two-thirds of a mile farther, across the bridge over Panthertown Creek, then right on Granny Burrell Falls Trail. The second area includes an A-frame shelter.

Fee? No.

Water: The three campsites mentioned are all along water. Water is scarce once you leave the valley floor; plan accordingly.

Trip highlights: Spectacular views of the intimate valley from Salt Rock and Little Green Mountain; 8 significant waterfalls (Schoolhouse being the best-known); trout fishing in streams with more of a western feel.

Special considerations: As of December 2009, trails in Panthertown were not marked. A map (see above) is mandatory; pay close attention to it.

Night hike in? Yes, especially if you camp at the first recommended campsite, which requires no water crossings to get to.

Solo? Yes.

Family friendly? Yes. The backpack in is short and easy, there's lots of fun water (pools and falls) to explore, and the trails are generally short and offer good views.

Bailout options: No, but it's a short backpack out.

Seasons: Winter, Spring, Summer, Fall.

Weather: Wet weather can pose problems in Panthertown Valley. Panthertown Creek, running west to east across the valley floor, runs high after rain and can be tricky to cross where there aren't bridges (Mac's Gap Trail and Panthertown Valley Trail below Schoolhouse Falls both have bridges). Likewise, during the cold of winter stream crossings can be treacherous.

Solitude rating: 3.

Nearest outfitter: Highland Hiker, Cashiers, (866) 836-9920, www.highlandhiker.com.

Hunting allowed? Yes, local seasons apply.

More info: USDA Forest Service, Nantahala Ranger District, (828) 524-6441. Also, The Nature Conservancy website, www.nature.org/wherewework/northamerica/states/northcarolina/preserves/art5621.html, and Friends of Panthertown, www.j-mca.org/friends.asp.

Panthertown's dozen or so falls make the valley a good place to cool off come summer.

One of the valley's allures is also one of its challenges. Domestication has been slow to come to Panthertown Valley since it became part of the Nantahala National Forest, with the help of The Nature Conservancy, in 1989. The area is crisscrossed with old logging trails; some have been incorporated into the main map of the valley, but some have not. And very few of the trails are marked. But again, none is especially long, so if you do become . . . displaced, you won't be for long.

FIRES CREEK

The 21,000-acre Fires Creek area is a backpacker's playground—and not one of those newfangled U.S. Consumer Product Safety Commission–approved playgrounds that have had the fun sanitized out of them. Rather, it's a good old-fashioned playground that forces you to rely on your imagination and wits, the kind with sharp edges, splinters, and metal surfaces that could cause trouble if you're not paying attention.

Actually, at Fires Creek if you aren't paying attention, the worst you can get is lost, and even if you do, it won't be for long. Fires Creek is a neatly contained forested island in the Nantahala National Forest. It's formed by a horseshoe-shaped 25-mile ridgeline of the Valley River Mountains, a Southern Appalachian box canyon, of sorts. Rimming this box canyon is the 25.5-mile Fires Creek Rim Trail; another 20 miles of trail descend from the ridge to the valley floor, creating a multitude of backpacking circuits—more if you include the 3 Forest Service roads that penetrate Fires Creek.

About those "sharp edges": Your main "danger" is getting lost. In addition to some 45 miles of official trail are at least twice that many miles of old roadbeds that can deceive even the savviest pathfinder. The local Mountain High Hikers have done a good job of marking official trails with blue blazes, but wrong turns still happen. If they do, the key to righting yourself is not to follow conventional wisdom and track a stream down the mountain, but to make your way up it: It's hard to miss the circumventing Rim Trail, in part because the backside of the Fires Creek bowl frequently consists of dangerously sharp drop-offs. Travel up the mountain is accommodated by a curious lack of undergrowth. In general, you'll find hardwood forests up-slope, rhododendron tunnels along the rim. And you likely won't have that far to go to reach the rim. The Southern Appalachians are beginning to wind down as they approach the Georgia border; unlike the Black Mountains and Great Smoky Mountains to the north, which exceed 6,600 feet, the Fires Creek rim tops out between 4,500 and 5,000 feet (base elevation is around 3,300 feet).

Here are three trip options.

29 **Fires Creek** Rim Trail

HAYESVILLE

25.5 MILES

NO. OF DAYS: 2–5

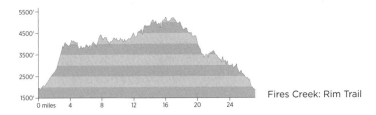

Fires Creek: Rim Trail

If you *really* want to explore the Fires Creek area and have at least 3 days, take the Rim Trail option.

Trekking the Rim Trail is a 2-day hike if you're into covering ground as quickly as possible; a 3-day journey if you're into stopping and smelling the roses (or in this case, spring wildflowers, including trillium, lady slipper, and Solomon's seal); and 4 days or longer if you use it as a launching pad to explore the valley below. Stick to the rim and you'll miss some of the best of what Fires Creek has to offer. (See trips 30 and 31.) You'll also be challenged to find water. Thus, dropping down from the rim on occasion is not only entertaining, it's essential.

Your best bet for planning a long exploration of the Fires Creek area is to score a copy of *Chunky Gal Trail and Fires Creek Rim Trail: Detailed Trail Guide with Maps of the Trails in the Nantahala National Forest in Clay County North Carolina*, by John R. Ray, Malcolm J. Skove, and Bill Kenyon. John Ray has run a measuring wheel over more than 45 miles of trail in Fires Creek. Plus, he and his Mountain High Hikers club have spent considerable time blazing trails and searching for sources of water on high. Those efforts are reflected in his comprehensive guide.

Thus, what you get here is an overview of the Rim Trail and trails that

Views from spots on the rim are remarkably devoid of signs of human activity.

drop into Fires Creek that might provide good side trips. With that in mind, we'll focus on camping spots near trail intersections and nearby spots where you *might* find water. I say *might*, because near the ridgeline most sources are intermittent, flowing only after recent rains. Distances are starting from the Fires Creek Picnic Area and hiking clockwise.

5.3 miles, Will King Gap, intersection with Phillips Ridge Trail. Phillips Ridge is a gentle, 5-mile descent to Laurel Creek. Campsites can be found just below the trail intersection on an old roadbed that heads west. There's an intermittent spring about 50 feet down the center of the cove. Another mile and a half along the Rim Trail is a nice campsite with a great nighttime view to the northwest, toward the town of Andrews.

7.9 miles, Rockhouse Creek Trail. After a short, deceptive gradual decline, Rockhouse Creek Trail drops like a rock, losing 1,000 vertical feet in less than a mile. At the beginning of the drop, less than two-tenths of a mile down the trail, is a spring, about 10 yards left of the trail.

13.1 miles, Sassafras Ridge Trail. There's water, from a tributary of Long

29 Fires Creek Rim Trail

Key

🚶 Trailhead

Elevation
5800
5200
4600
4000
3400
2800
2200
(in feet)

Shinbone Ridge/
Old Road Gap
Trail Intersection

*Tusquitee
Bald*

Chunky
Gal Trail
Intersection

Far Bald
Spring Trail
Intersection

Fires Creek Rim Trail

Sassafras Ridge
Trail Intersection

*Johnson Bald
4,908 ft.*

Little Fires
Creek Trail
Intersection

Rockhouse Creek
Trail Intersection

Tusquitee Mountains

340

*Squirrel
Spring Gap*

**Carver
Gap/
Bristol
Cabin Trail**

Will King Gap/
Phillips Ridge Trail
Intersection

Omphus
Ridge Trail
Intersection

Fires Creek Rim Trail

Fires Creek

Fires Creek Rim Trail

N

Miles
0   2

Kilometers
0   2

Fires Creek
Picnic Area
🚶

29 Fires Creek Rim Trail

Trailhead: From the west: From NC 141 go 4.7 mi. east on US 64 to Hillbrook Road and turn left. From the east: From the junction of US 64 and US 69 in Hayesville go west on US 64 for 4.9 mi. and turn right on Hillbrook Road. Once on Hillbrook, go 3.4 mi. to Fires Creek Road and go left. After 2.4 mi., enter Fires Creek Picnic Area, the trailhead.

Loop/one-way: Loop.

Difficulty: Moderate.

Campsites: See text.

Maps: *Chunky Gal Trail and Fires Creek Rim Trail: Detailed Trail Guide with Maps of the Trails in the Nantahala National Forest in Clay County, North Carolina*, by John R. Ray, Malcolm J. Skove, and Bill Kenyon, www.geocities.com/j3hnr3y. Includes detailed descriptions of all trails on this hike, including water sources just off the ridgeline. USGS: Hayesville, Andrews.

Follow the trail: From the trailhead in the Fires Creek Picnic Area head north and west on the blue-blazed Rim Trail. The trail takes a 25.5-mi. loop back to the trailhead.

Fee? No.

Water: See text.

Land manager: USDA Forest Service, Nantahala National Forest, Tusquitee Ranger District.

Trip highlights: Views from assorted knobs and balds.

Special considerations: This is a ridgeline trail; there are few reliable water sources. If you plan a side trip on one of the trails descending into Fires Creek, you should be able to find water within a quarter of a mile.

Night hike in? No.

Solo? Yes.

Family friendly? No. Length and potential lack of water could take the fun out of this trip for smaller hikers.

Bailout options: Yes. To cut your hike short, take one of the side trails down the ridge and take a Forest Service road (340 or 340A) back to the trailhead.

Seasons: All.

Weather: Ridgeline hiking: Watch for afternoon thunderstorms in summer.

Solitude rating: 3.

Nearest outfitter: Nantahala Outdoor Center, Wesser, (888) 905-7238, www.noc.com.

Hunting allowed? Yes; local seasons apply.

More info: USDA Forest Service, Nantahala National Forest, Tusquitee Ranger District, (828) 837-5152, www.cs.unca.edu/nfsnc.

Branch Creek, a half mile down Sassafras Ridge Trail. A quarter mile beyond the intersection is a secluded campsite surrounded by rhododendrons on a small knob to the right of the trail.

14.1 miles, Shinbone Ridge Trail/Old Road Gap Trail. Old Road Gap Trail comes in from the left; it heads about 2 miles north. Using Forest Service roads, you can connect with the Junaluska and Bartram trails. Shinbone Trail drops 1.7 miles inside Fires Creek; there's an intermittent spring 150 feet down the trail, right along the trail.

15.6 miles, Chunky Gal Trail intersection. Chunky Gal climbs steeply for a tenth of a mile to Tusquitee Bald, then continues for 21.5 miles to the Appalachian Trail. There's room for a tent on Tusquitee Bald; a better bet is a clearing under mature hardwoods a tenth of a mile before the Chunky Gal intersection, accessible via a narrow passage through rhododendrons on the right side of the trail. Opposite the Chunky Gal intersection is a trail marked "H2O"; take it for more than a tenth of a mile to a spring.

15.9 miles, Far Bald Spring Trail. There's water two-tenths of a mile down the trail. Trail descends 1.7 miles to FS 340.

17.6 miles, Johnson Bald. Notable for the wreckage of a small plane that crashed here in 1974.

18.2 miles, Little Fires Creek Trail. Another 0.2 miles down the Rim Trail is a gap with good campsites.

22.1 miles, Squirrel Spring Gap. Descend into a cove about a tenth of a mile to an intermittent spring in a rhododendron copse.

22.8 miles, Carver Gap, Bristol Cabin Trail. Possible campsites on an old road veering left. Trail descends 1.1 miles to Bristol Horse Camp.

23.2 miles, Omphus Ridge Trail. Drops one mile to FS 340.

25.5 miles, back to trailhead.

30 Fires Creek East Rim

HAYESVILLE

6.8 MILES

NO. OF DAYS: 2

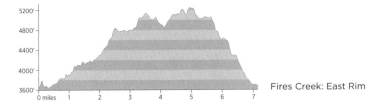

Fires Creek: East Rim

Old Road Gap Trail comes up to the rim from the north.

This route begins with a nice warm-up, a gradual (420 feet of vertical gain), 0.6-mile climb up the tail end of FS 340, which runs the length of the Fires Creek Canyon. Then it's Forest Service trail as usual, as the ensuing 1.5-mile climb up Sassafras Ridge Trail to the rim heads straight up the mountain, taking its cue from the accompanying Long Branch Creek. The good news: It gets you up to the Rim Trail posthaste.

Nearly all of the 2.8-mile stretch of the Rim Trail on this circuit is shrouded in rhododendrons. That creates a natural block from the blazing sun in summer and protection from cold northern winds come winter. As an added incentive, when there is a break, there's often a stellar view of mountain ranges extending as far as the Smokies to the northwest. These breaks also give you the opportunity to appreciate the precipitous drop off the backside of rim.

The best view comes near the end of your time on the Rim Trail. At mile 2.5 on the rim, the Chunky Gal Trail intersects on the right. Take it for 0.1 miles (a stout climb) to 5,240-foot Tusquitee Bald. Unlike some of the state's more notable balds—Max Patch and Grassy on the AT come to mind—Tusquitee is a heath bald, and all but a portion of it is covered by a tight collection of low-growing evergreens and briars. What is clear allows for a small campsite and a big view to the east. Something you should savor from the views on this trail: They are nearly devoid of human impact, a rare occurrence in North Carolina's mountains.

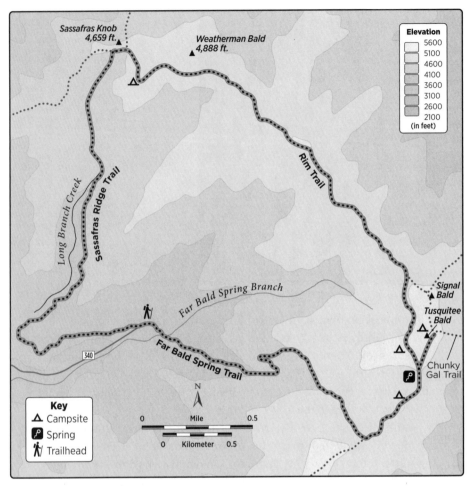

30 Fires Creek East Rim

30 Fires Creek East Rim

Trailhead: From the west: Go 4.7 mi. on US 64 east from NC 141 to Hillbrook Road and turn left. From the east: From the junction of US 64 and US 69 in Hayesville go west on US 64 for 4.9 mi. and turn right on Hillbrook Road. Once on Hillbrook, go 3.4 mi. to Fires Creek Road and go left. After 2.4 mi. enter Fires Creek Picnic Area; road becomes FS 340. Continue 10 mi. on FS 340 to Far Bald Springs trailhead. (Note: FS 340 is a gravel road, well maintained at first, less so as it nears the trailhead. Low-clearance cars may have trouble the last 2.5 mi., past the split for FS 340C.)

Loop/one-way: Loop.

Difficulty: Moderate.

Campsites (with GPS coordinates): 2.4 mi. (N35 09.542 W83 44.959), 4.6 mi. (N35 08.495 W83 43.674), 5.2 mi. (N35 08.330 W83 43.705).

Maps: *Chunky Gal Trail and Fires Creek Rim Trail: Detailed Trail Guide with Maps of the Trails in the Nantahala National Forest in Clay County, North Carolina,* by John R. Ray, Malcolm J. Skove, and Bill Kenyon, www.geocities.com/j3hnr3y. Includes detailed descriptions of all trails on this hike, including water sources just off the ridgeline. USGS: Hayesville, Andrews.

Follow the trail: From the trailhead, continue past the gate on FS 340 for 0.6 mi. to Sassafras Ridge Trail. Continue for 1.5 mi. to the Rim Trail and go right. Travel the Rim Trail for 2.8 mi. (with a 0.1-mi. side excursion up to Tusquitee Bald at mile 2.6), then go right on Far Bald Spring Trail; the trailhead is 1.7 mi.

Fee? No.

Water (with GPS coordinates): At the 3/4-mi. mark the trail picks up Short Branch, then Long Branch for about 1.3 mi. Shortly, the trail reaches the ridgeline, and the only source of water is a spring at the 4.8-mi. mark (N35 08.402 W83 43.643), opposite the intersection of the Chunky Gal Trail. (Follow the faint trail less the 0.2 mi.) Water is available for the remainder of the hike from Far Bald Spring, beginning at mile 5.5.

Land manager: USDA Forest Service, Nantahala National Forest, Tusquitee Ranger District.

Trip highlights: Ridgeline hike through rhododendron tunnels; rare North Carolina mountaintop views nearly devoid of development.

Special considerations: There are only 2 good campsites and 1 source of water on the Rim Trail.

Night hike in? No. If you arrive after dark, there is a camping area on FS 340 about a quarter mile from the trailhead.

Solo? Yes.

Family friendly? Yes. The 0.6-mi. climb up Sassafras Ridge Trail has a steep section; otherwise, it's easy hiking.

Bailout options: No.

Seasons: All.

Weather: Includes a ridgeline section; watch for afternoon thunderstorms in summer.

Solitude rating: 3.

Nearest outfitter: Nantahala Outdoor Center, Wesser, (888) 905-7238, www.noc.com.

Hunting allowed? Yes; local seasons apply.

More info: USDA Forest Service, Nantahala National Forest, Tusquitee Ranger District, (828) 837-5152, www.cs.unca.edu/nfsnc.

Speaking of camping, your best options are on the rim. Atop Sassafras Knob, 2.5 miles into the hike, is a good spot for a couple of tents. Your next option is 2.2 miles down the trail; watch for an opening in the rhododendron tunnel on your right, duck through, walk 15 yards, and you'll find a sizable clearing under the hardwoods. There's Tusquitee Bald, as mentioned earlier, and a spot 0.1 miles beyond the Chunky Gal intersection. Opposite the Chunky Gal Trail intersection is a sign indicating "H2O." Follow the path a little more than a tenth of a mile to a spring.

Camping at Sassafras Knob gives you the option of a day hike from your base camp west along the Rim Trail; camping on Tusquitee Bald or at the site just before gives you a chance to explore the 21.6-mile Chunky Gal Trail, which connects to the Appalachian Trail at Deep Gap.

Return to the trailhead along the 1.7-mile Far Bald Spring Trail.

31 Fires Creek West Rim

HAYESVILLE

9.4 MILES

NO. OF DAYS: 2

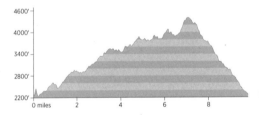

Fires Creek: West Rim

This trail begins with a math problem. Phillips Ridge Trail and Rockhouse Creek Trail start from the same location. It takes Phillips Ridge 5.0 miles to reach the Rim Trail, while it's only a 1.7-mile trip on Rockhouse Creek. Which trail will you take up the mountain and which will you take down?

With one brief exception, Phillips Ridge Trail is the ideal way for a backpacker to hike up a mountain. The trail begins along Laurel Creek, then makes a hairpin turn at mile 0.7, switching partners to follow Hickory Cove Creek. A little more than a mile later it changes course again, abandoning Hickory Cove and tracking west. Less than 3 miles into the trip it buddies up to Phillips Ridge, tracking its western flank. All of this occurs along old roadbeds that take their time reaching the top. The lone exception is a stark tenth-of-a-mile climb just after you cross the headwaters of Laurel Creek 4 miles into the hike.

Trails in the Fires Creek area are well marked. If you haven't seen a blaze in a while, odds are you're on an old roadbed that's not part of the trail network.

After 5 miles, you reach the Rim Trail at 3,715-foot Will King Gap and a view to the northwest. Unlike the views northeast from the Rim Trail on trip 30, this view takes in the town of Andrews and the distant crawl of traffic on US 19/74/129 against a backdrop of the Snowbird Mountains. The Rim Trail on this section is different as well. It's more rolling, with a nice climb up the west flank of Big Stamp, and it's more exposed, with passages through hardwood forests sprinkled amid the rhododendron tunnels. Camping options are few: Your best bet is a small platform at mile 6.4 that accommodates one tent and offers a stellar nighttime view of the afore-mentioned 19/74/129 valley.

After 2.7 miles it's time for the 1.7-mile portion of this equation. The descent down Rockhouse Creek Trail is gradual for the first couple hundred yards, then it becomes a real knee-burner, losing 1,000 vertical feet in less than a mile. Hiking poles are highly recommended.

The last three quarters of a mile of this hike is a pleasant stroll along frisky Rockhouse Creek. The surrounding terrain—stately hardwoods on clean slopes with little understory—is serene. Rockhouse Creek, however, has scoured its way through a narrow drainage, unearthing reading-chair-sized and smaller rocks as it makes its way over drops and spillovers to Laurel Creek. It's a good companion for the end of your trip.

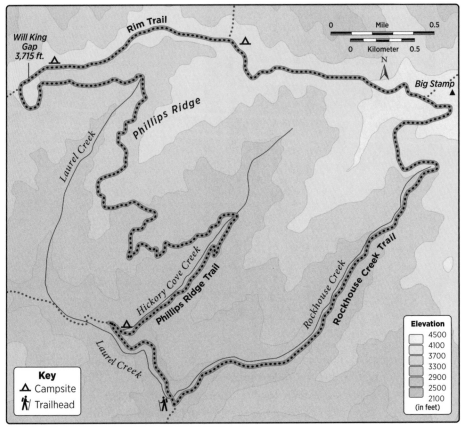

31 Fires Creek West Rim

31 Fires Creek West Rim

Trailhead: From the west: Go 4.7 mi. on US 64 east from NC 141 to Hillbrook Road and turn left. From the east: From the junction of US 64 and US 69 in Hayesville go west on US 64 for 4.9 mi. and turn right on Hillbrook Road. Once on Hillbrook, go 3.4 mi. to Fires Creek Road and go left. After 2.4 mi. enter Fires Creek Picnic Area; road becomes FS 340. Continue 1.8 mi. and go left on FS 340A. Trailhead is 1.0 mi., at gate.

Loop/one-way: Loop.

Difficulty: Moderate.

Campsites (with GPS coordinates): 1.0 mi. (in a pinch) (N35 07.344 W83 50.568), 5.2 mi. (N35 08.339 W83 51.106), 6.4 mi. (N35 08.576 W83 50.079), 7.2 (N35 08.412 W83 49.425).

Maps: *Chunky Gal Trail and Fires Creek Rim Trail: Detailed Trail Guide with Maps of the Trails in the Nantahala National Forest in Clay County, North Carolina,* by John R. Ray, Malcolm J. Skove, and Bill Kenyon, www.geocities.com/j3hnr3y. Includes detailed descriptions of all trails on this hike, including water sources just off the ridgeline. USGS: Hayesville, Andrews.

Follow the trail: From the trailhead, take Phillips Ridge Trail 5.0 mi. to the Rim Trail; go right. After 2.7 mi., go right for the return 1.7-mi. trip on Rockhouse Creek Trail.

Fee? No.

Water (with GPS coordinates): The trail follows Laurel Creek for the first three quarters of a mile, then follows Hickory Cove Creek for another three quarters of a mile. There are 4 stream crossings within a half mile beginning at mile 2.2, and another crossing at mile 4.0, the last potential water source before the Rim Trail. You won't find water again until a spring 10 yds. left of the trail on Rockhouse Creek Trail, at mile 7.8 (N35 08.210 W83 49.119). At mile 8.4 the trail picks up Rockhouse Creek, your companion for the rest of the hike.

Land manager: USDA Forest Service, Nantahala National Forest, Tusquitee Ranger District.

Trip highlights: Ridgeline includes a mix of rhododendron tunnels and hardwood forest; return on Rockhouse Creek Trail is a treat along its namesake creek.

Special considerations: Upper portion of Rockhouse Creek Trail loses 1,000 vertical feet in less than a mile; hiking poles are strongly advised.

Night hike in? Yes. Hike in is along a mellow roadbed; a couple sites about a mile in are good in a pinch.

Solo? Yes.

Family friendly? Yes. Good stretches along water, entertaining rhododendron tunnels, no particularly demanding stretches, and young knees will enjoy the aforementioned drop on upper Rockhouse Creek Trail.

Bailout options: No.

Seasons: All.

Weather: Includes a ridgeline section; watch for afternoon thunderstorms in summer.

Solitude rating: 3.

Nearest outfitter: Nantahala Outdoor Center, Wesser, (888) 905-7238, www.noc.com.

Hunting allowed? Yes; local seasons apply.

More info: USDA Forest Service, Nantahala National Forest, Tusquitee Ranger District, (828) 837-5152, www.cs.unca.edu/nfsnc.

Joyce Kilmer–Slickrock Wilderness

JOYCE KILMER-SLICKROCK WILDERNESS

If North Carolina were to hold a wildest of the wild contest, the Joyce Kilmer–Slickrock Wilderness would get at least one key vote, that of wilderness guide Burt Kornegay. "I tell people that when we get into the middle of Slickrock that's as far as you can get into woods. It has a real sense of wild forest." Pretty good endorsement coming from a guy who's spent the last 25 years leading more than 400 expeditions into the wild. So fond of this area is the Cullowhee-based wilderness guide that he named his guide service—Slickrock Expeditions—after the 17,394-acre wilderness.

The area is best known as home of the 3,800-acre Joyce Kilmer Memorial Forest, "perhaps the single most impressive growth of eastern virgin forest in the United States," according to Wilderness.net. Strolling among trees dating back to near the time of Columbus and tulip poplars more than 100 feet high and 20 feet around is indeed a memorable, even reverential experience. But it's once you leave the memorial forest that you get a sense of Kornegay's Slickrock: of trail encased in subtropical rhododendron and mountain laurel jungles, of creeks that bang through narrow gorges, and of long ridgelines that exchange the wild below with a realization that, when you reach a clearing and can view forested mountains disappearing in every direction, you truly are in a remote place.

Naked Ground Loop (trip 32) gives you a taste of the wildness; Slickrock Creek Loop (trip 33) thrusts you into the thick of it.

32 Joyce Kilmer-Slickrock Wilderness Naked Ground Loop

ROBBINSVILLE

9.8 MILES

NO. OF DAYS: 2; LONGER WITH DAY-HIKE OPTIONS

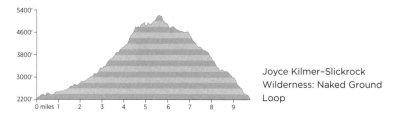

Joyce Kilmer–Slickrock Wilderness: Naked Ground Loop

You're standing next to a tree along Little Santeetlah Creek in the Joyce Kilmer–Slickrock Wilderness, and it's no ordinary tree. It's a massive yel-

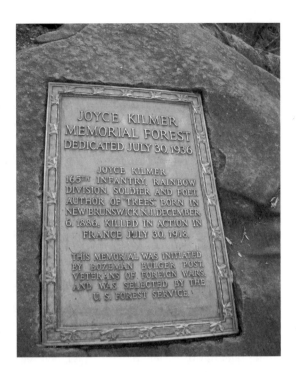

Be sure to swing by the adjoining Joyce Kilmer Memorial Forest after your Naked Ground expedition.

low poplar, ramrod-straight, its trunk 10 feet around at the base and its crown disappearing 125 feet into the sky. You stand and marvel not just at its sheer size but at its longevity: This tree could be more than 450 years old. To put that in chronological perspective, this tree might have existed, as a sapling, when Hernando De Soto, the first European known to have penetrated this far into the New World, passed not far from here in 1539. This tree has lived through all of recorded U.S. history.

You're standing on the north side of the Joyce Kilmer Memorial Forest, celebrated as one of the country's few remaining stands of virgin forest. Though the surrounding area was logged vigorously by the Babcock Lumber Company beginning in 1915, a series of fortuitous events spared this particular 3,800-acre tract. The greatest concentration of behemoths Joyce Kilmer is known for resides on the south side of Little Santeetlah, but the north side of the drainage has its share of towering hemlocks and poplars as well. And few of the tourists who invade the Joyce Kilmer Memorial Forest step foot on this side, part of a 33,285-acre wilderness that spills into Tennessee (that state's portion is called the Citico Creek Wilderness, part of the Cherokee National Forest).

You'll notice this as soon as you get to the parking lot trailhead. Ninety-

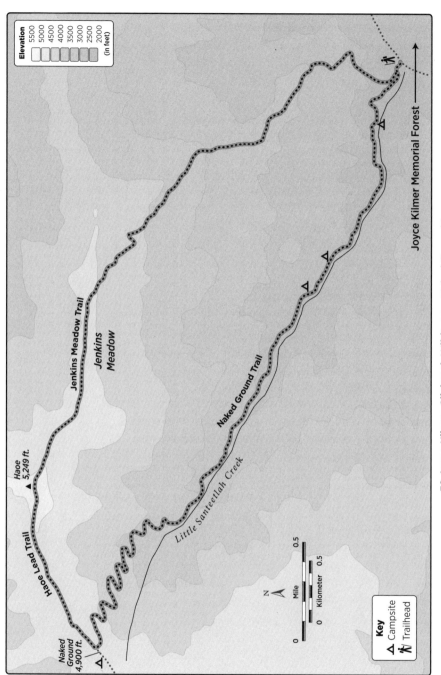

Elevation
5500
5000
4500
4000
3500
3000
2500
2000
(in feet)

Haoe Lead Trail

Haoe
▲ *5,249 ft.*

*Naked
Ground
4,900 ft.*
△

Jenkins Meadow Trail

*Jenkins
Meadow*

Naked Ground Trail

Little Santeetlah Creek

△

△

△

🏃

Joyce Kilmer Memorial Forest

N
↑

Mile
0.5

Kilometer
0.5

0

0

Key
△ Campsite
🏃 Trailhead

32 Joyce Kilmer–Slickrock Wilderness Naked Ground Loop

32 Joyce Kilmer–Slickrock Wilderness Naked Ground Loop

Trailhead: From Robbinsville, go west on US 129; just outside town, go left on NC 143. After 12 mi., go right on Joyce Kilmer Road/SR 1134. Go 2.3 mi.; the entrance to the Joyce Kilmer trailhead and parking area is on the left. Park at the far end of the lot; the trailhead is off the right side of the lot.

Loop/one-way: Loop.

Difficulty: Moderate.

Campsites (with GPS coordinates): 0.9 mi. (N35 21.518 W83 56.275), 2.2 mi. (N35 21.766 W83 56.702), 2.4 mi. (N35 21.863 W83 56.960), 5.0 mi. at Naked Ground (N35 22.801, W83 59.111).

Map: "Joyce Kilmer–Slickrock Wilderness and Citico Creek Wilderness in the Nantahala and Cherokee National Forests," USDA Forest Service, 1:24,000, 40-ft. intervals.

Follow the trail: From the trailhead, take the Naked Ground Trail 5.0 mi. to Naked Ground Gap and the Haoe Lead Trail. Go right for a mile along the ridgeline trail, then go right on the Jenkins Meadow Trail. Stay on Jenkins Meadow Trail for 3.0 mi., then go right on Naked Ground for 0.8 mi. to the trailhead.

Fee? No.

Water (with GPS coordinates): There is water along the trail, from Little Santeetlah Creek, for the first 3 mi., and a spring at Naked Ground, at mile 5.0 (N35 22.801, W83 59.111). There is no reliable water the rest of the trip.

Land manager: USDA Forest Service.

Trip highlight: Old growth trees, poplars in particular, along Little Santeetlah Creek.

Special considerations: This is a wilderness: Though there are signs at most trail intersections, the trails are not blazed. It is easy to lose the path with a little inattention.

Night hike in? No. Campsites are not obvious and can be difficult to find in the dark.

Solo? Not advised because of wilderness status.

Family friendly? No.

Bailout options: No.

Seasons: All.

Weather: Includes ridgeline hiking; watch for afternoon thunderstorms in summer.

Solitude rating: 3. The Joyce Kilmer Memorial Forest spur 0.9 mi. into the trip will siphon off 95 percent of foot traffic.

Nearest outfitter: Nantahala Outdoor Center, Wesser, (888) 905-7238, www.noc.com.

Hunting allowed? Yes; local seasons apply.

More info: USDA Forest Service, Nantahala National Forest, Cheoah Ranger District, (828) 479-6431, www.cs.unca.edu/nfsnc.

five percent of visitors will park and take the footbridge over Little Santeetlah onto the Joyce Kilmer Memorial Trail; the backpackers will pick up a nondescript footpath on the right side of the lot and head into the wild.

Though this is a wilderness and the trail is not blazed, it is relatively easy to follow. For the first 3.7 miles, it follows the north bank of Little Santeetlah, crossing it a half dozen times, none of which are cause for concern. There are 3 campsites along the way, but your best bet is at Naked Ground Gap. The gap has room for multiple tents, and because 4 trails converge here, it's an ideal base camp for day trips. One option is to take the trail southwest out of camp to the 5,341-foot Bob Stratton Bald, a hike of about a mile and a half. (The Bob Stratton Bald Trail continues for another 7 miles, looping back to the Joyce Kilmer trailhead.) Another option is to probe deeper into the wilderness on the 13-mile Slickrock Creek Trail, which heads north from Naked Ground Gap and descends, sharply at times, to its namesake creek.

To continue on this loop, head northeast from 4,900-foot Naked Ground Gap along the Haoe (think Ed McMahon: "Hey-o!") Lead Trail, which follows a gradually rising, mile-long ridge to a high point of 5,249 feet before splitting. Take the Jenkins Meadow Trail to your right for a 3-mile descent back to Naked Ground Trail and another three quarters of a mile back to the trailhead.

Be advised that the Little Santeetlah and a spring at Naked Ground are the only reliable sources of water on this trip. In a mix of good news, however, this part of the state is especially wet, and intermittent sources of water can often be found higher up. Just don't plan on it.

33 Joyce Kilmer–Slickrock Wilderness Slickrock Creek Loop

ROBBINSVILLE

15.8 MILES

NO. OF DAYS: 2–4

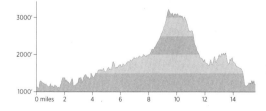

Joyce Kilmer–Slickrock Wilderness: Slickrock Creek Loop

Sixteen crossings of frisky Slickrock Creek and its more significant tributaries are required by the time you reach Big Fat Gap Trail and the climb out of the canyon.

Your first encounter with Slickrock Creek isn't entirely friendly. After hiking a narrow shelf trail along Calderwood Lake for just over a mile, you'll hear the ominous sound of feisty Slickrock. Round a bend and you'll come upon a vibrant mountain creek trying to squeeze through a narrow passage of Volkswagen-sized boulders. As if the roiling whitewater weren't enough, the creek plays hide-the-trail with you.

But once you navigate the trail (stay on your side of the creek, to the far left) and push through this 75-yard gauntlet, it's as if you've passed a test. Slickrock Creek, which defines the North Carolina/Tennessee border, quickly changes character, becoming a mild-mannered mountain stream that would like nothing better than for you to pull up to one of its languid pools, tie on a dry fly, and go after one of its native brown trout.

Don't be taken in: Slickrock has plenty more tricks to perform.

Sixteen, to be exact. That's the number of times the trail will cross the creek and its more significant tributaries in the 7 miles before reaching Big Fat Gap Trail. Crossings aren't accomplished by a wooden footbridge or strategically placed rocks, not in this wilderness. Rather, these are take-off-the-boots-put-on-the-river-sandals crossings, some of which are crotch deep—invigorating, especially in winter.

A journey up Slickrock Creek is true adventure. There are 2 named waterfalls—Lower Falls 3 miles into the hike and Wildcat Falls at mile 7.2; dozens of notable spillovers; and those deep, dark pools, good for dropping a line or, in summer, taking a dip.

Tired of the water? Feeder trails along the way let you explore higher ground. On the Tennessee side, Stiffknee Trail 3.4 miles in takes you up Little Slickrock Creek to Farr Gap (3.4 miles). Just over 3 miles upstream, Big Stack Branch Trail climbs 1.8 miles to Fodderstack Trail, which taps into the trail network in the adjoining Citico Creek Wilderness. (Combined, Joyce Kilmer–Slickrock and Citico Creek comprise 33,285 acres of wilderness.)

At the 8.1-mile mark, the trail meets up with Big Fat Gap Trail, a good place to set up camp after a day of creek crossings. If you plan to extend your trip, continue 4.6 miles up Little Slickrock Creek to Naked Ground. From there, you can loop back on the Haoe Lead (6.7 miles) and Hangover Lead (5.4 miles) trails. You can also hike to Stratton Bald, drop down the Naked Ground Trail to the Joyce Kilmer Memorial Forest, or head over to Jenkins Meadow, among other options.

If you're keeping your trip to 2 days, return with a 1.7-mile climb up to Big Fat Gap, where you'll have two options. Hangover Lead is probably

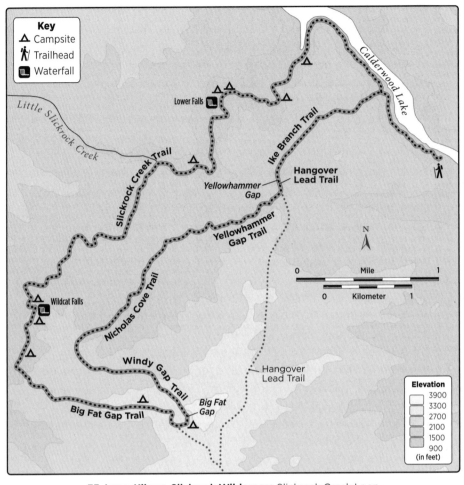

Key
- △ Campsite
- 🚶 Trailhead
- 🌊 Waterfall

Little Slickrock Creek

Slickrock Creek Trail

Lower Falls

Calderwood Lake

Ike Branch Trail

Yellowhammer Gap

Hangover Lead Trail

Yellowhammer Gap Trail

N

Nicholas Cove Trail

Wildcat Falls

0   Mile   1

0   Kilometer   1

Windy Gap Trail

Hangover Lead Trail

Big Fat Gap

Big Fat Gap Trail

Elevation
- 3900
- 3300
- 2700
- 2100
- 1500
- 900
(in feet)

33 Joyce Kilmer–Slickrock Wilderness Slickrock Creek Loop

33 Joyce Kilmer–Slickrock Wilderness Slickrock Creek Loop

Trailhead: From the intersection of NC 143 and US 129 in Robbinsville, go west on US 129 for 16.2 mi. Just before crossing the bridge over the Little Tennessee River (just below the Cheoah Dam), turn left on a short gravel road and park. The trailhead is 50 yds. down the road.

Loop/one-way: Loop.

Difficulty: Hard.

Campsites (with GPS coordinates): 1.8 mi. (N35 27.479 W83 57.780), 2.3 mi. (N35 27.356 W83 57.918), 3.3 mi. (N35 27.094 W83 58.395), 4.3 mi. (N35 26.912 W83 58.800), 5.9 mi. (N35 26.397 W83 59.533), 6.9 mi. (N35 25.793 W83 59.950), 7.3 mi. (N35 25.628 W83 59.955), 9.1 mi. (N35 25.110 W83 58.893), 9.8 mi. (N35 25.090 W83 58.413).

Map: "Joyce Kilmer–Slickrock Wilderness and Citico Creek Wilderness in the Nantahala and Cherokee National Forests," USDA Forest Service, 1:24,000, 40-ft. intervals.

Follow the trail: From the trailhead, take Slickrock Creek Trail 8.1 mi. to Big Fat Gap Trail; go left. Climb 1.7 mi. to a parking area at Big Fat Gap, then catch Windy Gap Trail at the west end of the parking area. Take Windy Gap Trail 1.5 mi. to Nicholas Cove Trail; go right. After 0.8 mi. go right on Yellow-hammer Gap Trail. Continue for 1.6 mi. to Ike Branch Trail; take Ike Branch another 1.6, then go right on Slickrock Creek Trail for the 0.5-mi. return to your car.

Fee? No.

Water: There is water along the trail from Slickrock Creek, from mile 1.5 to 8.5, and for another half mile to mile 9.0 from Big Fat Branch. Water sources are intermittent after that.

Land manager: USDA Forest Service.

Trip highlight: Slickrock Creek, with its 16 stream crossings, offers a true expedition quality to this hike.

Special considerations: This is a wilderness: though there are signs at most trail intersections, the trails are not blazed. Along the 7-mi. stretch of Slickrock Creek are 16 water crossings; the more significant crossings, of Slickrock Creek, are marked with signs (the smaller, sidecreek crossings are obvious). Many of these crossings may require wading in water up to your crotch. Do not assume that the best crossing is where the sign is; depending on water levels, you may find better options 10 yds. up- or downstream. Be patient.

Night hike in? No.

Solo? Not advised because of wilderness status.

Family friendly? No.

Bailout options: No.

Seasons: All.

Weather: Watch for quickly rising water during heavy rains.

Solitude rating: 4.

Nearest outfitter: Nantahala Outdoor Center, Wesser, (888) 905-7238, www.noc.com.

Hunting allowed? Yes; local seasons apply.

More info: USDA Forest Service, Nantahala National Forest, Cheoah Ranger District, (828) 479-6431, www.cs.unca.edu/nfsnc.

faster, but a more scenic option is to drop down Windy Gap Trail along an old roadbed to Nicholas Cove Branch, then take the Yellowhammer Gap Trail to Ike Branch and the beginning of Slickrock Creek Trail, a 7.4-mile trip.

It's a dry return with maybe a half dozen crossings of intermittent creeks. You—your feet especially—will welcome the change.

Piedmont

34 South Mountains State Park

MORGANTON

11.8 MILES

NO. OF DAYS: 2-3

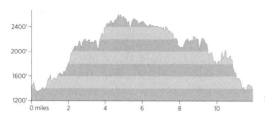

South Mountains State Park

Alan Nechemias, my frequent accomplice in adventures, and I were hiking along the Lower CCC Trail trying to justify being tired after only backpacking about 5 miles. We knew we were tired because we were more than willing to settle for a campsite 0.4 miles away rather than the site where we had planned to camp—which was only 0.2 miles farther.

"I think this is why a lot of people get turned off to backpacking," he said. I sensed a rationalization coming on. Instead, he made sense.

"I used to think it wasn't a good backpacking trip unless we covered 15, 20 miles in a day. Then I'd get through the trip and think, 'Geez, I'm done with that. That's crazy.' I'd much rather do a shorter backpack and then do longer day hikes from camp."

"Less sweat, more exposure" is the philosophy behind this book. It was also the reason behind our trip to South Mountains State Park, where a 12-mile trip with a 35-pound pack can easily expose you to twice as much hiking with a 5-pound day pack. That's especially good at a place such as South Mountains, where the ridgelines and peaks may not be high (2,894-foot Benn Knob is the highest point in the park) but the slopes are steep.

When we approached a park ranger at the trailhead and said we wanted to escape the madding crowds (the short hike up to 80-foot High Shoals Falls from the trailhead attracts the vast majority of park visitors), he didn't think twice before recommending Murray's Branch, one of South Mountains' 6 backcountry campgrounds. "People hardly ever go back there," he said.

Murray's Branch was 5.4 miles in (and up, it turned out), and we weren't hitting the trail until shortly before the park's winter closing time of 6:00 P.M. Instead, we set our sights on the Shinny Creek campground a mile and a half in. The next morning we climbed up Possum Trail to Horse

Kathy Creek is one of few stream crossings at South Mountains.

Ridge, a ridge that subtly proceeded to climb more. By the time we hit the split for the Lower CCC Trail to Murray Branch, at that mystifying 5-mile mark, we were ready to reconsider our destination for the evening. The Fox Trail camp two-tenths of a mile shy of Murray Branch was looking plenty remote to us (and it was; we had the spacious campground to ourselves). Which isn't to say we shorted ourselves on hiking. On the contrary.

With what remaining daylight we had after pitching camp the first night, we worked in a 4.3-mile day (and night) loop hike taking in portions of the H.Q., Upper Falls, and High Shoals Falls trails. And after breaking camp the second day and hiking back to the trailhead via the Upper Falls and High Shoals trails, we still had time to shed our packs and do the tourist thing with a hike up to High Shoals Waterfall.

We'd covered 20 miles in two and a half days, and nearly half of that had been without full packs. And we didn't feel at all bad about it—our legs, especially.

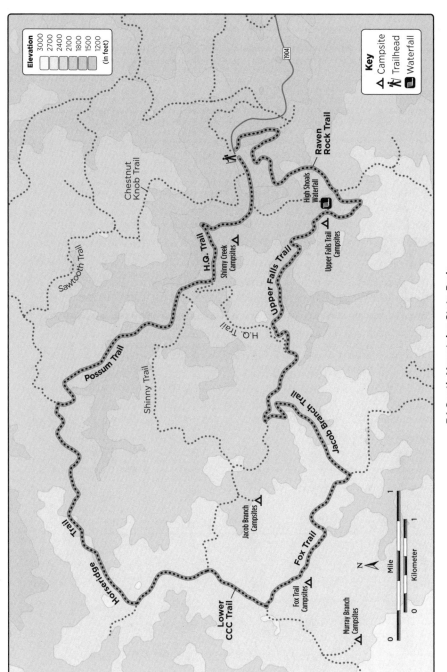

Elevation
3000
2700
2400
2100
1800
1500
1200
(in feet)

Key
△ Campsite
🚶 Trailhead
▥ Waterfall

1904

Raven
Rock Trail

High Shoals
Waterfall

Upper Falls Trail
Campsites

Chestnut
Knob Trail

H.Q. Trail

Shinny Creek
Campsites

H.Q. Trail

Upper Falls Trail

Sawtooth Trail

Possum Trail

Shinny Trail

Jacob Branch Trail

Jacob Branch
Campsites

Horseridge Trail

Lower
CCC Trail

Fox Trail

Fox Trail
Campsites

Murray Branch
Campsites

N

0   Mile   1
0   Kilometer   1

34 South Mountains State Park

34 South Mountains State Park

Trailhead: From NC 18 south of Morganton go west on Old NC 18 for 4.0 mi., then go left on Wards Gap Road. After 1.4 mi., go right on SR 1904 (State Park Road). The trailhead and parking is 3.5 mi.

Loop/one-way: Loop.

Difficulty: Moderate.

Campsites (with GPS coordinates): 1.2 mi. Shinny Creek camp (N35 36.246 W81 38.646), 6.2 mi. Fox Trail camp (N35 35.680 W81 40.580), 8.8 mi. Upper Falls camp (N35 35.658 W81 38.299).

Maps: Park map available at trailhead. USGS: Benn Knob, Casar, South Morganton.

Follow the trail: For the backpack portion of the trip, take the H.Q. Trail for 1.2 mi. to the Possum Trail split; go right on Possum Trail for 1.8 mi. to Horseridge Trail. Go left on Horseridge for 2.2 mi., then go left on Lower CCC Trail for 0.4 mi. to Fox Trail; go left. After 1.2 mi. on Fox Trail, go left on Jacob Branch Trail for 1.1 mi., right on Upper Falls Trail for 2.1 mi., then left on Raven Rock Trail. After 1.5 mi., go left on River Trail for the remaining 0.3 mi. to your car.

Fee? $13 per night camping fee.

Water (with GPS coordinates): Water is available for the first 1.5 mi. along Shinny Creek, at 6.0 mi. at Fox Trail camp (N35 35.680 W81 40.580), at 7.5 mi. (N35 35.862 W81 39.530), and at 9.7 mi. (N35 35.614 W81 38.280).

Land manager: N.C. Division of Parks and Recreation.

Trip highlights: A taste of the mountains without driving to the mountains; High Shoals Waterfall.

Special considerations: Hiking around waterfalls can be dangerous, especially during winter when trails can ice up.

Night hike in? Yes, to Shinny Creek camp, but be advised that the park gates close at 6:00 P.M. Nov.–Feb.; 8:00 P.M. Mar.–May, Sept., and Oct.; 9:00 P.M. June–Aug.

Solo? Yes. This is N.C. State Park–friendly hiking.

Family friendly? Yes. Diversions (waterfalls, streams, ridgeline views) get kids' minds off the moderate climbs.

Bailout options: No.

Seasons: Year-round.

Weather: A fair amount of ridgeline hiking; be aware of afternoon thunderstorms in summer.

Solitude rating: 3. The farther you get from High Shoals Waterfall, the higher your solitude rating soars.

Nearest outfitter: REI, Asheville, (828) 687-0918, www.rei.com.

Hunting allowed? No.

More info: South Mountains State Park, (828) 433-4772, www.ncparks.gov/Visit/parks/somo/main.php.

ASHEBORO

7.4 MILES

NO. OF DAYS: 2

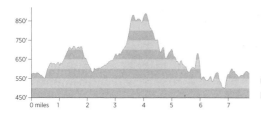

Uwharrie National Forest:
Birkhead Wilderness

Think of the 5,160-acre Birkhead Wilderness as something of the Grandpa of North Carolina backpacking. Back in its day—and this would be more than 400 million years ago—the Uwharries were a force to be reckoned with. There were rugged peaks approaching 20,000 feet, active volcanoes, and critters you won't find in your Audubon Guide to Eastern Forests. It was rockin'.

But, as is wont to happen, time has taken its toll. Four hundred million years of the forces of nature have mellowed the once-crazy Birkhead area. Today, its ridgelines top out at 750 feet, and its once chiseled features have been replaced by gentle, rolling ones (though you will find a rocky spine here and there). The spitfire of those volcanoes has been replaced by the overwhelming urge, on a crisp winter's day when the sun penetrates the cold, to sit against a hickory and nap. And the whole wilderness thing? It's more of an honorary title. Though technically a wilderness—it was designated in 1984—the trails are marked, there's at least one trail plaque (noting the Christopher Bingham plantation dating to around 1780), and the main camping area 3.5 miles in has stone and mortar fire pits.

Just because Gramps no longer spews molten lava doesn't mean he doesn't deserve a visit. An overnighter to the Birkhead is an oddly comforting, tranquil experience, not unlike a trip to Grandpa's for the holidays. The lack of stark features, the relatively predictable weather (at least compared with the Appalachians to the west), and the quiet that pervades make the Birkhead a particularly attractive destination for first-timers. (Adding to that aura is the curious absence of wildlife; in a half dozen trips to the Uwharries, I'm hard-pressed to recall seeing so much as a squirrel.)

It's the kind of place you'll return from with good memories, if not a

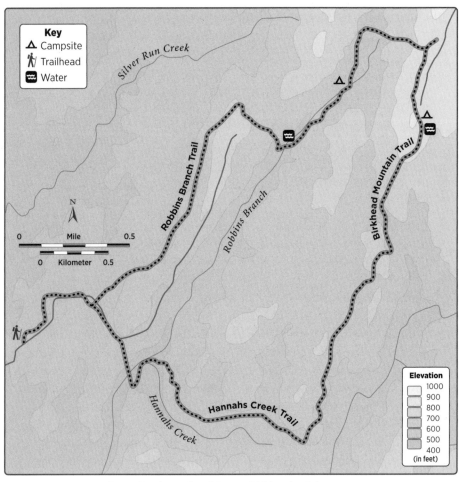

35 Uwharrie National Forest Birkhead Wilderness

35 Uwharrie National Forest Birkhead Wilderness

Trailhead: From NC 49 a little more than 6 mi. west of Asheboro, go south on Waynick Meadow Road. Shortly, Waynick Meadow Ts into Lassiter Mill Road/SR 1107; go right. Continue 5 mi., then go left on the gravel access road (there's a sign), which ends after a half mile, at the trailhead.

Loop/one-way: Loop.

Difficulty: Easy.

Campsites (with GPS coordinates): 2.4 mi. (N35 36.256 W79 55.526), 3.5 mi. (N35 36.256 W79 55.526).

Maps: "Uwharrie National Forest," USDA Forest Service, 1:126,720. USGS: Eleazer, Farmer.

Follow the trail: From the trailhead, take Robbins Branch Trail for 3.2 mi. (after 0.5 mi. Robbins Branch splits with Hannahs Creek Trail; stay left on Robbins Branch). Robbins Branch Ts into the Birkhead Mountain Trail, go right. After 2.1 mi., go right on Hannahs Creek Trail, which Ts into Robbins Branch Trail after 1.6 mi. Go left on Robbins Branch for the 0.5-mi. return to your car.

Fee? No.

Water (with GPS coordinates): 2.0 mi. (N35 36.071 W79 55.807), 3.5 mi., then walk down Camp 3 Trail for 1 mi. (N35 36.256 W79 55.526).

Land manager: USDA Forest Service.

Trip highlight: Gently rolling trail makes for an especially nice winter trip.

Special considerations: None.

Night hike in? Yes. Nothing tricky here.

Solo? Yes. (See above.)

Family friendly? Yes. Short distance and gentle terrain make for a good starter trip for kids.

Bailout options: No.

Seasons: Winter, fall, spring.

Weather: Typical Piedmont weather, with few extremes.

Solitude rating: 2. Located within an hour to an hour and a half of the Triad, Triangle, and Charlotte, the trail can be popular, especially with scout troops.

Nearest outfitter: Eldorado Outpost, 4021 NC 109, Eldorado, (910) 572-3474.

Hunting allowed? Yes.

More info: USDA Forest Service, Uwharrie National Forest, Uwharrie Ranger District, (910) 576-6391, www.cs.unca.edu/nfsnc/.

Wayfinding is aided in the Birkhead Wilderness by helpful signs.

compelling campfire tale about the bear that roared into camp (no bears) or being swept downstream and barely surviving a raging river crossing (Robbins Branch and Hannahs Creek work up a pleasant burble at best after a good rainstorm).

A reliable trip that won't disappoint. Just like going to Grandpa's.

36 Uwharrie National Forest Uwharrie Recreation Trail

TROY

22.9 MILES

NO. OF DAYS: 2

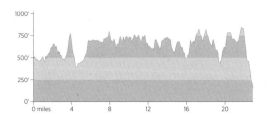

Uwharrie National Forest: Uwharrie Recreation Trail

Three miles into the Uwharrie Recreation Trail you hit your first true climb that reminds you that while you may be in the Piedmont, this nest

Gravel roads throughout the Uwharries make bailouts easy if the need arises.

of ancient mountains called the Uwharries doesn't feel like the Piedmont. The paradox becomes even more obvious as you crest the second of these climbs, 719-foot Dennis Mountain. About three quarters of the way up the mountain's eastern flank you leave a traditional mixed Piedmont forest dominated by hickories and oaks for one dominated by chestnut oaks, more common to higher, dry rocky slopes. Then, on top, another transition: a small clearing featuring ankle-high meadow grass and a stretch of exposed, weathered granite, a remnant of the days millions of years past when the Uwharries rose 20,000 feet. Adding to the feel of higher climes is a small stand of short-needled Virginia pine and a lone, towering cedar.

Backpacking the 22.9-mile Uwharrie Recreation Trail is a series of such crests followed by intimate interludes with holly- and mountain laurel–choked draws. These ascents are generally gradual—though there is the occasional journey into The Land That Switchbacks Forgot—wrapping around these long-dormant conical volcanic domes. Summiting is less a peak experience. Rather, you're greeted by a rounded dome weathered by eons of wind and rain leaving only a few stalwart chunks of exposed granite.

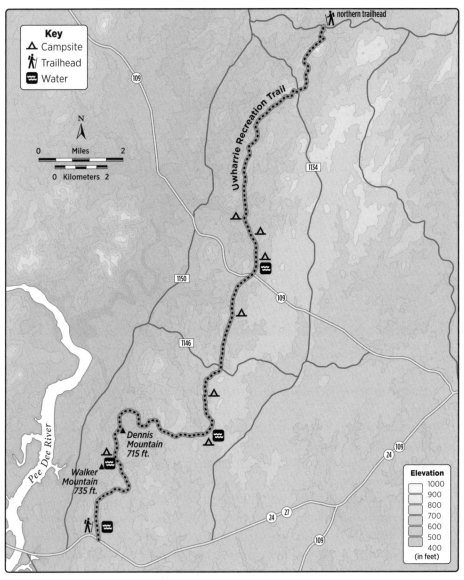

Key
△ Campsite
🚶 Trailhead
〰 Water

N

Miles
0 — 2

Kilometers
0 — 2

northern trailhead

Uwharrie Recreation Trail

109

1134

1150

109

1146

109

24

109

24 27

109

Pee Dee River

Dennis
Mountain
715 ft.

Walker
Mountain
735 ft.

Elevation
1000
900
800
700
600
500
400
(in feet)

36 Uwharrie National Forest Uwharrie Recreation Trail

36 Uwharrie National Forest Uwharrie Recreation Trail

Trailhead: From Troy, go 9.3 mi. west on NC 24/27. Trailhead parking is on your right.

Loop/one-way: One-way. To set up a shuttle from the southern trailhead parking lot: Turn left out of the lot on NC 24/27. Go 3 mi., turn left on Liberty Hill Road/SR 1134. (The road turns to gravel at mile 12.6 and stays as such for 3 mi.) At mile 16.8, go right on Tower Road (the continuation of SR 1134). Go three-tenths of a mile and turn right on Flint Hill Road/SR 1306. The northern trailhead is 1.8 mi. on your right.

Difficulty: Moderate.

Campsites (with GPS coordinates): Abundant, though generally concentrated on the north and south ends of the trail. Some recommendations throughout: mile 4.5, with water (N35 21.209 W80 02.002); mile 8.7, with water (N35 20.799 W80 00.171); mile 12.3, with water (N35 23.149 W79 59.330), mile 14.6, with water (N35 24.333 W79 58.855); mile 15.9, with water (N35 25.189 W79 58.936); mile 18.7, ridgeline (N35 26.609 W79 58.608).

Maps: "Uwharrie National Forest," USDA Forest Service, 1:126,720. USGS: Troy, Morrow Mountain, Lovejoy.

Follow the trail: From the trailhead, take the white-blazed Uwharrie Recreation Trail north until it ends 22.9 mi. later, at Flint Hill Road/SR 1306.

Fee? No.

Water (with GPS coordinates): Trail crosses at least a dozen creeks and draws, though not all run year-round. Most reliable sources: Woodrun Creek, 1.2 mi. (N35 19.435 W80 02.758); Big Island Creek, 4.5 mi. (N35 21.162 W80 01.803); Dutchman's Creek, 8.5 mi. (N35 20.799 W80 00.171); Cattail Creek, 14.7 mi. (N35 24.333 W79 58.855).

Land manager: USDA Forest Service.

Trip highlight: This is a young forest, but one stretch, through a draw 12.5 mi. into the trip, offers a trek through a more mature hardwood forest. It's a stark, noticeable contrast. This is about the point where the trail is the most isolated.

Special considerations: In 15 years of hiking the Uwharries, I've seen—or heard—surprisingly little wild-life. Camp overnight in one of the few midtrail campsites and you'll be surprised by the silence.

Night hike in? Yes. First campsite, accommodating 4 tents, is within 0.2 mi. of the trailhead (GPS: N35 18.947 W80 02.782).

Solo? Yes. There's cell phone reception the length of the trail.

Family friendly? Yes, especially considering that the trip can be shortened (see "Bailout options").

Bailout options: Three main roads cross the trail: SR 1146 at mile 10.9, NC 109 at mile 13.7, and SR 1134 at mile 20.1.

Seasons: Fall, winter, spring.

Weather: Especially good winter escape due to generally mild temperatures; summers get hot and sticky.

Solitude rating? 4.

Nearest outfitter: Eldorado Outpost, 4021 NC 109, Eldorado, (910) 572-3474.

Hunting allowed? Yes.

More info: USDA Forest Service, Uwharrie National Forest, Uwharrie Ranger District, (910) 576-6391, www.cs.unca.edu/nfsnc/.

Despite, or perhaps because of, the domed summits, vistas are few in the Uwharries, even in the naked days of winter. Occasionally you may be able to peer through the legions of gray tree trunks and catch a glimpse of a neighboring ridgeline, but by and large those long climbs let you know you're in some semblance of mountains.

Passage between these domes is along various creeks dominated by basketball- to beachball-sized chunks of granite and creeks perceived to contain fortunes by prospectors who took part in the local gold rush of the mid-1800s. (Some prospecting is still done in the region.) The abundance of creeks would suggest that water is plentiful, but most creeks appear to run only after a good rain. When you do find a creek running, take advantage and top off your water supply.

At 22.9 miles, the Uwharrie Recreation Trail would seem an easy 2-day trip. Although this is a National Forest and camping is permitted anywhere beyond 200 feet of a water source, "established" primitive campsites are few. You can go long stretches and not find a suitable sight. Same goes for water.

37 Umstead State Park

RALEIGH

18.1 MILES

NO. OF DAYS: 2

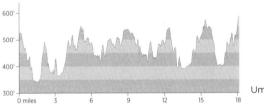

Umstead State Park

Umstead State Park, smack dab in the middle of the populated Triangle, may seem a curious choice for a backpack trip. With 800,000 visitors a year it's one of the State Park system's most popular venues, and the lone place where camping is allowed is a 28-site campground less than a mile from a busy runway at neighboring Raleigh-Durham International Airport. Not exactly getting away from it all.

But it is a place where you can do some goal-oriented backpacking. Got a friend or family member interested in giving backpacking a try but not at

Civilization intrudes occasionally on the hike at this urban park in the Triangle.

the expense of driving 5 hours to bear country? Got a new tent, camp stove, or other piece of gear you're dying to break in? Training for a weeklong trip out West? Or maybe you've got a hankerin' to head to the hills but are on a tight schedule. Umstead can serve a variety of backpacking needs.

Umstead is typical of many North Carolina state parks. Explored initially by Native Americans thousands of years ago, the area was settled by Europeans beginning in the 1770s; it was cleared and farmed to exhaustion by the 1920s. As part of the country's efforts to pull out of the Great Depression, about 5,000 acres of depleted farmland were bought by the government and put to pasture. As any armchair naturalist knows, when land goes to pasture, it often passes through a successional metamorphosis that restores it to something resembling its original arbored roots. Today, Umstead—encompassing 5,579 acres—is a mature Piedmont forest penetrated by 35 miles of trail.

This trip utilizes three of the park's most popular trails, starting with the most popular: Company Mill. Don't let that alarm you. Most hikers are only interested in the trail's first mile, which traverses three modest ridgelines down to Crabtree Creek. Cross Crabtree and go right (you'll be returning on the trail to your left) through a bottomland forest that soon takes an upland

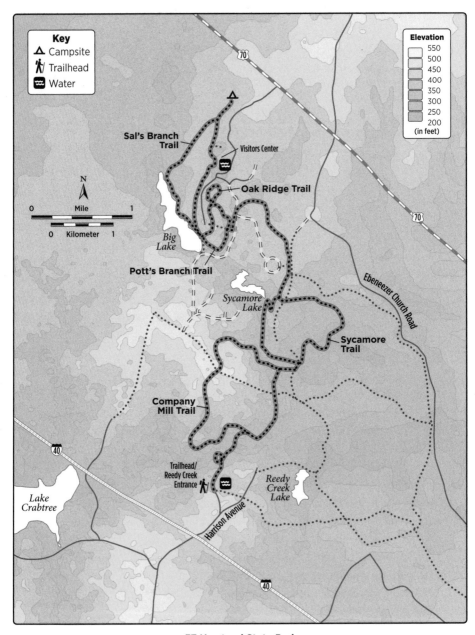

Key
△ Campsite
🚶 Trailhead
🌊 Water

Elevation
550
500
450
400
350
300
250
200
(in feet)

N

Mile
0   1

Kilometer
0   1

Sal's Branch
Trail

Visitors Center

Oak Ridge Trail

Big
Lake

Pott's Branch Trail

Sycamore
Lake

Sycamore
Trail

Company
Mill Trail

Ebeneezer Church Road

Lake
Crabtree

Trailhead/
Reedy Creek
Entrance

Reedy
Creek
Lake

Harrison Avenue

70

70

40

40

37 Umstead State Park

37 Umstead State Park

Trailhead: Parking lot off the Harrison Avenue entrance, exit 287 off I-40 (north side of highway). Company Mill Trail begins at the far opposite end of the lot.

Loop/one-way: Loop.

Difficulty: Moderate.

Campsites (with GPS coordinates): Campground with 28 sites, restrooms, and water, is at mile 8.6 (N35 53.128 W78 45.581). Campground is closed Dec. 16 through Mar. 14.

Maps: Trail map available at kiosk in parking lot. USGS: Cary, Raleigh West.

Follow the trail: From the trailhead, take Company Mill Trail 1.2 mi.; after crossing Crabtree Creek, go right and continue another 1.3 mi. to the spur (marked) to Sycamore Trail. Take the spur 0.2 mi., taking a quick left on the gravel road, then a right after crossing the bridge, to the Sycamore Trail. Go 1.8 mi.; here, Sycamore Trail splits—go right. After 1.9 mi., go left on Pott's Branch Trail. After 0.7 mi., go right on Sal's Branch Trail. After 1.5 mi., go right on the 0.3-mi. spur to the campground.

To return from the campground: Take the 0.3-mi. spur back to Sal's Branch and go right. Continue on Sal's Branch for 1.2 mi., then go straight on Pott's Branch. After 50 yds. or so, follow Pott's Branch left up the stairs to the parking lot, cross the lot, pick the trail up on the opposite side and take it past the large picnic shelter down to the trail's namesake creek, a total distance of 0.5 mi. Cross the bridge and go left on Sycamore Trail. After 1.9 mi., the trail splits. To the left is the way you came in; continue straight for another 1.1 mi. to the 0.2-mi. spur back to Company Mill Trail. At Company Mill, go right. Stay on Company Mill for the remaining 4.0 mi. back to your car.

Fee? $18 per night for campsite.

Water (with GPS coordinates): Treated water is available from a fountain at the trailhead parking lot. Creek water is at mile 1.1, Crabtree Creek (N35 50.687 W78 45.396); mile 2.5, Sycamore Creek (N35 51.227 W78 44.860); mile 7.9, treated, at visitors center (N35 52.856 W78 45.525); mile 8.6, treated, at campground (N35 53.128 W78 45.581). Return trip: mile 1.4, treated, drinking fountain (N35 52.254 W78 45.757); mile 4.8, Sycamore Creek (N35 51.218 W78 44.812); mile 7.7, Crabtree Creek (N35 50.687 W78 45.396).

Land manager: N.C. Division of Parks and Recreation.

Trip highlights: Being a novelty backpacker in a park dominated by urban hikers; access to a state park at night (North Carolina state parks close at dusk).

Special considerations: If you leave a car overnight at the trailhead parking lot, be sure to notify the park office (see "More info" below for contact). Campground is not far from Raleigh-Durham International Airport; prepare to be serenaded.

Night hike in? No (park closes at dusk).

Solo? Yes.

Family friendly? Yes.

Bailout options: Midway point campground is off US 70/Glenwood Avenue park entrance, making for a midpoint abandon.

Seasons: Fall, spring (campground is closed Dec. 16–Mar. 14).

Weather: Summers are hot and humid; sleeping can be a challenge.

Solitude rating: 1.

Nearest outfitter: Great Outdoor Provision Co., (919) 833-1741, http://greatoutdoorprovision.com; REI, (919) 233-8444, www.rei.com.

Hunting allowed? No.

More info: Umstead State Park, (919) 571-4170, www.ncparks.gov/Visit/parks/wium/main.php.

route, makes a steep climb, then levels out before gradually descending to its connection with the Sycamore Trail. Sycamore follows its namesake creek before another climb resulting in another gradual descent to the north side of the park. A short encounter with the Pott's Branch Trail hooks you up with the third loop in the set, Sal's Branch Trail. Midway through Sal's Branch is your overnight destination. The return trip is a similar cycle of relatively moderate climbs and descents.

The trip is long, but mellow. If you're looking to dial in a new pack to get the fit just right, Umstead is a good bet. If you're looking to get comfortable with having a pack on your back for 4 to 5 hours, Umstead is a good bet. And if you want a trip that will give a curious friend a taste of what it's like to travel with 35 pounds of life support on her back, Umstead is a good bet.

Umstead isn't about getting away from it all. It's about helping you prepare to get away from it all.

38 Falls Lake Mountains-to-Sea Trail

RALEIGH/DURHAM

38.8 MILES

NO. OF DAYS: 2–3

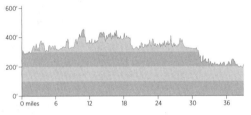

Falls Lake: Mountains-to-Sea Trail

This is one of those good news/bad news trips.

Good news: This is a 39-mile backpack trip in a major urban area that, for the most part, does manage to escape surrounding suburbia.

Bad news: Because the trail hugs the south shore of Falls Lake, the main drinking supply for Raleigh, camping is tightly restricted to two campgrounds along the path. One of those campgrounds is just 3.8 miles from the trailhead; the other is 18.4 miles down the line. Some quick math tells you this computes to some long days in the boots.

Good news: Because the trail hugs the main drinking supply for Raleigh, you might think water wouldn't be an issue.

Bad news: Water is an issue. While Falls Lake typically holds about

A rare overlook on section 14 of the Mountains-to-Sea Trail along Falls Lake.

115,000 acre feet of water, that's water before it goes through the city of Raleigh treatment plant below the dam—water that contains pollutants your personal water filter can't weed out. Thus, your safest bets for water are at 5 park facilities along the way (see info box). And while that water may be treated, it's not always a treat. (On one trip we asked the receptionist at the park office 14.9 miles into the hike if she drank water from a fountain 15 feet away. She gave us a look typically reserved for people who ask if they can clean your windshield at a stoplight. "No.")

Good news: The Mountains-to-Sea Trail through the Triangle could grow to more than 100 miles by 2012, believes Kate Dixon, executive director of the Friends of the Mountains-to-Sea Trail, the 1,000-mile statewide trail-in-progress, of which the Falls Lake Trail is a part.

Bad news: The camping opportunities will be slow to keep pace.

The rest is good news because despite its limitations, the Falls Lake Trail is a good resource for regional backpackers to have in their backyard. It's great training for longer treks, and not simply because of its length. The trail is constantly dipping into and climbing out of coves, providing a surprising amount of up-and-down. Because it runs from the Falls Lake dam in Wake County northwest to Durham, it's quickly accessible to most of the Triangle.

And don't get the impression that you have to be a superhiker to try this trail. The Falls Lake Trail may be long, but it's divided into 14 sections ranging in length from 0.5 to 5.6 miles. The sections are divided by roadways, allowing for easy access and letting you create shorter trips. Here's one 2-day option covering 8.6 miles:

Park at the park office off NC 50/Creedmoor Road and hike 3.6 miles southeast to the Shinleaf campground. This stretch includes a particularly lush cove passage around mile 1.8 that lasts about a half mile. Shinleaf, with walk-in camping only (no car camping), offers quiet with amenities (showers, and a picnic table and grill at each site). Day 2 is a 5-mile hike along the lake and through quiet forest to the Barton Creek boat ramp.

That's just one example. Use the accompanying trail breakdown to create your own trip.

SECTION 14: (3.8 MILES)
From Santee Road to the Rolling View State Recreation area.

SECTION 13: (3.0 MILES)
From Rolling View State Recreation area to NC 98 at Lick Creek.

SECTION 12: (1.4 MILES)
From NC 98 at Lick Creek to the dead end of Boyce Mill Road.

SECTION 11: (5.6 MILES)
From the dead end of Boyce Mill Road to NC 50 (Creedmoor Road).

SECTION 10: QUAIL ROOST SECTION (2.2 MILES)
From NC-50 (Creedmoor Road) to Ghoston Road (SR 1908).

SECTION 9: TWIN CREEK SECTION (0.5 MILES)
From Ghoston Road to New Light Road (SR 1907).

SECTION 8: SHINLEAF RECREATION SECTION (3.6 MILES)
From New Light Road to NC 98.

SECTION 7: UPPER BARTON CREEK SECTION (2.4 MILES)
From NC 98 to Six Forks Road (SR 1005).

SECTION 6: BLUE JAY POINT SECTION (3.1 MILES)
From Six Forks Road to Six Forks Road.

SECTION 5: LOBLOLLY POINT SECTION (1.3 MILES)
From Six Forks Road to Bayleaf Church Road (SR 2003).

SECTION 4: CEDAR CREEK SECTION (2.8 MILES)
From Bayleaf Church Road to causeway on Possum Track Road (SR 2162).

SECTION 3: NEUSE BEND POINT SECTION (3.0 MILES)
From Possum Track Road causeway to dead end of Possum Track Road.

SECTION 2: HONEYCUTT CREEK WEST SECTION (2.6 MILES)
From dead end of Possum Track Road to Honeycutt Creek causeway on Raven Ridge Road.

SECTION 1: HONEYCUTT CREEK EAST SECTION (3.5 MILES)
From Honeycutt Creek causeway on Raven Ridge Road to Falls Lake Dam on Falls of the Neuse Road.

38 Falls Lake Mountains-to-Sea Trail

Elevation (in feet)
550
500
450
400
350
300
250
200

N

Miles
0   2

Kilometers
0   2

Falls of the Neuse Road

Falls Lake

Falls Lake Dam

S1

S2

S3

Road

Honeycutt Creek Causeway

Track

Raven Ridge Road

S4

Bayleaf Church Road

S5

Possum

S6

Six Forks Road

Blue Jay Point

S7

Snaleaf Campground

S8

New Light Road

S9

Ghoston Road

S10

50

Creedmoor Road

50

S11

Boyce Mill Road

Carpenter Pond Road

98

S12

Rolling View Campground

S13

Mountains-to-Sea Trail

Lick Creek

S14

Santee Road

Baptist Road

Falls Lake

98

Key
△ Campsite
⚲ Trailhead
🚰 Water

38 Falls Lake Mountains-to-Sea Trail

Trailhead: From NC 98, go north on Baptist Road (which is 5.3 mi. west of NC 50/Creedmoor Road and 4.7 mi. east of US 70 in Durham). After 1.2 mi., veer left on Santee Road. Take Santee 1.4 mi. until it ends, at the trailhead. There's roadside parking. For the shuttle, head back to NC 98 and go left. Go 12.8 mi., then turn right on Falls of the Neuse Road. Go 4.0 mi. and turn right into the Falls Lake Recreation Area. Park in the lot on your immediate left.

Loop/one-way: One-way.

Difficulty: Moderate (due to length).

Campsites (with GPS coordinates): 3.8 mi., Rolling View Recreation Area (N36 00.588 W78 43.715); 18.4 mi., Shinleaf Recreation Area (N35 59.695 W78 39.379). Be advised that the Falls Lake State Recreation Area, which operates both sites, closes some campgrounds in winter. Call the park office to confirm that campgrounds are open before heading out: (919) 676-1027.

Maps: Your best bet for an accurate, up-to-date map of the Falls Lake Trail, part of the Mountains-to-Sea Trail, is to download it from the Friends of the Mountains-to-Sea website. Go to www.ncmst.org, click on "Maps and Trip Planning," then click on "Plan Your Hike—Trail Maps." Pertinent maps for this trip are nos. 26 and 27.

Follow the trail: The entire trip is on the white-blazed Mountains-to-Sea Trail.

Fee? $23 per night for Rolling View (includes electrical hookups); $18 for Shinleaf (no electrical). Both camping areas have picnic tables, grills, water, and showers.

Water (with GPS coordinates): 3.8 mi., Rolling View Recreation Area (N36 00.588 W78 43.715); 14.9 mi., Falls Lake park office (N36 00.802 W78 41.237); 18.4 mi., Shinleaf Recreation Area (N35 59.695 W78 39.379); 24.6 mi., Blue Jay Point County Park (N35 58.251 W78 38.309); 27.4 mi., Falls Lake's Yorkshire Center, 8:00 A.M.–5:00 P.M., Mon.–Fri. (N35 57.909 W78 37.953).

Land managers: N.C. Division of Parks and Recreation; N.C. Wildlife Resources Commission.

Trip highlight: A long backpack trek in an urban area.

Special considerations: Limited water, limited camping.

Night hike in? Yes.

Solo? Yes.

Family friendly? Shorter versions are (see text).

Bailout options: Yes. The trail currently consists of 14 sections, ranging in length from 0.5 to 5.6 mi. The sections are divided by roadways, making for easy egress from the trail.

Seasons: Fall, winter, spring.

Weather: Trips during the heat of summer can be plagued by flying pests and lack of water along the trail.

Solitude rating: 3.

Nearest outfitter: REI, North Raleigh, (919) 571-5031, www.rei.com.

Hunting allowed? Yes. Consult N.C. Wildlife Resources Commission, www.ncwildlife.org, for local seasons.

More info: Falls Lake State Recreation Area, (919) 676-1027, www.ncparks.gov/visit/parks/fala/main.php. Or visit the Friends of the Mountains-to-Sea Trail at www.ncmst.org.

DURHAM

14.0 MILES

NO. OF DAYS: 2-3

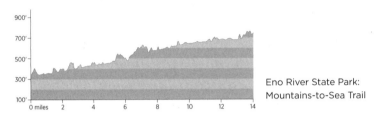

Eno River State Park:
Mountains-to-Sea Trail

In the mid-1960s, the city of Durham decided to build a dam on the Eno River to help slake the growing city's thirst. But the residents didn't like the idea of the rocky Eno, which resembles a mountain stream more than a Piedmont waterway, being at the bottom of a reservoir. Durhamites played in the Eno, they paddled on the Eno, and they sought out the Eno for escape.

The idea was scuttled after a coalition led by Margaret Nygard formed a formidable opposition. That opposition grew into the Eno River Association, whose mission has been to preserve land along the waterway, which begins above Hillsborough in Orange County and ends 40 miles later when it empties into Falls Lake. The group has helped to conserve more than 5,700 acres along the Eno, the vast majority of which has been put into 5 parklands: Eno River State Park, Occoneechee Mountain State Natural Area, West Point on the Eno city park in Durham, Penny's Bend Nature Preserve, and the Little River Regional Park, the latter of which is on an Eno tributary. Thanks to those efforts, it will one day be possible to backpack rather than water ski the length of the Eno. Today, 14 miles of that trip are reality—pretty much.

I say "pretty much" because there is one small caveat: There's still a small parcel or two (or three) in private hands. You can still backpack the 14-mile stretch, but in some spots—the spots yet to come under state parks control—the trail is indistinct. Here, let's take a walk:

We'll start at Durham's West Point on the Eno city park and walk upstream. The first 1.9 miles is in the park, on the Eagle Trail. At 4-lane Guess Road (a brief dalliance with civilization), jurisdiction changes over to Eno River State Park, where the trail continues on the opposite side of the river

Signs of the past mark the trail along the Eno River.

for 3.2 miles along the Laurel Bluffs and Pump Station trails. At the 3.2-mile mark, the distinct Pump Station Trail takes a left; you follow the less distinct fisherman's trail along the river. This trail gradually heads uphill and enters a meadow, where you pick up a dirt road, which shortly feeds into a paved road (go right), which Ts into Cole Mill Road. Take a right on

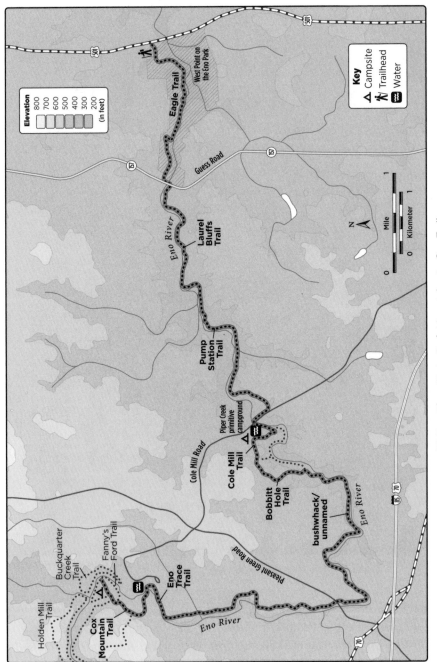

39 Eno River State Park Mountains-to-Sea Trail

Key
△ Campsite
🚶 Trailhead
▥ Water

Elevation
800
700
600
500
400
300
200
(in feet)

N

Mile
0   1

Kilometer
0   1

Eagle Trail

West Point on the Eno Park

Guess Road

Eno River

Laurel Bluffs Trail

Pump Station Trail

Piper Creek primitive Campground

Cole Mill Road

Cole Mill Trail

Bobbitt Hole Trail

bushwhack/ unnamed

Eno River

Buckquarter Creek Trail

Fanny's Ford Trail

Holden Mill Trail

Cox Mountain Trail

Eno Trace Trail

Pleasant Green Road

Eno River

501

501

57

57

70

70

70

39 Eno River State Park Mountains-to-Sea Trail

Trailhead: Pick up the trail from the gravel lot just inside the secondary entrance to West Point on the Eno city park, on the north side of the Eno River on US 15/501 a quarter mile south of Latta/Infinity roads. To set up a shuttle: Drive north on US 15/501 to Latta Road and go left. After 1.2 mi. go right on Guess Road for 0.2 mi., then left on Umstead Road. After 3.4 mi., go right on Cole Mill Road. Follow Cole Mill until it terminates in the park, after 2.4 mi.; park in the last parking lot.

Loop/one-way: One-way.

Difficulty: Moderate (due to length).

Campsites (with GPS coordinates): There are 2 designated primitive camping areas, the 8-site Piper Creek campground in the Cole Mill Access at 7.2 mi. (N36 03.236 W78 59.277) and at the end of the trip, in the 5-site Fanny's Ford campground in Fews Ford area (N36 04.891 W79 00.347). (Why would you want to camp at the end of the trip? Because maybe it's not the end of the trip. Read the story.)

Maps: Trail maps are available at the park office (you can pick them up when you set the shuttle). The trip is part of the statewide Mountains-to-Sea Trail, and up-to-date maps can be found on its website, www.ncmst.org. Click on "Maps and Trip Planning," then click on "Plan Your Hike—Trail Maps." Pertinent maps for this trip are nos. 25 and 26. Topo maps: Durham NW, Hillsborough.

Follow the trail: The description offered in the accompanying text is accurate as of April 2010. Volunteers from the Friends of the Mountains-to-Sea Trail have been blazing new trail on existing parkland, and the Eno River Association has been either buying or retaining access to the few small parcels of land along this route still in private hands. Odds are the trail will be better defined throughout by the time you read this. For up-to-date trail information, visit the Friends of the Mountains-to-Sea Trail at www.ncmst.org.

Fee? Campsite fee of $13 per night.

Water (with GPS coordinates): The Eno River runs through an urban area; while it is relatively clean, it does pick up pollutants that aren't weeded out by typical backpacking filters. Your best bet is to get treated water from fountains at 2 park sites: the Cole Mill Access at mile 6.2 (take the short spur to the parking area) (N36 03.385 W78 58.737); at the Fews Ford Access at mile 12.8 (N36 04.411 W79 00.584).

Land manager: N.C. Division of Parks and Recreation.

Trip highlight: A backcountry adventure in the midst of a metro area.

Special considerations: If leaving cars at the trailhead and/or end of the trail, let the appropriate park know that you will be leaving your car overnight: West Point on the Eno city park (919) 471-1623; Eno River State Park, (919) 383-1686.

Night hike in? No.

Solo? Yes.

Family friendly? Yes. For the most part, the trail is on easy-to-follow, state-park/friendly trail and is relatively flat.

Bailout options: Yes. The trail crosses 3 major roads: Guess Road at mile 2.0, Cole Mill Road at mile 5.7, and Pleasant Green Road at mile 10.3.

Seasons: Late fall through early spring. (Portions of the trail are not fully developed and become overgrown during warmer weather.)

Weather: Typical Piedmont weather, another reason not to hike it in summer.

Solitude rating: 1. Both parks attracts day hikers.

Nearest outfitter: REI, Durham, (919) 806-3442, www.rei.com.

Hunting allowed? No.

More info: Eno River State Park, (919) 383-1686, www.ncparks.gov/Visit/parks/enri/main.php. The Eno River Association website is a good resource for the flora and fauna of the Eno: www.enoriver.org. This trip is part of the statewide Mountains-to-Sea Trail; check for completion of additional trail at www.ncmst.org.

Cole Mill, cross the bridge over the Eno, then pick up the trail just past the bridge abutment on the west side of the road. You're back on state park trail, and after 1.3 miles you arrive at your destination for the evening, the Piper Creek primitive campground.

On Day 2 you leave the park after just less than a mile. You're on your own for the next two-thirds of a mile. In winter, wayfinding is easy, but if you're hiking in warmer weather, it can get overgrown. Just keep the Eno River in sight and you'll be fine. You're in the state park's Cabe Lands section for the next mile and a quarter, followed by another mile of freelancing. The last 3 miles are on park land. (Note: This trip also follows the statewide Mountains-to-Sea Trail; see "Follow the trail" in the information box.)

It's an easy 2-day trip, but I recommend extending it to 3 by staying a second night, at the Fanny's Ford campground at trail's end. This makes for a nice base camp for exploring the Fews Ford Access and some of the best hiking on the Eno. In particular, the 3.75-mile Cox Mountain Trail, which takes you through an upland hardwood forest, and the combined 4.1-mile Buckquarter Creek/Holden Mill figure-eight loop, which offers equal parts ridgeline hiking and rambles along particularly rocky stretches of the Eno.

40 Raven Rock State Park

LILLINGTON

5.0 MILES, WITH DAY-HIKE OPTIONS

NO. OF DAYS: 1–2

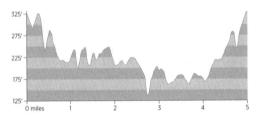

Raven Rock State Park

Late one November night several years back, I heard an odd noise building outside my tent in a remote section of Raven Rock State Park. I crawled out in time to see, not 100 yards to the north, the moonlit silhouettes of two army Blackhawk helicopters from nearby Fort Bragg heading up the Cape Fear River, perhaps 50 feet above the river's surface. It was a curious sight made curiouser by the fact that this was a work night and I had to be in

Checking out the old Native American fish traps on the Cape Fear.

the office by 9:00 A.M. I figured the helicopters would make for good water-cooler talk the next morning.

That's part of the allure of Raven Rock, located within an hour or so of 2 million people in the Triangle, Fayetteville, and the Sandhills region. Have a bad day and need to get away, even if for just a night? Raven Rock awaits. While the park's 5-site Family Wilderness campsite may fill on weather-perfect fall and spring weekends, the rest of the time you're likely to have the campground, with sites well-spaced for privacy, to yourself.

The campsites are located midway on the 5.0-mile Campbell Creek lolli-pop loop trail. From the visitors center, head northwest on the trail through rolling forest that's Piedmont with a touch of high country tossed in. Holly and mountain laurel are prominent in the mellow coves that carve their way down to the Cape Fear, coves that add a bit more up-and-down than you might expect in a park on the cusp of North Carolina's coastal plain. Fortunately, it's just a 2.7-mile hike to the campsites, which are primitive

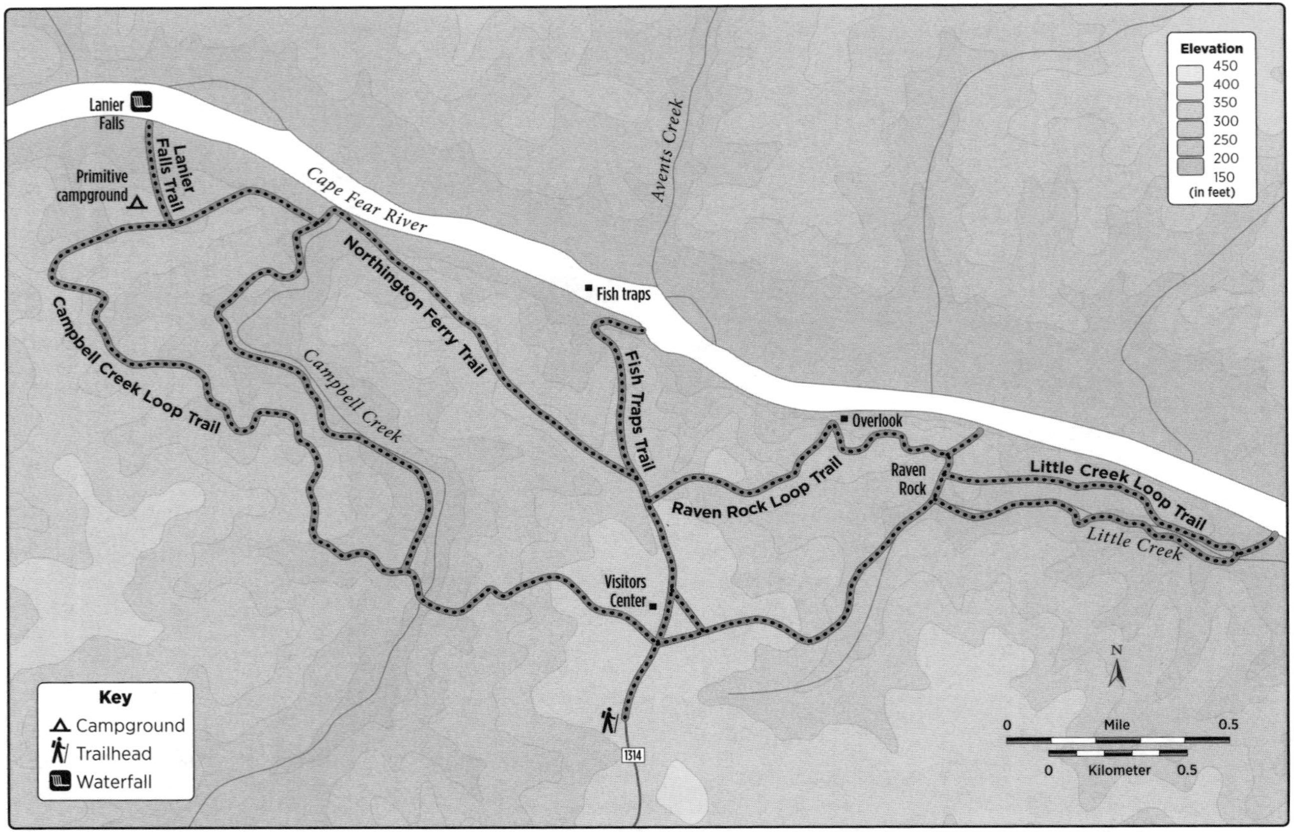

40 Raven Rock State Park

Key
△ Campground
🏃 Trailhead
📖 Waterfall

Elevation
450
400
350
300
250
200
150
(in feet)

N

Mile
0   0.5

Kilometer
0   0.5

Cape Fear River

Avents Creek

Fish traps

Little Creek

Little Creek Loop Trail

Overlook

Raven Rock

Raven Rock Loop Trail

Fish Traps Trail

Northington Ferry Trail

Visitors Center

1314

Campbell Creek

Campbell Creek Loop Trail

Lanier Falls Trail

Lanier Falls

Primitive campground

40 Raven Rock State Park

Trailhead: From US 421 9 mi. west of Lillington, turn north on Raven Rock Road. After 3 mi., Raven Rock Road dead-ends in the park, at the visitors center. Campbell Creek Trailhead is just west of the center.

Loop/one-way: Lollipop loop.

Difficulty: Moderate.

Campsites (with GPS coordinates): Five primitive backcountry sites located 2.7 mi. from the trailhead (N35 28.587 W78 55.759).

Maps: Trail map available at visitors center. USGS: Mamers.

Follow the trail: The entire trip is on the Campbell Creek Loop Trail, a lollipop loop you can pick up at the visitors center.

Fee? $13 a night campsite fee. Register at park office.

Water (with GPS coordinates): Treated water at visitors center trailhead. Creek water at mile 1.0, Campbell Creek (N35 27.854 W78 55.275); mile 2.8, Cape Fear and Lanier Falls (N35 28.748 W78 55.853); and for a little over a mile beginning at mile 3.0 (N35 28.590 W78 55.455) along Campbell Creek.

Land manager: N.C. Division of Parks and Recreation.

Trip highlight: Being on a surprisingly empty trail in an otherwise busy park.

Special considerations: If you decide to make this a quick mid-workweek overnight trip, be advised of the park's hours (and thus your egress and ingress): The park opens daily at 8:00 A.M. and closes at 9:00 P.M. June–Aug.; 8:00 P.M. Mar.–May, Sept., Oct.; 6:00 P.M. Nov.–Feb.

Night hike in? No (see hours).

Solo? Yes.

Family friendly? Yes.

Bailout option: No, but at worst you're never more than 2.5 mi. from the car.

Seasons: Fall, winter, spring.

Weather: No special considerations.

Solitude rating: 2.

Nearest outfitter: Walmart, Sanford.

Hunting allowed? No.

More info: Raven Rock State Park, (910) 893-4888, www.ncparks.gov/Visit/parks/raro/main.php.

save for a fire ring and privy. (Tip: If you need to make a cell phone call, stand in the doorway of the latrine; it's got the best reception in the campsite.)

Hike the loop clockwise and save the best of the trail for your hike out. A 0.2-mile diversion to Lanier Falls (more of a "drop," actually) on the Cape Fear offers a rare look at a frisky spot on this big river. A mile and a half of the return trip is along Campbell Creek, whose sandstone bottom gives the impression of a clear mountain stream. A mature canopy enhances the effect.

While Raven Rock makes for a nice overnight getaway, there's reason to linger. The park has 6.5 miles of additional trail south of the Cape Fear worth exploring. From the visitors center, take the 0.6-mile Fish Traps Trail to the river and check out the ingenious rock channels the area's first human inhabitants—Siouan and Tuscarora Indians—built to funnel fish into wooden traps. The 1.5-mile Little Creek Loop Trail offers one of the greenest year-round hikes in the region (thanks to an abundance of creek-loving holly and mountain laurel), and the 2.6-mile Raven Rock Loop Trail takes in the park's namesake attraction, a mile-long bluff 400 million years in the making that rises 150 feet above the Cape Fear. An elaborate staircase offers safe footing on the passage to Raven Rock's base, where you can gaze up and appreciate the full splendor of this high bluff on the cusp of the coastal plain.

You may even see a helicopter or two.

41 Crowders Mountain State Park

GASTONIA

12 MILES

NO. OF DAYS: 2–3

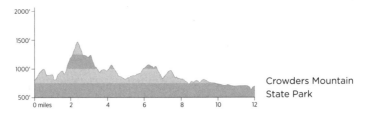

Crowders Mountain
State Park

Sometimes when you strap on a backpack you don't mind venturing down a faint trail into an overgrown wilderness unsure of whether you'll find

The rocky top of Kings Pinnacle has a Wild West feel and views in all directions. Photo courtesy N.C. Division of Parks and Recreation.

water and a decent campsite, let alone return without the aid of the local search and rescue.

Sometimes, though, you like to park your car in a secure, paved lot that will be gated after dark. You like running into a ranger who will assure you that things are exactly as they appear on the map, that after 1.0 miles you will arrive at a reserved campsite with a tent pad, a fire pit, cut firewood, a pit toilet, and water from a pump—the "primitive" campsite equivalent of a mint on your pillow. Sometimes when you strap a pack on your back you want to feel like you're getting into the wild, but you also want to know what you're getting into.

Sometimes you want the new Ridgeline Trail, which connects Crowders Mountain State Park in North Carolina with Kings Mountain State Park to the southwest in South Carolina. Because the trail, opened in April 2009, connects two state parks, you can expect it to be well marked and well maintained. But just because there's a degree of comfort and convenience doesn't mean you'll be sacrificing the backwoods experience.

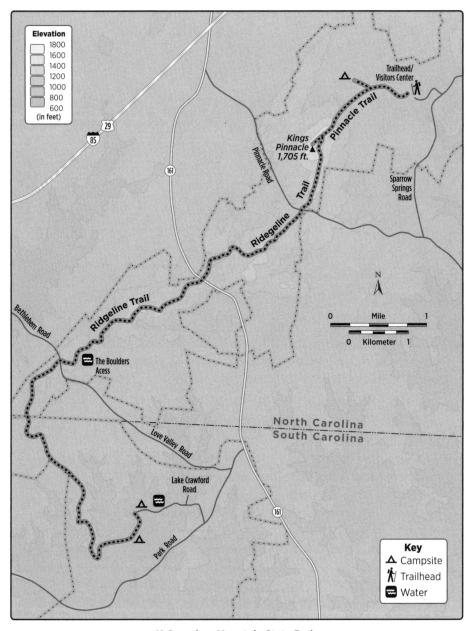

Elevation
1800
1600
1400
1200
1000
800
600
(in feet)

29
85

161

Pinnacle Road

Pinnacle Trail

Kings Pinnacle 1,705 ft.

Ridegeline Trail

Ridegeline Trail

Bethlehem Road

The Boulders Acess

Trailhead/ Visitors Center

Sparrow Springs Road

N

0   Mile   1

0   Kilometer   1

North Carolina
South Carolina

Love Valley Road

Lake Crawford Road

Park Road

161

Key
△ Campsite
🏃 Trailhead
〰 Water

41 Crowders Mountain State Park

41 Crowders Mountain State Park

Trailhead: From I-85 in Gastonia, take Edgewood Road (exit 13) south. From there go 0.6 mi., then turn right on US 74. After 2.1 mi., turn left on Sparrow Springs Road; stay on Sparrow Springs, which veers right, 3.7 mi. (Freedom Mill Road goes straight). At 4.2 mi., park entrance is on the right; at 4.3 mi., trailhead parking.

Loop/one-way: One-way. If you're hiking one way, set up a shuttle by parking one car at Kings Mountain State Park and driving the second back to the Crowders Mountain trailhead. From Kings Mountain: Go left on SR 705 (which becomes SR 1100 after crossing into North Carolina); at 2.4 mi., turn left on Unity Church Road; at 2.43 mi., turn right on Lewis Road/SR 1126; at 3.7 mi., turn left on Sparrow Springs Road; at 4.9 mi., park entrance is on the left; at 5.0 mi., trailhead parking.

Difficulty: Moderate (due to length).

Campsites (with GPS coordinates): Camping is restricted to 2 sites in both state parks: 1.0 mi., Crowders Mountain State Park primitive campground (N35 12.978 W81 18.321); 12.0 mi., Kings Mountain (S.C.) State Park campground (N35 08.986 W81 20.908). Additional camping is planned along the trail.

Maps: Trail maps for the Ridgeline Trail are available at both the Crowders Mountain and Kings Mountain state park visitors centers. USGS: Kings Mountain, Gastonia.

Follow the trail: From the trailhead, hike 0.2 mi.; at the T, go left on the orange-blazed Pinnacle Trail. After 0.3 mi. on Pinnacle is the 0.5-mi. spur (r) to the primitive camping area. Continue 0.3 mi. to Turnback Trail (which returns to the visitors center), and 0.8 mi. to the short but steep spur (r) up to the pinnacle. This is where the Ridgeline Trail (red blaze) begins. On the Ridgeline Trail: at 0.9 mi. is the Pinnacle Road crossing; 2.7 mi., NC 161 crossing; 5.0 mi., Bethlehem Road crossing; 5.5 mi., spur (r) to Boulders Access area; 6.1 mi., South Carolina border. At 8.5 mi., the trail Ts; go left 8.8 mi. to a picnic area; 9.2 mi. to a picnic area with shelters. At 9.5 mi., the trail ends in Kings Mountain State Park.

Fee? $13 per night at Crowders Mountain; $10 at Kings Mountain.

Water (with GPS coordinates): Treated water is available at the trailhead; at the Crowders Mountain campground at mile 1.0 (N35 12.978 W81 18.321); at the Boulders Access area, mile 8.1 (N35 10.212 W81 22.129); at the Kings Mountain picnic area, mile 11.4 (N35 08.711 W81 21.205); and in the Kings Mountain campground, mile 12.0 (N35 08.986 W81 20.908).

Land managers: N.C. Division of Parks and Recreation; S.C. Department of Parks, Recreation and Tourism.

Trip highlight: Rocky ridgeline hiking with 360-degree views from atop Kings Pinnacle.

Special considerations: Three paved road crossings: Pinnacle Road (3.5 mi.), NC 161 (5.2 mi.), Bethlehem Road (7.5 mi.). All are moderately busy; look both ways before crossing.

Night hike in? Yes, but keep in mind the park gate at Crowders Mountain closes at 6:00 P.M. Nov.–Feb.; 8:00 P.M. Mar., Apr., Sept., Oct.; 9:00 P.M. May–Aug.

Solo? Yes. Trails are well marked and well maintained.

Family friendly? Yes, although the length may be a challenge—both physically and from an entertainment standpoint—for younger hikers. A good, short, overnight option: Hike the mile in to the Crowders Mountain primitive campground, set up camp, then do a day hike to Kings Pinnacle.

Bailout options: Possible bailouts at the three road crossings (see "Special considerations").

Seasons: Fall, winter, spring. (Buggy and muggy in summer, especially the 3.4-mi. South Carolina section, which is flatter and runs through lowland forest.)

Weather: Afternoon thunderstorms on the ridgeline are possible in summer.

Solitude rating: 3. Potential for crowds on both ends; otherwise, you're on your own.

Nearest outfitter: REI, Charlotte, (704) 921-0320, and Pineville, (704) 341-7405, www.rei.com. Trading post at Kings Mountain campground has some provisions, but hours are limited.

Hunting allowed? No.

More info: Crowders Mountain State Park, (704) 853-5375, www.ncparks.gov/Visit/parks/crmo/main.php; Kings Mountain (S.C.) State Park, (803) 222-3209, http://southcarolinaparks.com. Both have information about the Ridgeline Trail.

Near the northern trailhead in Crowders Mountain State Park you can take a short spur to the top of 1,705-foot Kings Pinnacle. Seventeen hundred feet may not sound like much, and it's certainly a fraction of how high the ancient Kings Mountain Range once reached. From this rocky perch you'll get 360-degree views (okay, so about 320 of those degrees are consumed by Gastonia to the north, Charlotte to the east, and assorted other development to the south and west). You'll also get a chance to see at least 2 species not often found in the Piedmont: Bradley's spleenwort fern and the Carolina pygmy rattlesnake (appreciate the latter—which has the classic diamond-shaped head, rattler, and dark spots running down its back and sides—from afar).

A prolonged ramble along the range's spine allows for introspection (though be sure to pop back to reality when you hit the 3 roads the trail crosses) and the chance to hike amid the storied American chestnut. The American chestnut is commonly thought to have become extinct following a blight in the early 1900s. In fact, sprouts of the American chestnut can live up to 15 years and reach 30 feet in height before succumbing to the fungus that eventually kills them. (FYI, efforts are under way to reintroduce the American chestnut with blight-resistant nuts. The success of the program won't be known until 2015 to 2020, according to the American Chestnut Foundation, http://www.acf.org.)

After passing into South Carolina (a gas line easement serves as the border), the trail flattens and passes through a lowland forest on its final 3.3 miles to the Kings Mountain Campground. Thrill seekers may wish to end the hike here, amid such typical campground comforts as lake swimming, horseshoes, and a trip for provisions (I recommend the 24-oz. Mountain Dew Code Red after a long day on the trail) at the campground trading post. If you're into mileage, the 12-mile return trip gives you an impressive 24-mile weekender for your backpacking résumé.

Coast

HAVELOCK

20.1 MILES

NO. OF DAYS: 2–3

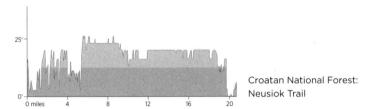

Croatan National Forest:
Neusiok Trail

You don't need a better explanation for why this trip is done in winter than the name of the Neusiok's northernmost shelter: Copperhead Landing. Not only does the venomous copperhead inhabit the area, but so do its viperous buddies the cottonmouth and the timber and pygmy rattlesnakes. Being cold-blooded types, they're less likely to be out and about come winter, when the daytime highs in this coastal forest are typically in the mid-50s. Those cool daytime temperatures, coupled with overnight lows around freezing, help with the other reason you should only do this trail in winter: flying pests that bite, sting, and make a general nuisance of themselves by buzzing about your every facial orifice.

All that said, this is the ideal trip for when you're sitting around post-holidays, lethargic, aching to get out for the weekend, but not aching enough to strap a 40-pound winter pack on your back and gain 3,000 vertical feet on a potentially icy Appalachian trail. Two days on the Neusiok Trail are the perfect antidote for the first-of-the-year blues. Hit it on a crisp, sunny day—a frequent occurrence at the coast—and a Neusiok trip could become an annual winter ritual.

From the northern trailhead at the Pine Cliffs Recreation Area, the Neusiok briefly travels a sand beach along the Neuse River, which at this point in its 275-mile journey from the Piedmont is 2.5 miles wide and more resembles a sound. A prevailing north wind this time of year will send a stiff chill down your backpacked spine (a main reason I suggest doing this trail north to south).

After a mile and a half of beachcombing between the Neuse to your north and an ancient bluff to your south, the trail heads inland. At times the trail rambles through a pine savannah; at times it dips into a coastal swamp. Winter afternoons are generally quiet, save for the occasional rat-a-tat of a

The wide Neuse River is a companion on the north end of the trail.

woodpecker, including the endangered red-cockaded woodpecker. You'll pass signs of old folklore, including an intertwined pin oak and loblolly pine about two miles in that supposedly represents the forbidden love of two Native Americans from opposing tribes. You'll pass signs of a more recent and colorful past in the rusted remains of old stills that are slowly dissolving into the landscape. And during those moments when the Neusiok lulls you into a winter reverie, you'll snap to at the sight of holly and galax and wonder whether you're at the coast or on the crest of a mountain ridge. All of this is within the first 7 miles of the trip.

An overnight at the Dogwood Shelter, where there's also plenty of room to pitch tents, divides this trek into a tidy 2-day trip. With drinkable well water at the 3.7-, 11.3-, and 19.3-mile marks, and with the snake and pest population safely tucked in, the Neusiok Trail makes for a worry-free weekend in the woods.

Again, provided you hike it in winter.

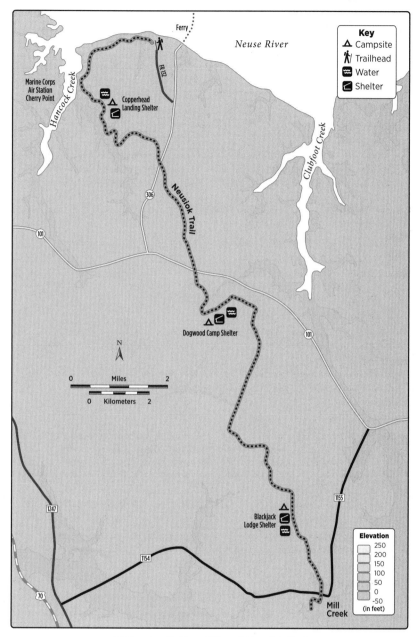

42 Croatan National Forest Neusiok Trail

42 Croatan National Forest Neusiok Trail

Trailhead: From US 70 in Havelock, take NC 101 east. After 5.3 mi., go left on Ferry Road/NC 306. Go 3.3 mi. to the gravel FR 132 and turn left. The Pine Cliff Picnic Area and Neusiok Trail's northern trailhead are 1.7 mi. To set up a shuttle, return down NC 306 to NC 101 and turn left. Turn right on Old Wimberly Road and go 3.8 mi. to Mill Creek Road (you'll pass the turn for the northern end of this loop road after about 2 mi.; resist the urge to turn left here). Go right, then take a quick left to the southern trailhead parking lot.

Loop/one-way: One-way.

Difficulty: Easy (long, but flat).

Campsites (with GPS coordinates): There are 3 main camping areas. All include shelters, accommodating about 5 hikers, and water pumped from a well: 3.7 mi., Copperhead Landing (N34 54.780 W76 50.441); 11.3 mi., Dogwood Camp (N34 51.497 W76 47.784); 19.3 mi., Blackjack Lodge (N34 46.909 W76 45.801).

Maps: "Croatan National Forest," USDA Forest Service, 1:126,720. USGS: Cherry Point, Core Creek, and Newport quads.

Follow the trail: The entire trip is on the white-blazed Neusiok Trail.

Fee? No.

Water (with GPS coordinates): Drinkable water pumped from a well can be found at the three shelters: 3.7 mi., Copperhead Landing (N34 54.780 W76 50.441); 11.3 mi., Dogwood Camp (N34 51.497 W76 47.784); 19.3 mi., Blackjack Lodge (N34 46.909 W76 45.801).

Land manager: USDA Forest Service.

Trip highlights: Stretches, especially north of the NC 306 crossing, where galax and other flora associated with the mountains give this coastal trek an oddly montane feel; nice pine savanna near northern trailhead.

Special considerations: Only if you hike it in warm weather, when you'll be forced to deal with flying things and venomous slithering things—bad for hiking, really bad for trying to sleep.

Night hike in? Yes.

Solo? Yes.

Family friendly? Trail is flat but long and could try the patience of small hikers. Suggest a truncated version, backpacking the first day from the Pine Cliff Recreation area to Copperhead Landing, a distance of 3.7 mi., then hiking 3.2 mi. the next day to NC 306, where you can park a shuttle vehicle or make the relatively easy 2.7-mi. hike back to the trailhead. (Go north on NC 306 for 1.2 mi., then left on the gravel FR 132 for 1.5 mi.)

Bailout options: Yes, after 6.8 mi., at NC 306 (see "Family friendly?" above for directions back to car).

Seasons: Winter.

Weather: Winter weather is generally mild, with daytime temps in the mid-50s and overnight lows dipping to around freezing.

Solitude rating: 4.

Nearest outfitter: Walmart, Havelock.

Hunting allowed? Yes; local seasons apply.

More info: Croatan National Forest Service, (252) 638-5628, www.cs.unca.edu/nfsnc/recreation/neusiok_trail.pdf.

43 Hammocks Beach State Park Bear Island

SWANSBORO

2.7-MILE PADDLE; BACKPACK OF NO MORE THAN A HALF MILE

NO. OF DAYS: 2-3

So, you must be wondering, why is there a trip that requires a boat in a guide to backpacking?

Okay, it's a good question, since you aren't sitting next to me outside my tent on a November evening watching as the darkening heavens slowly shed a week's worth of clouds and reveal a brilliant night sky you don't see on the mainland. You can't look out past a small spit of sand and see the vast Atlantic as it gets swallowed by the night.

It's a fair question, since you can't look out at the inky horizon and see the blinking lights of buoys and fishing vessels trying to milk the ocean of its bounty. You can't look to the east and see the distant blinking lights of Emerald Isle, a sign of civilization that somehow makes you feel even more remote, a reminder that you are the lone human on this 3 1/2-mile-long, 892-acre barrier island. And you won't be in my tent later as the waves coming ashore serve as a lullaby sending me into a very deep sleep.

You won't wake with me just before dawn and scramble out of the tent to be among the first in the country to welcome the sun, a sun that signals its intentions with a deep crimson burst that slowly evolves into rich reds, oranges, and yellows. You won't be with me as I walk the deserted beach to see what the Atlantic has brought ashore overnight. And as the morning unfolds, you won't realize that you truly are alone, since the ferry that brings the vast majority of visitors to Bear Island suspends operation between November 1 and March 31.

It's a good question, since you won't be with me to experience what truly is the essence of why we pack a life support system on our backs and venture into the wild. In the search for anyplace wild in North Carolina, it's hard to top a barrier island that's eluded development. Save for a handful of picnic shelters and the bathhouse mid-island, Bear Island isn't much different than it was 6,000 years ago when the first Americans began visiting. (I say "visiting" because with no source of fresh water, it wasn't until the advent of pottery around 1000 B.C. that people were able to come out for extended stays.) And it's a place where you still run the risk, as a sign at the bathhouse warns, of finding unexploded ordnance dating to the Civil War.

An extra piece of equipment is required for the trip to Bear Island.

That, in a nutshell, is why a trip that requires a boat is in a book about backpacking.

Any more questions? I thought so. You should find most of your answers for how to get here in the info box.

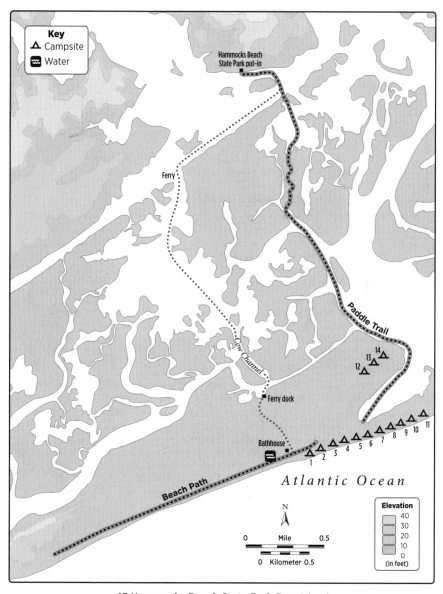

43 Hammocks Beach State Park Bear Island

43 Hammocks Beach State Park Bear Island

Trailhead: From NC 24 in Swansboro, go east on Hammocks Beach Road for 2.5 mi. Just before the road ends, go right, into the park. The canoe and kayak put-in is to the left of the visitors center. Take the canoe and kayak trail marked with white signposts (the yellow posts will take you to Huggins Island).

Loop/one way: One way.

Difficulty: Easy hike. The paddle is relatively easy, through wetlands behind the barrier island. Requires a short crossing of the Intracoastal Waterway; pay attention to motorboat traffic.

Campsites (with GPS coordinates): Campsites 12–14 are located along the inlet, to your right (N34 38.557 W77 07.489). Continue paddling another 0.4 mi. to the takeout for sites 1–11, which is on your left (N34 38.236 W77 07.716). Sites 7 and 8 are are just a few steps from the takeout; sites 1–11 are within a quarter mile in both directions along the beach, nestled, for the most part, in protective dunes.

Maps: Maps of the canoe trail and the island are available on the park website (see below).

Follow the trail: The only trail on this trip is the 2.6-mi. paddle trail from park headquarters to the Bogue Inlet end of Bear Island; it is blazed with white markers on orange posts. Once you're on the island, the best exploring is done along the beach. If you explore inland, beware the prickly-pear cactus, which considers your ankles its natural habitat. Also watch for signs warning of unexploded ordnance on this onetime military outpost dating back to the Civil War.

Fee? $13 per night camping fee.

Water (with GPS coordinates): Treated water is available at the bathhouse (N34 38.018 W77 08.290), which is within a mile of all campsites. (Note: access to the bathhouse from campsites 1–11 is along the beach. Access from campsites 12–14 requires walking through the middle of the island, which is peppered with prickly- pear cactus (the natural habitat for which appears to be your ankles). Also, there is no defined trail.

Land manager: N.C. Division of Parks and Recreation.

Trip highlight: Do this trip between Nov. 1 and Mar. 31, when there is no ferry service from the mainland, and there's a good chance you'll have the entire island to yourself.

Special considerations: Although the paddle over is through a typically calm wetland, some paddling experience is preferred. The paddle can be particularly challenging in storms and when the wind kicks up. Check the tide table for Swansboro when planning your trip; try to time your paddle out to coincide with low tide, and your paddle back to take advantage of high tide. It's also a good idea to pack your gear in dry bags for this trip. Dry bag backpacks start at about $50.

Night hike in? No.

Solo? Yes, but only for experienced paddlers.

Family friendly? Yes, provided everyone is comfortable on—and in—the water.

Bailout options: No.

Seasons: All. (In summer you must contend with a host of flying pests that can make sleeping, in particular, a challenge.)

Weather: Generally mild, almost always a wind of some kind blowing.

Solitude rating: 5, provided you go when the ferry isn't running.

Nearest outfitter: Barrier Island Kayaks, Swansboro, (252) 393-6457, www.barrierislandkayaks.com, which rents boats if you need one.

Hunting allowed? No.

More info: Hammocks Beach State Park, (910) 326-4881, www.ncparks.gov/Visit/parks/habe/main.php.

Index

About the Author

Joe Miller grew up in Colorado but didn't become addicted to outdoor adventure until moving to North Carolina in 1992. For seventeen years, he wrote about his passion for adventure for the *News & Observer* of Raleigh, featuring endeavors that ranged from winter backpacking in the high country to a Fourth of July bike race on the bottom of the Atlantic Ocean. Today, Joe is an outdoors and fitness writer based in Cary, N.C., where he produces the outdoor recreation blog GetGoingNC.com. He is also the author of *100 Classic Hikes in North Carolina*. In addition to being a hiker and a backpacker, Joe is an avid cyclist, participating in cross-country and endurance mountain bike races; a skier-turned-snowboarder; a paddler (flat water, mostly); a certified scuba diver; and the owner of a longboard skateboard, which he rides with the utmost respect. In 2009, he rekindled a long-dormant love of running, trading the faster 10Ks of his youth for half marathons and trail running.

Other **Southern Gateways Guides** you might enjoy

Wildflowers and Plant Communities of the Southern Appalachian Mountains and Piedmont A Naturalist's Guide to the Carolinas, Virginia, Tennessee, and Georgia

TIMOTHY P. SPIRA

A habitat approach to identifying plants and interpreting nature

A Field Guide to Wildflowers of the Sandhills Region
North Carolina, South Carolina, and Georgia

BRUCE A. SORRIE

The first-ever field guide to the wildflowers of this vibrant, biodiverse region

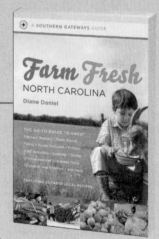

Farm Fresh North Carolina The Go-To Guide to Great Farmers' Markets, Farm Stands, Farms, Apple Orchards, U-Picks, Kids' Activities, Lodging, Dining, Choose-and-Cut Christmas Trees, Vineyards and Wineries, and More

DIANE DANIEL

The one and only guidebook to North Carolina's farms and fresh foods